Quality Performance Assessment: A Guide for Schools and Districts

By Center for Collaborative Education

Foreword by Jay McTighe

www.qualityperformanceassessment.org

Lead Authors: Christina Brown and Amy Mednick

Foreword: Jay McTighe

Contributors*

- Laurie Gagnon
- Dan French
- Maggie Ward
- Austin Mueller
- Julia Moskowitz
- Olivia Biagetti
- Pascale Mevs
- Amy Woods
- Liza Duddy

*In order of contribution.

Permissions

- Some of the tools and strategies used or adapted for this guide are drawn from the work of Karin Hess (as cited in context). Permission is given to QPA and schools using this guide to reproduce and use these materials as long as authorship is fully cited. All rights for the original materials remain the intellectual property of Karin Hess and cannot be copyrighted by others. This work includes:
    - o *Local Assessment Toolkit:* Hess Cognitive Rigor Matrix; Great American Chocolate Chip Cookie Taste Test; Student Work Analysis Protocol; Assessment Development & Validation Protocols
    - o Tools for Examining Text Complexity (with S. Hervey, 2011)
- eSchool News for *A Window into Performance Assessment at Frances W. Parker Charter Essential School:* Copyright © February 2012, eSchool News (www.eschoolnews.com); reprinted with permission.
- National Writing Project for Friedman, T. (2006). Developing a culture of inquiry for equity: One school's story. In L. Friedrich, C. Tateishi, T. Malarkey, E. R. Simons, and M. Williams (eds.), *Working toward equity: Writings and resources from the Teacher Research Collaborative* (pp. 129–139). Berkeley, CA: National Writing Project.
- Microlabs and Text-Based Seminar protocols are copyrighted by the National School Reform Faculty® (NSRF®) and adapted/used with permission. For more information, call 812-330-2702 or visit http://www.nsrfharmony.org.

QPA website: www.qualityperformanceassessment.org
CCE website: www.ccebos.org

Please contact us at QPA@ccebos.org

Second printing 2013

ISBN: 978-0-9883116-0-2

TABLE OF CONTENTS

Foreword

Jay McTighe
Co-author, *Understanding by Design*

Throughout North America, high-stakes, accountability tests have influenced the nature and practice of district and classroom assessments. Since these external, standardized tests rely primarily on selected-response (and sometimes, brief constructed-response) formats, it is too often the case that local assessments mimic their form. Indeed, an entire cottage industry of "practice tests" has emerged with the promise of helping to raise the scores.

While there is nothing wrong with multiple-choice or short-answer formats, they are inherently limited in the outcomes that they can appropriately assess. Indeed, some of the most valued educational outcomes (e.g., creative thinking, ability to construct and support an argument, experimental inquiry, oral communication) do not lend themselves to standardized "bubblesheet" responses. Moreover, students quickly learn a truism of schooling – "what is assessed signals what is important." The things that are not tested are less likely to be seen as important.

Quality Performance Assessment (QPA) offers a timely and refreshing alternative to a fixation on standardized test methods. The book makes a strong case for the importance of including performance assessments as part of a balanced assessment system. Like the game in athletics or the play in theater, quality performance assessment tasks provide clear and relevant targets for learning. Rich performance tasks engage students in applying their knowledge and skills to a realistic issue or challenge.

Quality performance assessments get at essential questions of curriculum and instruction: *What content is most important? What do we want learners to be able to do with their learning? What evidence will show that students really understand and can apply learned content? How good is "good enough"? What can we do to improve performance?* They encourage a "backward design" approach to curriculum by identifying a worthy end in mind from which teaching is planned. In fact, teaching to rich performance tasks should occur without apology, just as effective coaches practice with the game in mind. In addition to assessing traditional subject matter, QPAs provide a natural vehicle for integrating the so-called 21st century skills (e.g., critical thinking, technology use, creativity, teamwork) with academic content – skills that can easily "fall through the cracks" of conventional teaching and multiple-choice assessments.

The book clearly delineates the principles and practices needed to insure that performance assessments and companion rubrics are of high quality in order to provide fair and valid measures of targeted goals. These abstractions are brought to life through specific examples and memorable anecdotes featuring recognizable teaching situations. In addition, the authors champion the value of the process of developing, refining, and using performance assessments. The essential conversations and collaborations required (e.g., task and rubric design, peer reviews of drafts, group scoring and calibration) contribute to profound professional learning. Moreover, the subsequent analysis of student work and shared ideas for improvement lies at the heart of a professional learning community.

While the book focuses on summative assessments, the authors also make a case for the importance of diagnostic (pre-assessments) and formative (on-going) assessments and their benefits to teaching and learning. They offer tried and true, manageable methods by which teachers can effectively apply a range of assessments to enhance, not simply evaluate, the performance of their students.

Quality Performance Assessment is authoritative without being "ivory tower." Indeed, one of its greatest strengths lies in its practicality. The variety of proven tools and protocols will support educators in improving their assessments while concurrently engaging their students in meaningful learning. I am a long-standing advocate for performance assessment, and this book is music to my ears. I trust that you too will enjoy its melody and act on its lyrics.

Preface

"One thing I never want to see happen is schools that are just teaching the test, because then you're not learning about the world. . . ."
—President Barack Obama, March 28, 2011

Is it possible to heed President Obama's warning and create a student assessment and accountability system that actually does teach students about the world? Is it possible to prepare students for our global society and create a system that makes profound differences in student engagement and achievement? In such a student assessment and accountability system, students would demonstrate what they have learned, how they have learned, and how their knowledge can be applied to real-life situations.

Performance assessments allow educators to rethink the intersections of teaching, learning, and assessment through meaningful and transferable student learning. Quality Performance Assessment (QPA) seeks to demonstrate that performance assessments can be a powerful tool to drive and measure meaningful learning in the 21st century at the school, district, and state levels.

QPA began in 2008 when the Center for Collaborative Education (CCE) partnered with the Nellie Mae Education Foundation with the goal of demonstrating that rich performance assessment systems can play a vital role in preparing diverse students for attending college, achieving success in their careers, and participating in the 21st century global society. CCE launched the initiative by conducting a review and analysis of seven large-scale performance assessment initiatives, seeking to identify successes and challenges (Tung & Stazesky, 2010). Out of this study emerged the building blocks of the QPA initiative—quality performance assessment systems need to be supported by three critical components: technical quality, robust professional development, and leadership support. In a second study, QPA interviewed almost 100 graduates from three Boston Public schools with strong performance assessment systems. Interviewees reported strong preparation for the demands of complex thinking and understanding in college and career (Gagnon, 2010). QPA concluded that there is strong evidence to support promotion of performance assessment as a key measure of student learning in the 21st century.

In 2009, QPA recruited twelve Massachusetts public secondary schools to form the QPA Network. The network aimed to collaborate in the design of valid and reliable common performance assessment tasks in English language arts, to strengthen local performance assessment systems to build technical quality, and to develop a robust professional development model to train school educators in the design of quality local performance assessments. While the network encompassed mainly ELA teachers, the professional development conducted in QPA Network schools included teachers of social studies, science, mathematics, the arts, and all elective subjects, concentrating on interdisciplinary performance assessments and integrating literacy across the disciplines. Another eight schools joined the cohort one year later, including schools from Rhode Island and New Hampshire. Over the course of three years, extensive fieldwork and field testing enabled QPA to create a model for building strong school, district, and state performance assessment systems.[1]

An independent evaluation conducted in spring 2011 on CCE's performance assessment work found that "the project has contributed in significant ways to the ongoing development of teachers' assessment literacy and their schools' assessment processes. In addition to supporting the development of teachers' technical knowledge about assessment, it has helped school teams sharpen and focus their assessment work and modeled processes for local adoption and adaptation" (Gallagher, 2011, p. 1).

QPA enters the conversation about student assessment with the following premise:

> Embedding high-quality performance assessments throughout the core academic curriculum will result in an increased use of curriculum aligned to Common Core State Standards, robust assessment data, and enhanced student learning. We believe these outcomes will lead to higher student achievement, the closing of achievement gaps, higher graduation and lower dropout rates, and higher college-going and persistence rates.

[1] While the QPA Common Performance Assessment Tasks focused primarily on English language arts Common Core standards, the Common Core stipulates that the standards are interdisciplinary in nature, covering ELA and literacy across disciplines. QPA Common Tasks were also implemented in history and humanities classes.

Students collaborate in science class.

QPA believes that performance assessments add a fuller, more in-depth picture of student learning, lead to more rigorous and relevant learning experiences, and result in greater equity of access to postsecondary skills, knowledge, and credentials for all students. QPA helps school and district leaders develop performance assessments where:

- The design of the assessment is engaging and meaningful to students.
- The assessment measures real-world skills and knowledge.
- The assessment provides feedback that motivates students to continue learning.
- The assessment allows students to demonstrate mastery of the content and skills they have learned.

To succeed, these assessments must be valid and reliable, accompanied by robust professional development, and provided with strong leadership and policy support. When teachers become assessment literate and experienced in developing quality tasks and rubrics that are aligned with the Common Core, they will design and deliver more meaningful, standards-aligned learning experiences.

Comments from QPA teacher participants consistently illustrate the power of teacher learning in QPA.

> "These (scoring) conversations are very important because they help us all consider how we make judgments about student work, what consistency means, and how to create prompts and rubrics that are clear."

> "The process took my understanding of looking at student work to a new level—I did not really get what calibration and reliability looked like with performance assessment until today."

QPA defines performance assessments as: *Multistep assignments with clear criteria, expectations, and processes that measure how well a student transfers knowledge and applies complex skills to create or refine an original product.* The QPA approach to performance assessments is guided by the research-based and field-tested QPA Framework:

1. **Aligned instruction**
2. **Task design**
3. **Data analysis**

QPA's overarching goal is to demonstrate the viability of creating performance assessments with high technical quality at the school, district, and state levels in order to establish an effective student assessment policy. This guide is intended to provide educators with a practical how-to manual for designing quality performance assessments. QPA believes that systemic use of performance assessments will lead to a rigorous pre-K–12 education with more relevant student-centered learning experiences, as well as greater equity of access to postsecondary opportunities.

Dan French

Executive Director
Center for Collaborative Education

Acknowledgments

- QPA Team: Christina Brown, Laurie Gagnon, Rosann Tung, Maggie Ward, Susan Westlund
- QPA Interns: Olivia Biagetti, Jennifer Hanson, Stephanie Lloyd, Pascale Mevs, Julia Moskowitz, Austin Mueller, Carolina Prieto, Erica Schwartz
- CCE Editorial Group: Robert Frank, Dan French, Anne Marshall, Sarah Ottow, Alethea Pratt, Leah Rugen, Lynn Stuart
- Design and Layout: Meena Mehta, Two M's Design

We wish to thank the following people for their contributions to this book and the Quality Performance Assessment (QPA) Initiative:

- We would like to thank the dedicated faculties and leadership of the QPA Network, who gave of their time and wisdom with students as well as with the QPA team during the QPA research period. Without their efforts, this guide would not exist. The story of Quality Performance Assessment cannot be told without the work of the students, teachers, and school leaders of the QPA Network, QPA clients, and QPA Summer Institute participants who have served as a high-caliber peer-editing team for QPA's work.

- We would like to extend our deepest gratitude to Dr. Karin Hess of the National Center for the Improvement of Educational Assessment for providing support to QPA since fall 2009 in the areas of project design and technical quality of performance assessment development and implementation. Dr. Hess is a recognized national leader in developing practical approaches for designing and using learning progressions as a foundation for formative, interim, and performance assessments. Dr. Hess has provided invaluable feedback, support, guidance, tools, and wisdom to the QPA team and has helped us to make technical quality accessible to QPA Network schools. Her tools and wisdom fill this guide and make the work of QPA possible.

- We are grateful to all external reviewers of this guide: Ceronne Daly, Lori Digisi, Karen Engels, Megan Lewis, Cindy Lung, and Amy Woods. Each reviewer contributed valuable perspectives and feedback.

- We are grateful to the QPA Advisory Board, which has provided guidance and insight throughout the project that has deepened the quality of our work: Theresa Austin, Katie Bowler, Doug Christensen, Chris Gallagher, Cindy Gray, Stuart Kahl, Sharon Lee, Beth Miller, Ray Pecheone, Charlie Toulmin, and Kit Viator. Special thanks to Katie Bowler, Cindy Gray, Stuart Kahl, and Beth Miller for their review of this guide.

- We are grateful to the state departments of education in Massachusetts, Rhode Island, and New Hampshire for their support and feedback.

The research, fieldwork, and production of this guide were generously funded by the Nellie Mae Education Foundation.

Center for Collaborative Education

Quality Performance Assessments is an initiative of the Center for Collaborative Education. The mission of the Center for Collaborative Education (CCE) is to transform schools so that all students succeed. We believe schools should prepare every student to achieve academically and to make a positive contribution to a democratic society. CCE partners with public schools and districts to create and sustain effective and equitable schools.

For additional tools and information, see the CCE and QPA websites.

CCE: www.ccebos.org
QPA: www.qualityperformanceassessment.org

How to Use This Guide

Quality Performance Assessment: A Guide for Schools and Districts builds on the paper *Harnessing the Power of Teacher and Student Learning* (Brown & Mevs, 2012) to delineate the process of crafting performance assessments of consistent technical quality supported by school-based professional development. When performance assessments are of high quality, they are aligned to standards, embedded in curriculum, and drive student learning. The guide contains a collection of research-based and field-tested tools that educators can use in building strong performance assessment systems. Technical quality is a complex and collaborative journey, not a destination. Continual refinement is part of the process. The story of improved professional practice and student learning forms the foundation for this guide and serves as a model from which other educators may learn as they begin a journey of their own.

Read this guide collaboratively and systematically, taking the time to digest the material, and discussing its implications with colleagues. After reading chapter 1, school and district leaders might want to flip to chapter 5 before going to the other chapters. One school's faculty might decide, after reading the first chapter, that it would be best to begin with aligning instruction and assessment. A district might want to begin with data analysis. Just as the work of QPA is cyclical in nature, the guide does not necessarily need to be read in a linear fashion.

Chapter 1 of this guide presents a rationale for widening the parameters and practice of assessment. It demonstrates how performance assessment at the school, district, and state levels can be a driver of professional development and student achievement. The chapter describes the shifts in the Common Core, focusing on an increased level of rigor and alignment to college and career readiness. It introduces the QPA Framework as a tool for implementing performance assessments.

The **QPA Framework** guides school and district leaders in the design of a local performance assessment system with three key elements: instruction aligned to college- and career-readiness standards; assessments with clear criteria and appropriate levels of content and cognitive complexity; and data analysis that informs instruction and assessment in a collaborative professional community. In the QPA Framework, student learning is at the center; it is meaningful to students and offers opportunities for ownership and decision making in real-world situations.

Chapters 2 through 5 provide a road map to the QPA Framework, with stories from the QPA Network schools about doing the work. Each of these chapters starts with an illustrative vignette, as well as two organizing elements that guide readers through putting that element of the QPA Framework into practice:

- Process: What are the steps for implementing this element of the QPA Framework?
- Decoding the Jargon: What are the technical words and definitions that the reader needs to understand this element of the QPA Framework? Words in italics throughout the guide are defined in this section.

Chapters 2 through 5 close with three organizing elements:

- Let's Get Started: Entry points for the work that allow educators to jump right in.
- Refining Our Work through Self-Assessment: Questions that help readers reflect on where their school or district is on the journey.
- Tools: A list of tools that are included in the chapter.

Chapter 5 concludes with an examination of the power of networks of educators using performance assessments collaboratively, and presents examples of the structures that support this work at the state and district levels. While performance assessment takes place across all grade levels and in all disciplines, this guide focuses primarily on literacy in all content areas in secondary schools, following the Common Core approach of embedding literacy and performance assessments across all disciplines. The design, practices, and tools are applicable across all grade levels and subject areas. As the work evolves and progresses, additional resources, including new tools, examples, and annotated student work samples, will be available on the QPA website: www.qualityperformanceassessment.org. Future QPA work, and subsequent editions of the guide, will include more performance assessments across disciplines and at elementary grade levels.

QPA teacher and coach set calendar for performance assessment goals.

The Tools Section encompasses a list of tools (in alphabetical order) and protocols referred to throughout the guide. Each tool is numbered and can be found in the chapters of the text by tool number and page number. It is not necessary to use every tool or to follow the steps in chronological order. If a certain tool or protocol fits the context of the school community, begin exploring that with colleagues as the school works simultaneously on building communities of practice. All tools are marked in the text with an icon.

In a final note, this is not a guide to implementing the Common Core standards. This is a guide for putting in place performance assessments of technical quality that QPA believes can result in the integration of the Common Core into practice and into teacher professional development. If teachers collectively learn to design, effectively use, and evaluate performance assessments with technical quality, the promise of college and career readiness contained in the Common Core might truly be achieved. Assessment systems led by assessment-literate teachers are the most effective way to guarantee that students will learn the skills outlined by the Common Core through curriculum alignment, student-centered learning, and meaningful assessments. To support this process, every chapter provides tools, tips, and research that support Common Core implementation through common performance assessments as marked by an icon.

Let's Get Started: Entry Points and a Sample Timeline for Quality Performance Assessment

"The rhythms of an assessment system reflect the cycles of learning, relearning, and extending learning that occurs in the daily lives of students and teachers. The power of an assessment system is that it weaves the interdependent elements of teaching and learning into a complex whole…. A system for assessing learning takes a school community on a journey of self-renewing improvement." —*Lynn Stuart, Assessment in Practice*

Implementing quality performance assessment is a dynamic, cyclical process that takes place over years. The journey of each school or district is unique, and there are multiple entry points and pathways, but the destination of increased student achievement should always focus the work. Matching local context, needs, and concerns is important, as there is not only one way to do this work, and it might look different in different places. QPA suggests entry points in the "Let's Get Started" section of each chapter, but these entry points are not prescriptive or exhaustive. The work starts when school and district leaders make a decision to make rich and complex student work the focus of professional development and teacher collaboration. Protocols provide the how-to once this decision is made. The QPA Guide provides many protocols to support professional development and adult learning. QPA protocols are designed to take between 30 and 60 minutes, so that they can be adjusted to fit in teacher planning periods or early-release days.

As Lynn Stuart lays out in *Assessment in Practice,* "Like the rhythms of the natural year, the rhythms of a school-based assessment system have routine cycles that are punctuated by special moments which mark important passages for students and teachers." This rhythm of learning and assessment includes important work for school and district leaders in laying the groundwork and creating the conditions that make the work possible. It also includes important work for faculties in moving through the learning cycle: Align, Design, Analyze. The time can be organized in the following buckets of work and can start in any part of the school year:

- **Laying the foundation:** Making the decision to implement common performance assessments and starting to build the assessment literacy and capacity of teachers and leaders to do this work with technical quality is the first step. It is important that leaders lead by making clear that a direction has been chosen and that "common" means all teachers will be part of the process.
- **Beginnings:** Committing to a process, setting goals, deciding how to allocate time and resources, and which teams will do what aspects of the work is the next step. Different collaborative groups within a school can be designated to take the lead: leadership team(s), grade-level teams, discipline area teams,

selected teacher-leaders, department heads, or entire faculties. Creative shifts in time and commitments can be made once commitments to the work are established.

- **Implementation:** Field testing and administering common performance assessments and scoring student work collaboratively are part of the process of implementation. Schools need to decide how many common performance assessments to administer. It might be two a year in the first year—one a semester—and grow over time to four a year—one each quarter—or even more, depending on what is sustainable based on the school's performance assessment design and the amount of time provided for teachers to work together.

- **Consolidating and expanding learning:** While the other aspects of the work focus on the process for adults, this aspect focuses on the process for students. Student learning is at the center, and it is critical that school leaders and teachers consider processes such as student goal setting and reflection and metacognition strategies, and how students will present and share their work with the school community and beyond. These processes consolidate and expand the learning as they promote student ownership and motivation.

- **Refining:** Collaboratively analyzing the results and making a plan for improvement continues the cycle. Intentionally designing a continuous feedback loop after the administration of each common performance assessment informs the work of the school and increases student achievement.

Schools can explore the QPA Framework for entry points for the work. The principles, processes, and ideas are consistent, but there is flexibility to innovate within the framework:

- **Alignment:** Start with backward planning that will lead to the creation of a performance assessment.

- **Design:** Start with implementation of an adapted or existing performance assessment in common across classrooms.

- **Analysis:** Start with analyzing and scoring student work.

- **Leadership and collaboration:** Start with collaborating in a community of practice focused on assessment, using protocols.

The sample timeline on the next page is provided as an example of one window into thinking about the path implementation might take.

SAMPLE TIMELINE FOR PERFORMANCE ASSESSMENT WORK

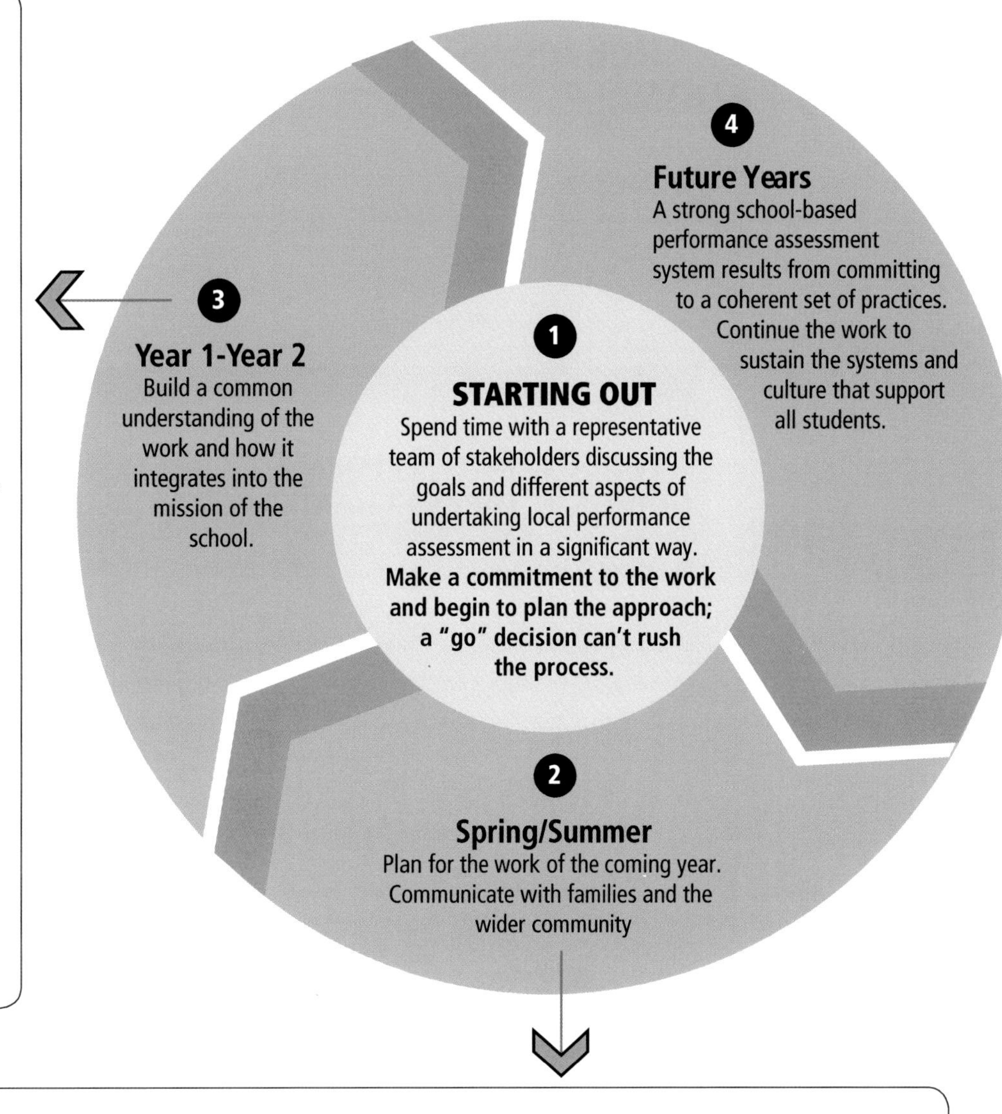

Year 1-Year 2

Teacher Role

Teachers who participated in the summer institute field test one or more common performance assessments and complete the cycle of technical quality by analyzing the results for implications for instructional practice and assessment design.

Communicate and share the work with the rest of the faculty and build their assessment literacy by looking at student or teacher work, using protocols.

Complete additional cycles of Align, Design, and Analyze and involve more people each time. Lead teams serve as a resource for teams experiencing the process for the first time.

Administrator Role

Observe the work and learn with faculty, asking what they need and observing points of confusion. Arrange for professional development or coaching as needed.

Gain input and build buy-in for shifts in school structures, policies, and culture.

Evaluate successes and challenges.

Spring/Summer

Teacher Role

Engage in a professional development and planning institute to develop assessment literacy and begin the teacher learning cycle through the aspects of technical quality: Align, Design, Analyze. During this institute, teachers work in a community of practice to design performance assessments to field-test in the fall. The institute might include all teachers or a smaller group (i.e. by discipline or grade level).

Administrator Role

Plan to create supportive structural and cultural conditions for the work. Assess current conditions and choose one or two key shifts to focus on in the first phase. Big changes might require more time and people to plan and implement. Some ideas to consider:

1. Are school assessment policies for graduation, promotion, and reporting on student progress aligned to your vision and performance assessment culture?
2. Are all students supported in learning rigorous standards such as through schedules with longer blocks of time, opportunities for student choice and out-of-school learning, and academic and social supports?
3. Do teacher teams have regular common planning time to work on defined assessment-related goals and share their efforts school-wide?
4. Is technology used to support effective teaching, learning, and assessment?

CHAPTER 1

PERFORMANCE ASSESSMENT: A FRAMEWORK AND RATIONALE

A WINDOW INTO PERFORMANCE ASSESSMENT AT FRANCIS W. PARKER CHARTER ESSENTIAL SCHOOL

by Dennis Pierce

In a darkened classroom at Francis W. Parker Charter Essential School in Devens, Massachusetts, 15-year-old Tom G. is giving a PowerPoint presentation on what he's learned in math this past semester—and how he's applied this knowledge to a project he designed.

"I can predict where the NASDAQ will be when I know where the 'Footsie' has ended up," he says, referring to the FTSE, an index of the 100 biggest companies on the London Stock Exchange.

He takes his audience through a series of slides that explain how to find the correlation between two random sets of data by using simple linear regression—pretty advanced stuff for a high school sophomore. In this case, his "audience" is just one person: his teacher, Nathan Soule, who scribbles notes on a sheet of paper as Tom is talking.

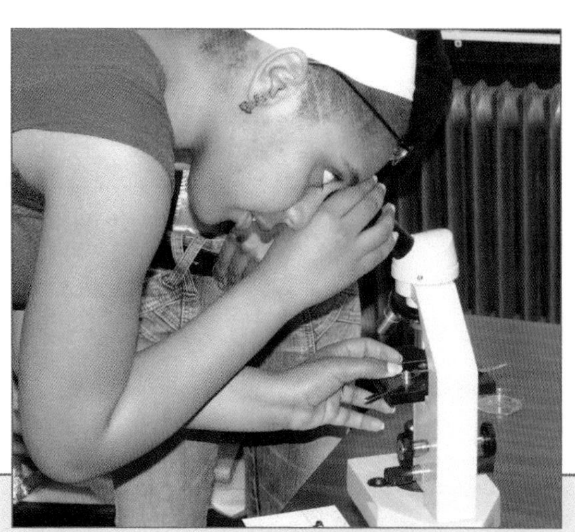

Performance Assessment gives students the chance to go deeper into their learning.

Tom is practicing for an exhibition, which the school calls a "gateway exercise," that he must complete before advancing to the next grade level—like a graduate student's oral examinations. Parker's gateway exercises are a classic example of performance-based assessments in which students show their understanding not by filling in bubbles on a standardized test but by producing actual work—an essay, a lab report, a presentation, a portfolio, or some other demonstration of competency.

Just as a driving test is a practical assessment of whether you can handle a car on the road, performance-based assessments are superior tools, their supporters say, for showing how well students have learned the higher-order thinking skills necessary in the Information Age—such as the ability to analyze, synthesize, and evaluate information.

That's obvious from watching Tom rehearse his gateway presentation at Parker Charter School. With Soule looking on, Tom describes how his gateway project stemmed from the question "How can I use math to make money?" He notes that linear regression can help analysts predict the future—which is an important skill for stockbrokers.

Soule is Tom's assessor for the gateway process. The event itself is more of a celebration than an actual assessment; all the heavy lifting has been done beforehand in class as Tom has been working on his project and discussing it with Soule. So, this practice run is held more to give Tom feedback on his presentation than to evaluate his work.

"You're going to have a slide on this part, right?" Soule asks at one point. Later, he tells Tom the presentation was really good, but a little short: 20 minutes, when it should be 30 to 45 minutes long.

Anyone watching Tom's presentation would clearly see that he understands not only how to find correlation using linear regression, but also why this knowledge is significant and how it applies outside of school.

Because performance assessment engages students in an activity that ultimately leads to a task or product that can be scored, students tend to go "way beyond the things they learn in class," Soule says. The result is a better understanding of students' skills by their teacher, but also a keener knowledge of the topic by the students themselves.

Performance assessment gives students "the chance to go deeper into their learning," says Sue Massucco, arts and humanities domain leader at Parker Charter School. "They get to know their content deeply, but they also get to activate their minds—which will last a lifetime."

When the word assessment comes up, most people think of testing. Billions of dollars are spent annually in this country on testing—U.S. students are the most tested in the world—and the success or failure of students and schools is increasingly tied to the single skill of test taking.... When we assess the growth and progress of our own children, when we assess the value of our co-workers, it's not test scores but rather character and accomplishments that are the basis of our measurement.

—Ron Berger, An Ethic of Excellence

Introduction

All students should have the opportunity to engage in meaningful work that matters and that equips them to thrive in the 21st century. Performance assessments allow educators to rethink the intersections of teaching, learning, and assessment, and to focus on deeper understanding and student learning.

The goal of this chapter is to present a framework and rationale for widening the parameters and practice of assessment to infuse performance assessments into teaching and learning at the district and school levels. In this context, performance assessment steers professional development and enhances student achievement.

Student Work Sample: 7th grade comparison between a cell and a fishing boat

DECODING THE JARGON

Defined terms, italicized on first reference in the text, are listed in alphabetical order.

Assessment literacy consists of understanding types and purposes of assessments and having the ability to apply one's technical knowledge about assessments in practice.

Common performance assessments consist of a carefully orchestrated learning plan composed of individual tasks in which a whole school, grade-level teams, or discipline-area teams work collaboratively to adapt, create, or implement tasks and rubrics, and then score student work reliably.

Performance assessments are multistep assignments with clear criteria, expectations, and processes that measure how well a student transfers knowledge and applies complex skills to create or refine an original product.

Quality Performance Assessment (QPA) is a set of practices and principles for implementing performance assessments with technical quality that requires educators to work together to align, design, and analyze performance assessments to increase student achievement and equity of outcomes.

Summative assessments determine whether or not students have mastered the standards in question, either at a classroom level, in the case of a performance assessment or exam at the end of a unit, or at the district or state level, in the case of standardized or performance assessments administered to measure the progress of an entire grade, school, or district.

Formative assessments are assessments for learning that continuously track each student's ongoing learning and mastery of target standards. Formative assessments provide the teacher with information on which students are making progress, which students need additional instruction, and which concepts are not clearly understood.

21st century skills are skills that take into account the global economy, technology, and changing workforce requirements. These skills include complex thinking, analytical skills, collaboration, computer skills, creativity, media literacy, and cross-cultural skills.

A Framework for Quality Performance Assessment Systems

The *Quality Performance Assessment* (QPA) Framework guides teachers and administrators on how to design and implement performance assessment systems with technical quality. The QPA approach focuses on performance assessment because performance assessment allows us to see whether students are able to apply their knowledge and skills. The QPA Framework addresses three factors of success for developing and sustaining performance assessment systems: (1) the technical quality of the assessments; (2) a robust professional development model to train district and school educators; and (3) leadership support (Tung & Stazesky, 2010).

QPA DEFINITION OF PERFORMANCE ASSESSMENT:

Performance assessments are multistep assignments with clear criteria, expectations, and processes that measure how well a student transfers knowledge and applies complex skills to create or refine an original product.

The QPA Framework elements include both the content and process for designing and evaluating performance assessments. The set of processes described in the framework is designed for development over time and is cyclical in nature. Many aspects of the QPA Framework can be integrated into an existing student assessment system without a comprehensive overhaul. The graphic illustrates how the elements form a cycle of teaching and learning, with student learning at the center.

Students and teacher build frame based on calculated dimensions.

QPA Framework

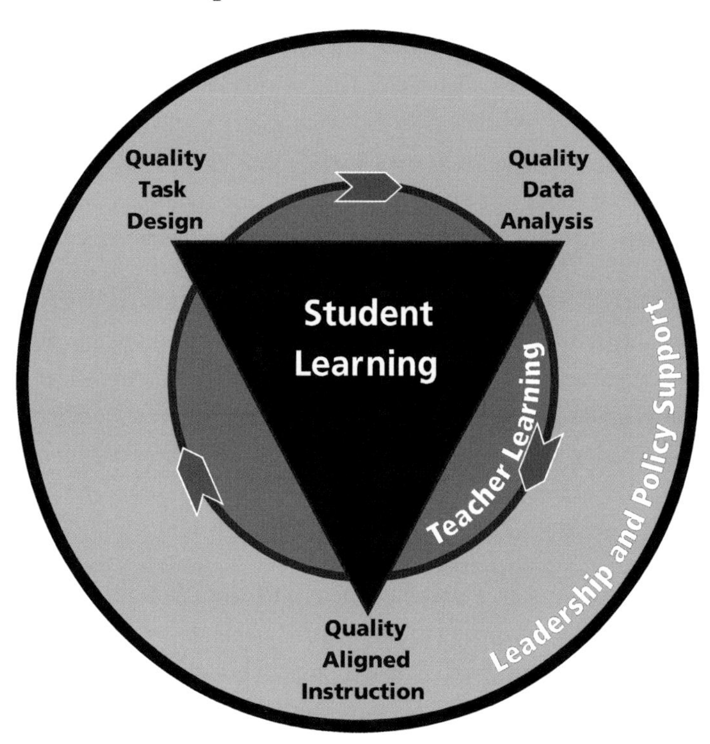

Student learning, at the center of the framework graphic, is the goal of this iterative cycle. QPA focuses on meaningful, student-centered learning, incorporating complex skills and content that are transferable to new situations. Learning is assessed in multiple modes and engages students through opportunities for ownership and decision making in real-world situations. The learning process supports college and career readiness by embedding *21st century skills.*

The three elements at the vertices of the triangle combine to create performance assessments with technical quality.* As assessment-literate practitioners cycle through the framework, assessments become aligned to standards, reflect high-level instruction in the classroom, and produce meaningful evidence of student learning resulting in the following aspects of technical quality:

- *Validity* ensures that learning assessments are clearly aligned to standards and that they measure student performance on the intended standards.
- *Reliable* refers to inter-rater reliability, where a group of teachers (or scorers) come to an agreement on how to interpret a rating and corresponding performance descriptors and score student work consistently.
- *Free of bias* means the assessment does not disadvantage the performance of certain groups of students.
- *Sufficiency* describes a combination of related, validated assessments that provide enough assessment evidence to accurately infer the level of proficiency of a student on a standard.

* The idea of using a triangle to arrange the criteria for technical quality was inspired by the three vertices of the National Research Council Assessment Triangle, which connects Cognition, Observation, and Interpretation (National Research Council, 2001).

Quality aligned instruction means instruction and assessment practices are interwoven and aligned to each other and to standards. All students need instruction that is accessible to their diverse learning strengths and needs based on a common vision for student success articulated clearly in standards and practice. This set of standards is based on appropriate national, state, district, and school standards that prepare students to be college and career ready. Effective instructional practice provides students with the opportunity to master these standards, and aligned assessments allow them to demonstrate what they know and are able to do.

Quality task design begins with clarity about what students at each grade level should know and be able to do. A common understanding among faculty about appropriate content and cognitive complexity in the grades they teach and in adjacent grades guides the design of prompts and scoring tools. Documentation of the assessment design and a validation process build awareness of expectations, allow appropriate performance levels to be set at each grade level, and help make the assessment accessible to all students.

Quality data analysis involves working in teams to examine teacher and student assessment work and score data to ensure that assessments are valid, reliable, free of bias, and provide sufficient evidence of learning. Conclusions from the data analysis provide information to practitioners about whether or not they are in fact teaching what is being assessed and whether patterns of student demonstration of mastery are equitable. Incorporating what they learn into practice enables teachers to plan future instruction and assessment accordingly.

Teacher learning in professional communities of practice, as represented in the cycle of teacher learning in the framework graphic, occurs when teachers engage in professional dialogue about aligned instruction, task design, and analysis of student work. Collaboration creates a synergy and provides the level of quality required for teacher and student learning through performance assessment. This process fosters ongoing conversations focused on expectations, requirements for proficiency, and practices teachers must implement to assist all students to demonstrate mastery. As it deepens professional knowledge and skills, this collaborative work requires a cultural shift that takes time and trust. Over time, teachers speak openly about their formerly private practice and reap the rewards of sharing their own teaching and their students' learning.

Leadership and policy support are represented by the outer circle of the framework. Support from teachers, families, community members, and school district officials is essential for the successful adoption of performance assessments. The more all stakeholders participate in building the foundation of a QPA system, the more school leaders will be able to draw upon this base of support in the future. The need for such support makes it especially important to field test, fine tune, and scale up the performance assessment system slowly, particularly if there are high stakes outcomes such as linking student performance to graduation and promotion or to teacher evaluation. District and school leadership can build support and sustainability for performance assessments through embedding them in graduation requirements, building performance assessments into the district's formative assessment system, and developing a web-based bank of validated common performance tasks that schools and teachers can access. Leaders also support the work by cultivating a collaborative school culture that establishes a comfortable and safe environment and teacher leadership that builds buy-in for the work.

Reclaiming a Broader Vision of Assessment

The advent of the Common Core State Standards requires a rethinking of the historical notions of how to assess student learning. The Common Core places a greater emphasis on knowledge and skills that are not as easily assessed through traditional, paper-and-pencil standardized tests. They "are designed to be robust and relevant to the real world, reflecting the knowledge and skills that our young people need for success in college and careers" (Council of Chief State School Officers [CSSO], 2010). These new standards include a stronger emphasis on critical and higher-order thinking skills, understanding complex texts, use of evidence, ability to engage in rigorous conversations, and real-life application of new concepts learned.

Teacher providing feedback

The Common Core reflects an increasing awareness that the tests of the future need to prepare students for their futures in college, career, civic participation, and living in a multicultural and global world. Yet, David Conley (2008), a professor at the University of Oregon and an expert on high school to college transition, notes: "For the most part, state high-stakes standardized tests require students to recall or recognize fragmented and isolated bits of information.... The tests rarely require students to apply their learning and almost never require students to exhibit proficiency in higher forms of cognition" (p. 12). According to one study, college faculty noted that first-year college students lack critical thinking and problem solving when they enroll (Lundell, Higbee, Hipp, & Copeland, 2005). This notion is reinforced by the Alliance for Excellent Education (2011): "Tasks and questions that ask students to apply their knowledge to solve complex problems, work in teams, and effectively communicate their knowledge and analysis are completely overlooked by most current statewide, standardized assessments" (p. 7).

Newmann, Bryk, and Nagaoka (2001) argue that any sound student assessment system should be based on a vision of what students should learn and be able to do. The "contemporary demands of productive work, responsible citizenship, and successful management of personal affairs extend well beyond giving correct answers and following proper procedures for the work traditionally assigned in school" (p. 13). These educators propose that any student assessment and accountability system must have as its foundation a conception of teaching and learning that is framed around students using their minds well in all aspects of living in a pluralistic, democratic, and multicultural society. These researchers pose three characteristics of "authentic intellectual work" (p. 2):

- Construction of knowledge that involves interpretation, evaluation, analysis, synthesis, and organization of prior knowledge or solving new problems or gaining new understandings;
- Disciplined inquiry, or using prior knowledge to gain in-depth understanding and communicate that knowledge and understanding in multiple ways;
- Knowledge that has "utilitarian, aesthetic, or personal value" (p. 15) beyond school.

In order to adequately assess students' mastery of the complex skills embedded in the Common Core and those enunciated by Conley (2007) and Newmann et al. (2001), additional assessments that measure students' proficiency over this new set of knowledge, skills, and dispositions are necessary. Increasingly, the role of performance assessments in school, district, state, and federal accountability is being considered as a strong measure of student learning for the more complex higher-order thinking skills required in the Common Core. This new thinking about assessment is in line with that of industry leaders, who indicate that successful preparation for the workplace and further education requires performance-based demonstrations and applications of knowledge (Kiker, 2007).

WHAT IS COLLEGE- AND CAREER-READY WRITING?

by Olivia Biagetti

As a student and writing tutor at Colby College, I am trained to navigate the college writing process, reorienting my peers when their papers' logic and coherence go astray. I have noticed that my tutees' greatest missteps occur when they try to synthesize primary and secondary sources to build arguments, particularly when they must complete career-based and research-heavy writing tasks such as briefs or proposals. My peers' difficulties with these assignments, however, are symptoms of a much larger issue: Students arrive at college without the skills needed to access and apply informational texts.

In response to students' difficulties with text comprehension, the Common Core standards in ELA place stronger emphasis on multidisciplinary and informational reading and writing. As the new standards are implemented, K-12 educators can visualize the challenges faced by college students attempting the leap from high school to postsecondary writing without a strong understanding of how to apply informational texts and present a clear argument to an authentic audience. These experiences reveal specific areas of writing that teachers can target to align with the Common Core, and also ensure their students are prepared for life after graduation.

An illustrative tutoring session began when a peer arrived at the writing center with an environmental policy brief. The brief was intended to present background facts about a current environmental law, argue for how courts should interpret the law, and propose a new application of the law. After extensive research, the student understood the content of his brief, but struggled to write the paper because he had never dealt with the task's format. He had sailed through high school writing only standard analytical essays for his English class, and had never encountered the career-preparing writing prompts assigned by college professors. We walked through each step together, outlining his brief and inserting his thoughtful evidence at every opportune turn. Once my tutee understood how to accurately organize his research, he could convey his ideas with force and clarity.

Professors also ask students to compose memoranda, lab reports, proposals, research papers, abstracts, and other assignments usually alien to high school curricula. These assignments are examples of performance assessments, or real-world tasks that develop a student's 21st century skill set. While tutors can do their best to rescue students during performance assessments, as I did with my tutee, students would benefit from completing these assessments in high school under the professional guidance of teachers.

This tutee's experience points to larger issues confronting students as they transition from high school to higher education and careers. The tutee lacked command of the format and obligations of a career-oriented task, hampering his ability to muster his knowledge in the most convincing way. My hope is that as teachers use performance assessments to implement the Common Core, these gaps will be narrowed, and students will arrive on campus better prepared for the cognitive demands that await them in college.

Using Performance Assessments to Support Student and Teacher Learning

There is a growing body of research and experiential evidence to indicate that the use of performance assessments is linked to building higher-order skills, as well as to improving classroom instruction and student outcomes. Performance assessments require students to demonstrate complex knowledge and skills, and they improve instruction by providing teachers with better information about student progress (Goldschmidt, Martinez, Niemi, & Baker, 2007; Pellegrino, Chudowsky, & Glaser, 2001; Stemler, Sternberg, Grigorenko, Jarvin, & Sharpes, 2009; Wood, Darling-Hammond, Neill, & Roschewski, 2007). Darling-Hammond and Rustique-Forrester (2005) came to similar conclusions—performance assessment improved instruction, largely due to the embedding of assessment in the curriculum, the immediate availability of results, and the authenticity of the tasks asked of students.

Grant Wiggins, in his 2006 article "Healthier Testing Made Easy: The Idea of Authentic Assessment," points out that, with good feedback built into the learning process, students are better able to transfer their learning effectively. "Assessment should determine whether you can use your learning, not merely whether you learned stuff," (para. 11) he writes. As a soccer coach, Wiggins says he learned the hard way about the importance of designing assessments that teach students how to transfer their skills to new contexts.

> The practice drills did not seem to transfer into fluid, flexible, and fluent game performance. It often appeared, in fact, as if all the work in practice were for naught, as players either wandered around purposelessly or reacted only to the most obvious immediate needs.
>
> The epiphany came during a game, from the mouth of a player. In my increasing frustration, I started yelling, "Give and go!" "Three on two!" "Use it, use it—all the drills we worked on!" At that point, the player stopped dribbling in the middle of the field and yelled back, "I can't see it now! The other team won't line up like the drill for me!"
>
> That's both a clear picture of the problem and the road to the solution: too many sideline drills of an isolated skill, and not enough testing of it; too great a gap between what the simplified drill was teaching and testing and what the performance demands. (para. 13-15)

There is a place to teach drills and isolated skills, but students will flounder in the coming decades without the experience of applying them in real-world situations. Learning the same content in different educational settings prepares people to transfer their newly acquired skills to different workplace contexts (Bransford, Brown, & Cocking, 1999). Students need the experience of applying the knowledge that they've learned in the context of new settings or problems.

Performance assessments of technical quality represent an opportunity for students to demonstrate transfer in an authentic task.

When teachers develop *common performance assessments,* the process generates the kind of feedback that is crucial to improving teacher learning and student achievement. To develop common performance assessments effectively, teachers must collaborate to explore: how students best learn content and skills aligned to standards; how to design assessments that elicit evidence of student competency; and how to reliably interpret student work. Participating in professional dialogue about aligned instruction, assessment design, and collaborative analysis of student work leads to *assessment literacy* and promotes the level of quality required for learning through student performances.

Teachers cannot accomplish the challenging work of developing performance assessments and learning to use them to make decisions about curriculum and instruction in isolation. Teachers and administrators need to have conversations around assessment. Teachers need opportunities to communicate ideas, express and debate opinions, and collaboratively determine what constitutes quality assessment practices and levels of proficiency. In his 1999 article, Stiggins suggests that teachers possess assessment literacy when they understand "the difference between sound and unsound practices in assessment, evaluation, and communication" (p. 17). The conversations that take place among teachers while building assessment literacy are critical to improving teaching and learning in our schools.

Ongoing, classroom-based assessments that generate timely teacher feedback permit students to reflect on, refine, and improve their work. In this process—called *formative assessment*—students learn as needs arise on a daily, or even hourly, basis. Assessment experts from the Forum for Education and Democracy note ongoing, formative assessments, including performance assessments, can be "responsive to emerging student needs and enable fast and specific teacher response, something that standardized examinations with long lapses between administration and results cannot do" (Wood et al., 2007, p. 4). Performance assessments can provide meaningful, real-time information for students, teachers, parents, and administrators, and can be a springboard for improving teacher practice.

Students learn more during performance assessments as they adjust their approach to a problem and make corrections in response to targeted feedback from their instructors or peers. A writing conference, for example, prompts a student to revise an essay; peer feedback offers a student a new strategy to consider a mathematics problem; and a rehearsal yields a successful performance of a play. This assessment *for* learning differs from traditional *summative assessments* that function as a separate measurement *of* learning.

Giving performance assessment a major role in a local assessment system will improve both student learning and teacher performance. Further, Wood et al. (2007) suggest that the benefits of assessment systems with embedded performance assessment include greater teacher buy-in, increased teacher collaboration, and increased capacity to make midcourse corrections based on formative data. When teachers are engaged as designers of performance assessments and skilled assessors of their students' performance, the impact on curriculum and instruction can be profound. By building school-wide assessment literacy, QPA lays the foundation for strong local assessment practice, creating a bridge to meaningful learning, and college and career readiness.

Conclusion

QPA is an approach to teaching and learning where teachers develop formative and summative performance assessments. Teachers use the results of these assessments to guide their daily instruction and larger revisions of curriculum, and to make high-stakes decisions related to graduation and promotion. Every activity or assignment teachers create is connected and aligned to the learning goals and standards of the curriculum. Students have the opportunity to express what they know and are able to do in a variety of ways. They are assigned rich and engaging work that requires them to demonstrate their understanding of important ideas.

How is this approach to assessment different from what has been done in many schools in the past? First, performance assessment measures the complex higher-order thinking skills that are increasingly paramount in a global and technological world. Second, assessment informs instruction in immediate ways. QPA is an ongoing approach to assessment that makes explicit use of all of the ways teachers receive information about what their students are learning. Third, with QPA, teachers pay close attention to the information they receive and use it to make adjustments in curriculum and instruction. Finally, performance assessment enables our increasingly diverse student population to demonstrate their competency in multiple, real-world ways that they will encounter in college and career, which can result in reductions in achievement gaps and dramatic gains in student learning of 21st century skills.

Fenway High School: Senior Position Paper

At Fenway High School, a diverse urban public high school with 300 students in Boston, Massachusetts, juniors and seniors are expected to complete a variety of performance assessments designed to prepare them for the world beyond school. Eleventh graders complete the Junior Review, a reflection on a series of assessments demonstrating mastery of their benchmark standards collected in a portfolio. Juniors who show readiness for senior year are inducted into the Senior Institute. During their senior year, students are again assessed on both academic and nonacademic criteria to determine their readiness for the next step—college and careers. Beyond traditional measures, students show that they are able to meet more authentic demands through a range of performance assessments, which include presenting a portfolio of work, completing a six-week internship, the college application process, and the Senior Position Paper.

As part of an overall examination of the assessment policy, faculty members took a critical look at ways to better assess and support the senior paper. In the assessment, all seniors write a paper that demonstrates their ability to argue their position and write effectively on a topic of their choice related to a person or an event. Learning goals for the position paper are aligned to the Common Core standards for English language arts as well as to the Fenway Habits of Mind—perspective, evidence, connection, relevance, and supposition. The task calls for careful thought and effort, as students are assessed both on what they say—that is, the quality of their ideas—as well as how they say it—that is, the quality of their writing. To graduate, seniors must conduct relevant research, use appropriate citations, revise and edit their work, present and defend their views on a key issue, write persuasively, and use appropriate voice.

During freshman year, teachers and staff at Fenway begin to lay the groundwork for the knowledge and skills students must master by building performance tasks, including portfolios, into their curricula. By the time students reach senior year, they have already spent three years fine-tuning their ability to think critically and reflectively about their learning. They have edited and revised pieces for portfolios, which provide evidence of their learning and progress. By senior year, students have had ample opportunity not only to show what they know and can do, but to reflect on their own learning in order to improve.

Graduates should be able to think critically and reflectively.

As a team, teachers regularly revisit the criteria and expectations for a proficient position paper, review guidelines for helping students accomplish that goal, and examine the directions to the students for clarity. Common rubrics support this work and shape teacher practice and student expectations at each grade level by fostering common understandings. Grade level expectations are further solidified through the creation of anchor papers, in which teachers at Fenway document evidence of what student work should look like at each performance level on the rubric. These anchor papers serve as models for students as they embark on their own senior journeys, so that they have a clear understanding of their target and can demonstrate mastery and meet the graduation benchmark.

In a collaborative review of the anchor papers, Fenway teachers opted to increase the level of proficiency required on the senior position paper. The proficiency requirement is evident in the expectation that students revise their senior position paper until it reflects a standard of quality that merits graduation. Teachers at Fenway have worked to align their instruction to the new standard for this assessment and, as one teacher reflected, to "vertically align the quality of the senior position papers students write each year in humanities to ensure that the quality of the senior position paper is at the level required for college success."

Part of this process included embedding a QPA Common Task as part of a larger unit on the history of slavery in the United States in a 10th-grade humanities class. The unit and task connect students to the present by requiring that they take a position on reparations for slavery. This task requires research, engaging in the writing process, and considering an authentic audience and purpose for the writing. This 10th-grade paper is one of many position papers students write throughout their four years at Fenway as they prepare for the high standards required by the senior position paper.

FENWAY HIGH SCHOOL POSITION PAPER TASK SUMMARY

- **Topic:** Reparations: Should the United States government make reparations to the descendants of slaves?
- **Genre:** Argumentative or persuasive writing: The goal of the position paper is to use evidence to convince the reader that your position for or against government reparations is correct.
- **Evidence sources:**
  - Text: At least three sources from the provided research packet.
  - Text: At least two articles found through individual research.
- **Audience:** Members of the United States Congress.
- **Time frame:** Three weeks for research and completing the writing process, including multiple drafts and peer and teacher editing.

Student success in this process requires commitment and considerable effort. Students and their parents must understand the value of creating portfolios, conducting presentations of learning, and revising student work multiple times. Fenway High School has demonstrated that this work can be explicitly linked to college- or career-ready outcomes so that it is a worthy investment of students' time and energy, as well as parents' support.

"For other classes at college where there were required presentations, or exhibitions, I excelled in those classes because at Fenway the science fair, or your Junior Review, or your senior projects, all of these required you to stand in front of an audience and talk about what you had learned, to put it into practice in front of a group of people who are assessing you." *—Fenway Graduate (Gagnon, 2010, p. 27).*

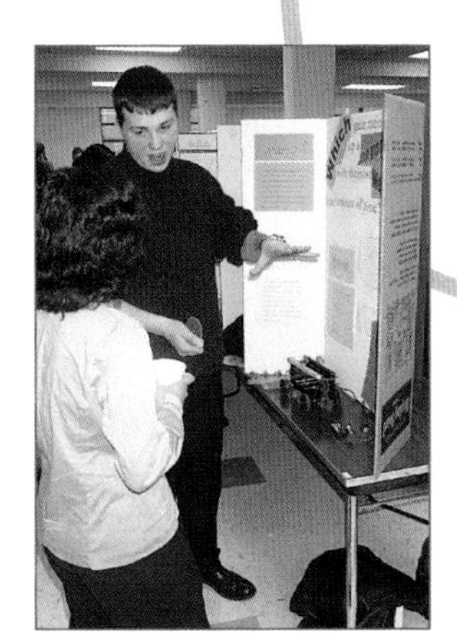

Student presents his work at the Fenway science fair

REPARATIONS POSITION PAPER TENTH-GRADE STUDENT WORK SAMPLE

The task of sorting out whom to pay for the reparations is too great. As Zinmeister writes in the article "Reparations Should Not Be Paid To The Descendants of African American Slaves", "...the identities of 'slave' and 'slaveholder' have blurred and melted away over generations to the point where it is now impossible to say who would pay and who would receive in the account of slavery" (3). African-Americans that do not know specifically who their slaves' ancestors are would have to complete the long and expensive process of tracing back their ancestry to slavery. In order to pay reparations, billions of dollars and hours of time would have to be spent for all investigations to identify who should receive the payments. People would need to discuss a plan over who would receive reparations, how would the payments change for recipients who have both slave and slaveholder ancestors, how much would reparations cost, who would pay them, in what form would they be paid (scholarships, welfare, etc.), over what time period would they be paid, and many more questions. With all this discussion, there is bound to be disagreements, further delaying payment to descendants until a compromise is made. The task of designing the reparation system undercuts the actual value of the reparation payments.

CHAPTER 2

ALIGN: INSTRUCTION AND ASSESSMENT

As I was reading about statewide assessment, I noticed that every element of quality performance assessment on a larger scale could be used in my classroom and with my colleagues. I started to think more carefully about the why behind what we were doing (in QPA and at Parker), rather than just the what.

—QPA Network Teacher Reflection

Japanese Rice Field

In the Aomori district north of Tokyo, Japan, the farmers of Inakadate present a model of the way a school community might develop a plan for aligned instruction. Each year, the town's 8,000 farmers and residents, working together, create exquisite, large-scale thematic works of art in the rice fields. In the beginning, a few farmers and residents would create simple rice field art, but each year the work has generated more interest and become increasingly complex. With years of experience, these agricultural artists design detailed images and then countless volunteers turn out to plant green-, purple-, and yellow-leafed rice. With the seeds arranged according to a computerized design, the colors create the pattern that brings the images to life. One year the fields depicted legendary warrior-monk Benkei and the warrior Ushiwaka-maru; another year, Napolean and a Sengoku-period warrior, both on horseback. Travelers enjoy the rice paddy art all summer. In September, the rice is harvested and plans begin for the next year's art (Campbell, 2010).

Throughout this guide, we refer to unpublished documentation and artifacts shared with QPA by educators, including validation feedback, PD evaluations, teacher reflections, personal communications, and teacher and student work. Because they are unpublished, they do not appear in the References section. For further information about these types of documentation, please contact QPA directly.

Just as the residents of Inakadate successfully plan the creation of a huge and elegant work of public art, school districts and schools beginning aligned instruction will achieve results with a clear plan agreed to by the whole community. The farmers of Inakadate plant with a specific end in mind. Similarly, aligning instruction begins by creating a vision of the graduate. Having the desired outcome in mind focuses the process of *backward design*.

PROCESS

The plan school leaders and teachers use as they align instruction is outlined in the following steps:

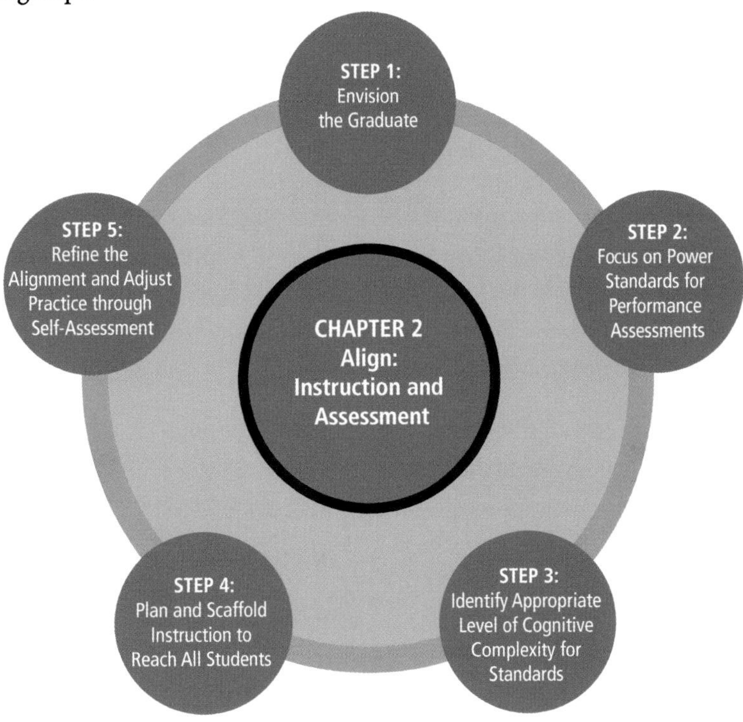

DECODING THE JARGON

Defined terms, italicized on first reference in the text, are listed in alphabetical order.

Backward design, is a way to plan curriculum with the end in mind, taking into consideration performance assessments, standards, level of rigor, and learning goals. In backward design, teachers identify the desired standards, skills, and habits they want students to master; create the assessment that will best measure whether students have reached proficiency; and then plan the instruction and curriculum that will help students optimally achieve the target standards (Wiggins and McTighe, 2005).

Depth of Knowledge (DOK) framework, is a model that allows educators to analyze the cognitive level, or depth of content understanding and complexity of thinking, implied by a learning goal or required to complete an assessment task (Webb, 1997).

Enduring understandings are important ideas that have lasting value beyond the classroom and are central to a discipline. As learners make deeper meaning of these enduring understandings they also become equipped to apply the learning to new contexts (Wiggins & McTighe, 2005).

Essential questions are overarching, inquiry-based questions that are used to frame the central understandings and content of a unit of study or performance assessment. Essential questions allow students to reflect and debate larger issues and themes and to thoughtfully uncover deeper meaning through exploration of possible answers.

Formative assessments are assessments for learning that continuously track each student's ongoing learning and mastery of target standards. Formative assessments provide the teacher with information on which students are making progress, which students need additional instruction, and which concepts are not clearly understood.

Habits are the critical skills, knowledge, and dispositions (i.e., the learner's feelings, attitudes, values, and interests) that give teachers information about how students approach learning. Schools refer to these habits in a variety of ways, for example: Habits of Mind, Habits of the Graduate, or Habits of Learning.

Power standards are the most essential standards selected to guide assessment work (Aimsworth, 2003).

Summative assessments determine whether or not students have mastered the standards in question, either at a classroom level, in the case of a performance assessment or exam at the end of a unit; or, at the district or state level, in the case of a standardized or performance assessments administered to measure the progress of an entire grade, school, or district.

Understanding by Design, developed by Grant Wiggins and Jay McTighe, is a three-stage structure designed to lead teachers through a process that focuses on designing curriculum, beginning with the student learning goals in mind (Wiggins, 1989; Wiggins & McTighe, 2005).

Universal Design for Learning, developed by David Rose and Jenna Gravel (2009), is a set of guidelines for tailoring curriculum to meet the needs of all students, including those with special needs, and to give them opportunities to demonstrate their learning in a variety of ways.

Introduction

This chapter is devoted to the process of aligning instructional practices to the principles of performance assessment. It begins with the school-level concepts of envisioning a school's graduates, identifying the most essential standards, and determining the level of rigor for standards. The second half focuses on the teacher's role in aligning instruction, providing tools and checkpoints, for the process, especially as it applies to literacy.

STEP 1

Envision the Graduate

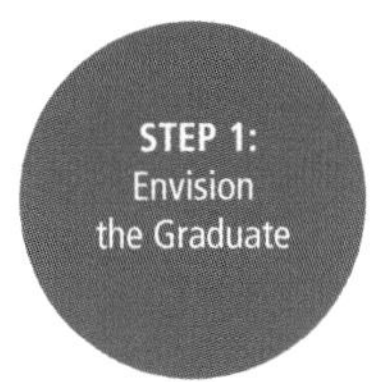

As a faculty, identify the understandings, skills, and habits graduates should develop and be able to demonstrate when they graduate (from elementary, middle, or high school), and align them to the school's vision.

> "I think [my school] taught me a lot more than just basic curriculum. It really taught me how to learn." —*Student from QPA Network School*

As an early step in planning performance assessments that are curriculum embedded, a teacher or team of teachers determines the most critical standards to assess and creates a final assessment that fits those standards. For example, a team of social studies teachers plans to assess standards on government content knowledge and communication skills. The teachers decide to end a six-week unit on government with a mock election and a political speech. During this planning process, initial questions include: What understandings, skills, and *habits* will students demonstrate by successfully completing these assessments? What will an excellent mock election and an excellent written speech look like? Given these assessments, what is the appropriate sequence for the whole unit? Every step of the unit—every lesson, reading, mini-lecture, and activity—should prepare students for success in the final, *summative assessments*. Much of the ongoing work of the unit will be building blocks for these summative assessments—research, drafts of writing, and practice performances.

The *Understanding by Design* framework developed by Grant Wiggins and Jay McTighe (2005) is a useful structure for creating aligned instruction. The three-stage structure guides teachers through a process that focuses on teaching and assessing for student understanding, on the ability to transfer learning to new situations, and on the *backward design* of curriculum with the student learning goals in mind. The process is embedded in the Common Performance Assessment Curriculum Planning Template (see Tool #8).

In Stage 1 of Understanding by Design, teachers decide on their long-term goals for the curriculum unit: they describe what *enduring understandings* students will need to have, which open-ended, active essential questions students will explore, and what knowledge and skills students will gain. These enduring understandings and essential questions that frame the performance assessment allow students to make deeper meaning and equip them with the ability to apply their learning to new contexts.

Once the understandings, essential questions, skills, and habits have been defined, teachers begin planning performance assessments. In Stage 2, teachers produce assessments that motivate students to provide evidence of their learning of the target understandings, skills, and habits. The assessments that teachers create offer students opportunities to work with scientific materials, analyze maps and primary sources, communicate using rhetoric and argumentation, and understand the tools of the given discipline. Teachers also develop ongoing *formative assessments,* such as reflective journals and teacher and peer critiques, which give students teacher feedback and opportunities to reflect on their own work, and which supply teachers with information on students' progress and gaps. "Over time, the student masters progressive levels of prerequisite learning that accumulate to mastery of the standard. Ongoing classroom assessment must track that progress in order to know, at any point in time, what comes next in the learning," according to Rick Stiggins and Rick Dufour (2009, p.641). Tracking progress permits the teacher to adjust instruction in order to validate student learning and to allow students to recognize their own progress and take responsibility for the next learning steps.

In Stage 3, teachers plan instruction aligned to the original learning goals as well as to the planned performance assessments. In a classroom with aligned instruction and assessment, teachers use resources beyond the textbook that fit the goals. They shape learning to be constructed and/or experienced by the student and respect different learning styles. Just as rice is cultivated all summer under the careful and watchful eyes of the farmers and community members of Inakadate, teaching and learning will take place during the entire unit under the guidance of the teacher, who strategically cultivates gradual release of responsibility to the students. The final performance assessment should celebrate the achievements of the students—the bounty of a carefully cultivated harvest.

At the Boston Arts Academy, a 430-student high school in Boston, Massachusetts, school leaders start with the end in mind. Decisions relating to students' lives are predicated on the school's vision for their graduates. The academy's handbook states its mission: "The Boston Arts Academy prepares a diverse community of aspiring artist-scholars to be successful in their college or professional careers and to be engaged members of a democratic society." The meaning and importance of this vision is encapsulated for students and faculty in the school's Habits of the Graduate: *Refine, Invent, Connect,* and *Own*. These young artists are treated as scholars, and they are educated in a purposeful way to serve their community as active, productive citizens.

EXAMPLE

BOSTON ARTS ACADEMY HABITS OF THE GRADUATE

Refine

Have I conveyed my message?
What are my strengths and weaknesses?

Invent

What makes this work inventive?
Do I take risks and push myself?

Connect

Who is the audience and how does the work connect?
What is the context?

Own

Am I proud of the work I am doing?
What do I need to be successful?

The importance of the habits to the school is exemplified in the senior grant project, in which students apply their scholarship, artistic credentials, and contributions as citizens to write a formal grant proposal. Several of these proposals are funded each year; that prospect impels seniors to produce their best work. Students begin the research for these grant proposals in their junior year. The stage is set for this culminating activity early on as underclassmen witness the success of the graduating seniors. The project is carefully designed, with each student expected to adhere to strict grant proposal guidelines and deadlines. As part of the proposal, students contact organizations or programs in the community and write detailed descriptions of their role in the community as well as biographies of the leaders of those programs. For example, one academy theater major proposed to lead teen women in improvisation. She wrote the following summary:

> "Fierce Girls of the Future is a one-week program that focuses on the empowerment and advancement of young teen women in society. I will lead five day-long workshops at the Boston Area Health Education Center, where young girls around Boston will learn about preventing and dealing with [negative] images pertaining to women through improvisational theater and present their findings in local schools, organizations, and community centers."

Students also describe the community they choose to serve, why they are serving that particular community, and how the proposal will help them grow as artists, scholars, and citizens. This reflection connects students to the school's mission and habits.

The young woman explained her motivation for working with teen girls in Boston:

> "For my senior grant project, I decided to work with girls throughout Boston between the ages of 13 and 18. I chose to work with young women because currently women are not as highly regarded as men, and I want to change this misfortune. . . . I want to empower girls at a young age so they can grow up to be successful and prominent in their future. I want to be a guide that will show girls that their image should be a reflection of themselves as opposed to the reflections of the society."

Along with the written proposal, students submit an updated resume, a timeline for the project, a budget, and appendices with supporting materials.

VISION OF THE GRADUATE PROTOCOL

The Vision of the Graduate Protocol (see Tool #39) breaks down the complicated process of creating a vision of the graduate for a school faculty. In this two-hour workshop, charts are posted at separate stations labeled with guiding questions and drawings representing the head, heart, hands, feet, and eyes of a student. Initially, each participant responds in writing to the question "What should a graduate from our school know, understand, and be able to do?" Those responses are posted. Then the teams rotate among the stations, read the previous teams' responses, build on existing comments using symbols, add ideas, and pose questions. The teams return to their initial station, synthesize responses, and post their ideas.

Participants then conduct a Gallery Walk, take notes, and leave sticky notes with "Wows" (impressive ideas) or "Wonders" (ideas that make you think or raise questions). The entire group reconvenes, discusses, and records the answers to the questions below:

1. **What did you notice?**
2. **What seems important?**
3. **Do our ideas promote equity in our schools?**
4. **Do our ideas align with what we know about teaching and learning?**
5. **How do you hope the information will be used?**
6. **What worked about the process, and what didn't work so well?**

Finally, the group completes a chart describing what needs to happen, who needs to be involved, a time scale, location, and resources needed, making sure to consider a list of questions, including:

1. **How coherent is our vision at this moment? What will it take to make it readable and understandable?**
2. **How can we tell if the vision is embedded in all the work of the school?**

This workshop sets the stage for schools to begin the process of thinking about performance assessment and the alignment of instruction and assessment with their vision for their graduates.

Boston Arts Academy tries to understand their graduates' postsecondary education needs and then refine its curriculum to suit those needs. Another QPA Network School in Boston that demonstrates alignment of their instruction, assessment system, and goals for students to succeed after graduation is Fenway High School. The Educational Policy Improvement Center included Fenway in a survey of 38 exemplary high schools from urban, suburban, and rural communities serving populations of traditionally underrepresented groups. Conley and a team of researchers arranged two-day site visits, collecting data, observing in classrooms, and conducting interviews.

Conley (2008) found that successful high schools "strove to align course expectations, assignments, goals, and activities vertically across grades 9–12, using a set of college readiness standards as the reference point" (p. 3). Conley's team found that Fenway exemplified the qualities of a college-going culture and embedded college readiness standards of content knowledge, cognitive strategies, and self-management skills in their curriculum. For example, Fenway students are required to complete a 30-hour per week internship during the second semester of the senior year. During the internship, students take a seminar at the school on Monday afternoons; undertake a large project at the internship site; complete a weekly log; and create a senior portfolio documenting their work (Conley, 2010). Fenway seniors also take a class that teaches them professional skills such as resume and cover-letter writing, and role playing.

A District's Approach: Aligning Instruction to Habits of Learning

In the Pentucket Regional School District in West Newbury, Massachusetts, five Habits of Learning—*thinking, communication, collaboration, independence, and creative exploration*—are an integral part of curriculum and instruction throughout the district. These habits are the critical skills and dispositions—the feelings, attitudes, values, and interests possessed by the learner—that give teachers information about how students approach learning. The habits provide students at all grade levels with a deeper understanding of content and prepare them with strategies to apply their learning to new situations. The Habits of Learning are used by the district as an entry point for aligned instruction and assessment.

District-wide performance assessments of the habits in fourth, sixth, eighth, and eleventh grades took place for the first time in the 2010–2011 school year. Students reflected on the integration of habits in their courses throughout the school year and then prepared portfolios, a collection of work samples, that demonstrated how they had used the habits throughout their courses. Student presentations varied in length, audience size, and preparation according to grade level.

During the school year, juniors at Pentucket Regional High School met monthly in small groups with faculty advisors to self-assess their progress. In preparation for the presentations, teachers and district leaders developed common rubrics to assess students' demonstrations of habits. Students practiced their presentations using the common rubrics as a guide. At the end of the year, juniors presented their portfolios to a panel of parents, teachers, administrators, and community members. These 20-minute capstone presentations play an important role in the district's graduation requirements.

Student presents final project

During his presentation, a junior at the high school described his outlook on the habit of communication:

> "It's listening, it's observing and it's becoming better through observing other people present. [In history class,] we had seven groups to observe and to watch before us...Ultimately, [we realized] they did a lot of slideshow and a lot of fact-based information and that didn't engage the audience at all...We wanted to engage the audience. We made a slide show and we posed questions to the audience throughout the entire slide show."

As a long-term goal, the district aims to have all teachers embed the habits in instruction and use formative assessments to inform practice. One Pentucket High School teacher remarked that using the Habits of Learning during instruction helped students improve their performance, thus demonstrating the power of performance assessment to function as assessment for learning.

> "Once students were introduced to the project, they were asked to consider how they could improve their creative exploration habits through the... assignment. Midway through, they again used the rubric to reflect on their progress. Finally, at the end, as part of their reflection, they evaluated themselves according to the rubric. The teachers were pleased with the result, as it was clear that the rubrics were helpful in directing students to push their thinking."

Students who use rubrics to reflect on their progress and observe and critique their peers' work have clear understandings of what it means to be proficient and have opportunities to revise and improve their work. This practice of student reflection on progress in relation to the rubric can lead to more equitable outcomes when students who might be the first in their families to attend college are provided with a clear vision of what college-ready looks like as described in rubric criteria. District leaders at Pentucket wish to foster this sort of teaching across subject areas and grade levels to develop an overall assessment system that creates more equitable outcomes as a result of its attention to formative as well as summative assessment. Building a local assessment system begins with a vision for what understandings, skills, and habits students should have mastered by graduation. Starting with that knowledge allows Pentucket district and school leaders to keep track of the greater goals they have for students as they create graduation and promotion requirements and common assessments in each grade level and subject area.

Focus on Power Standards for Performance Assessments

STEP 2:
Focus on Power Standards for Performance Assessments

Teams of teachers select the most essential standards to guide common performance assessment work.

> "After you have selected your essential content standards, replace the verbiage with your own language, questions, and prompts, perhaps reflecting on Conley's (2005) habits of mind or the upper end of Bloom's taxonomy."—*(Schmoker, 2011, p. 138)*

In Singapore, Japan, and China—where students are among the highest scoring on tests in the world—teachers are required to cover fewer than a third of the standards in comparison to teachers in the United States—about 15 to our 50 per grade level (Schmoker, 2011, p. 44). The state of Oregon cut its mathematics standards by two-thirds so that teachers could go into more depth and focus on real-world connections in mathematics class. The change has improved understanding of concepts and, consequently, achievement levels. "The typical [Oregon] eighth grader now performs at nearly the same level as most sophomores [across the nation]," Schmoker writes (p.46). Other states that have adopted this "less is more" approach have experienced similar success. "Clearly, we need to simplify curriculum—to drastically reduce the number of standards to those with the highest priority" (p.46). Schmoker describes a method for selecting only the *power standards,* which he says normally comes as a welcome respite. "Minus the 'clutter' of the less-essential standards, it reveals the opportunity for in-depth instruction of a potent core of agreed-upon topics" (p.47).

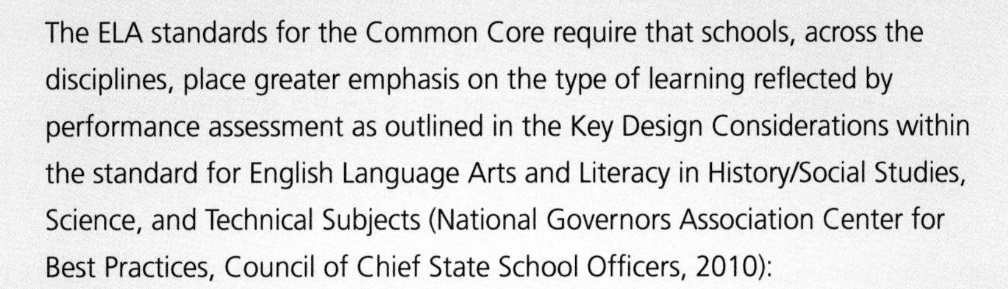

The ELA standards for the Common Core require that schools, across the disciplines, place greater emphasis on the type of learning reflected by performance assessment as outlined in the Key Design Considerations within the standard for English Language Arts and Literacy in History/Social Studies, Science, and Technical Subjects (National Governors Association Center for Best Practices, Council of Chief State School Officers, 2010):

- **An integrated model of literacy:** The standards ask for the integration of reading, writing, listening, and speaking. Schools need to integrate all four and not focus on reading and writing to the exclusion of listening and speaking.
- **Research and media skills blended into the standards as a whole:** The standards ask for students to conduct purposeful research in the role of both consumers and producers of media and research in a variety of forms. The Common Core calls for students to "create a high volume and extensive range of print and nonprint texts in media forms old and new" (Common Core State Standards Initiative, 2011, p.4).
- **Shared responsibility for student's literacy development:** The ELA standards are standards for literacy across all content areas and technical subjects, and the ELA standards are no longer the sole responsibility of the English department. Presentation and media skills can be more effectively scaffolded if there is a shared responsibility for their development as well as consensus about which skills to develop in which grades through particular common assessments.

In fact, one characteristic of the Common Core is a reduced number of standards across subject areas and grade levels. When teachers narrow the standards to the most essential standards that can be assessed at a higher level of complexity, they design deeper and clearer assessments, and students' understanding becomes more profound. QPA adapted Schmoker's process and created the Power Standards Protocol (see Tool #16), which allows teachers to select the most important standards to guide common assessment work. Initially, a team of teachers in a given discipline or across disciplines convenes with a prioritized list of standards and then selects roles. The facilitator reviews the protocol, and the group asks clarifying questions about the process and the standards in question. Team members pair up, for example by contiguous grades, and silently examine each other's standards using the following criteria:

Leverage: Knowledge and skills of value in multiple disciplines.

Endurance: Knowledge and skills beyond the test date or time in school.

Success in: Essential knowledge and skills for success in next grade level.

School/District: Essential knowledge and skills for the school/district's mission.

The pair has a brief conversation about which parts of the criteria the standards contain. The pairs then post on three separate charts each standard that receives a rating of three or more of the criteria, standards with two criteria, and any remaining standards with one criterion that they feel are essential. Each participant votes for their top 15 standards. In a discussion, the group addresses the following questions:

- What did we agree were the power standards for our discipline?
- What does a graduate of our school/district look like in our discipline?
- What agreements did we come to about our discipline's coherence from grade to grade?
- What are the next steps?

In a debrief session, the group then discusses questions that arose and what they noticed about the standards and the process, and implications for instructional practice. While the focus for this guide is on performance assessment, there are other types of assessments that would be incorporated into a local assessment system. Power standards, as they assess more rigorous levels of learning, lend themselves well to the skills assessed in complex performance assessments essential for college and career readiness.

The Maine School Administrative District 15 of Gray–New Gloucester, Maine, used the Power Standards Protocol at the beginning of a school year. Teachers were reluctant to give up standards, because every standard seemed crucial to different teachers. Over the course of the year, however, the teachers began to see how narrowing the focus helped their students. As Assistant Superintendent Karen Caprio said at the end of the year:

> "Teachers had to learn to embrace the power standards and to continue to deepen the focus of the common performance assessments we were creating. Teachers have come to realize the need to really own power standards. When we started this work, it took an entire gymnasium wall to show standards in ELA from K–8. We needed to figure out how to narrow our focus on power standards so we can focus on assessment creation. What are the standards we will assess with common performance assessments and what are the standards we will assess with more traditional assessments? We had to learn to trust the process."

Teachers have now created a list of power standards to apply to common performance assessments.

Identify Appropriate Levels of Cognitive Complexity for Standards

STEP 3:
Identify Appropriate Level of Cognitive Complexity for Standards

During planning of performance assessments, teachers gauge the level of rigor for the assessed standards and challenge students with a variety of levels of complexity.

> "As educators become more skilled at recognizing the elements and dimensions of cognitive rigor and analyzing its implications for instruction and assessment, they can provide learning opportunities that benefit all students, across all subject areas and all grade levels." —*Hess et al., 2009, p. 8*

Once teachers select power standards and are ready to begin planning performance assessments, they design cognitively complex and rigorous curricula. Rather than relying on intuition, teachers can evaluate the level of rigor as they align their curriculum and instruction to the standards. Norman Webb's *Depth of Knowledge* framework (Webb, 1997) stipulates four different ways students interact with content, leading from basic recall to problem solving. Karin Hess has developed sample descriptors for each of Webb's levels for alignment purposes in all content areas. The levels do not necessarily designate a degree of difficulty; rather, according to Hess, Carlock, Jones, and Walkup (2009), they help teachers "articulate how deeply students must understand the related content to complete the necessary tasks" (Hess, et al. 2009, p.3). Hess et al. (2009) describe Webb's Depth of Knowledge (DOK) levels in this way:

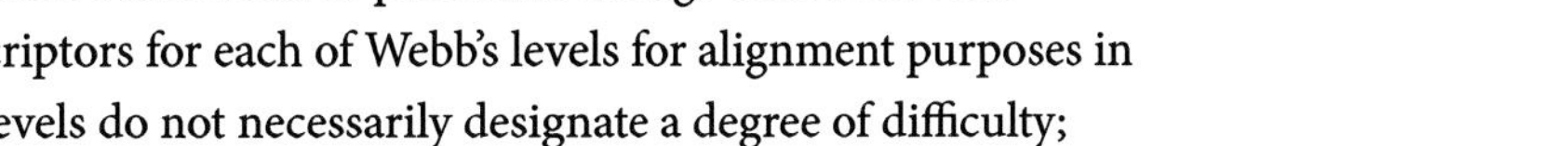

1. **Recall:** Recall of recognition of fact, information, concept or procedure.
2. **Basic Application of Skills/Concepts:** Use of information, conceptual knowledge; selection of appropriate procedures; implementation of two or more steps with decision points along the way; resolution of routine problems; organization and display of data.

Webb's Depth of Knowledge levels are based on Bloom's Taxonomy, a classification system developed in 1956 by a team led by educational psychologist Benjamin Bloom for the cognitive (knowledge), affective (attitude), and psychomotor (skills) domains. Within the cognitive domain, Bloom identified six levels, from simple recall to increasingly more complex levels of thinking. Educators assigned an action verb to each level to allow them to guide their questioning. For example, verbs such as "memorize, name, or define" are associated with simple recall.

3. **Strategic Thinking:** Requires reasoning, developing a plan or sequence of steps to approach a problem; requires some decision making and justification; abstract and complex; often more than one possible answer.
4. **Extended Thinking:** An investigation or application to real world; requires time to research, think, and process multiple conditions of the problem or task; use of non-routine manipulations, across disciplines/content areas/multiple sources (Hess, 2011, p. 3).

Hess et al. (2009) note that an activity aligned to level 1 is not always less difficult than an activity aligned to level 2. For example:

> "A DOK-1 activity might ask students to restate a simple fact or a much more abstract theory, the latter being much more difficult to memorize and restate. Neither of these DOK-1 tasks asks for much depth of understanding of the content. On the other hand, greater depth is required to explain how or why a concept or rule works (DOK-2), to apply it to real-world phenomena with justification or supporting evidence (DOK-3), or to integrate a given concept with other concepts or other perspectives (DOK-4) (p. 3)."

In order to address the true depth of students' understanding of content, Hess developed a method that allows teachers, school leaders, and districts to apply the Depth of Knowledge levels when they design instruction and create performance assessments. Combining the Webb DOK levels and Bloom taxonomy, with the Hess Cognitive Rigor Matrix (see Tools #5 and #6), teachers are able to examine and categorize tasks and assessments to their level of complexities. "When used to plot multiple assignments over time, the Cognitive Rigor Matrix can graphically display a unique view of instructional emphasis and ultimately reveal the focus on learning within a classroom, a grade level, or a school system" (Hess et al., 2009, p.2).

A starting point for exploring Webb's DOK levels and the expectations of the Common Core is the Looking at Assessment Work Protocol (see Tool #14). In this protocol, participants begin with the student work sample as they focus on the evidence they see in the work framed by a question posed by the presenting teacher. Only after close examination of the student work do participants hear more from the presenting teacher and see the task and rubric.

APPLYING DEPTH OF KNOWLEDGE: WRITING

According to Hess's work, the application of the levels looks slightly different in mathematics, reading, science, social studies, and writing.

In a writing class, for example:

Level 1 (Recall) requires a student to write/edit complete sentences or recite simple facts;

Level 2 (Basic Application of Skills/Concepts) asks the student to organize ideas in single paragraphs, requiring some mental processing (e.g., summarizing, connecting ideas);

Level 3 (Strategic Thinking) requires students to develop ideas in multiparagraph compositions or essays, demonstrating synthesis or analysis; and

Level 4 (Extended Thinking) demands synthesis, analysis, and/or evaluation of complex ideas or themes and drawing from multiple sources of evidence, resulting in products such as research reports.

APPLYING DEPTH OF KNOWLEDGE: SCIENCE

Level 1 (Recall) asks students to recall a science term, definition, or principle; use a well-known formula; or follow a set procedure;

Level 2 (Basic Application of Skills/Concepts) asks students to make observations, estimate, collect and organize data, or explain relationships (e.g., explain cause-effect predictions);

Level 3 (Strategic Thinking) involves multistep tasks requiring more demanding reasoning, such as conducting a designed investigation. Students would be required to cite data/evidence to support conclusions drawn; and

Level 4 (Extending Thinking) requires that the student apply complex reasoning, as when developing an experimental design requiring multiple data sets and conducting the investigation, usually over an extended time period (e.g., conducting a field study of local water quality).

At Pentucket Middle School, eighth-grade teachers aimed to address the higher levels of Depth of Knowledge as they planned a common performance assessment in which students would recognize Veteran's Day in a meaningful way. While explicitly focusing on two of the district's Habits of Learning, communication and independence, teachers expected students to use strategic thinking and reasoning, and extended thinking as they ventured into the world outside their school.

Teachers asked eighth graders to interview a person who had served in the United States Army, Air Force, Navy, or other branch of the armed services and to write a feature article based on the veteran's story. The assignment required students to locate a veteran themselves and prepare at least 20 questions to ask the veteran. It included guidelines for how to speak to and question the veteran. During the interview, students took notes and then wrote a news story based on the veteran's story.

The assessment required strategic thinking and reasoning (DOK 3) in that students needed to use reasoning to develop a plan and make decisions outside of their daily routine. It also demanded extended thinking (DOK 4) as students interviewed and conducted an interview and then pulled the information together to write a news story. The assessment also tested students' flexibility, self-reliance, and resourcefulness—characteristics of the independence Habit of Learning—because, in order to find a veteran and interview him or her, students had to venture into the community and use interpersonal skills to complete this task. Communication, as assessed in this interview, is about writing, speaking, listening, and expressing ideas, and, equally important, treating others with respect.

As a way to thank the veterans for their time and service, students presented each veteran with the final article after they completed it as part of a class collection of articles formatted in the style of a newspaper. Many students later included the work from this assessment in their Habits of Learning portfolios to illustrate proficiency in the Habits of Communication and Independence.

CCSS

As schools and districts align to the Common Core, it is important for practitioners to consider ways skills and content can be embedded in rich performance assessments such as the Veteran's Day article task. The Common Core requires that teachers of history/social studies and science and technical subjects provide meaningful instruction in reading and writing aligned to the skills and content of the discipline. The Veteran's Day article task could be aligned to history standards and become an interdisciplinary task if students interviewed, analyzed, and wrote about the historical time period and causes for the war in which the veteran they researched served. Students could also create a timeline that demonstrated their understanding of the events before and after in order to meaningfully place the veteran in history. The life of the veteran provides a meaningful connection that helps students to organize and remember historical dates and events. This interdisciplinary task simultaneously meets the demands of content literacy required by the Common Core, of skills required by life in the 21st century, and of student engagement.

EXPLORING STUDENT ENGAGEMENT AT THE HILLTOWN COOPERATIVE CHARTER SCHOOL

by Julia Moskowitz

Brightly colored displays about the evolution of camouflage and about Renaissance fashion filled the seventh/eighth-grade classroom at Hilltown Cooperative Charter Public School in Haydenville, Massachusetts. Students at Hilltown engage in performance assessments each year, culminating in the eighth-grade independent project, which gives students an opportunity for voice and choice in their work. Interdisciplinary study, experiential learning, community building, and critical thinking are all part of the K–8 school's mission. Hilltown's eighth-grade project is an example of the power of interdisciplinary performance assessment to allow sharing of students' interests and abilities with the entire school community.

The assignment requires students to use interactive and visual components in order to write and present an in-depth research topic. Projects are often inspired by a curiosity or connection to a topic. For example, one eighth-grade student visited the National Museum of American History in Washington, DC, which inspired him to study cantilevers and build a wooden model. Another eighth grader interested in art recreated Andy Warhol's studio, covering desks in shiny silver paper and adding visual elements documenting 1960's culture and Warhol's art. All presenters engaged their audience members using various interactive devices such as YouTube clips, coloring pages, cheese sampling, and Qi meditation exercises that deepened their understanding of the topic. The range of topics and breadth of knowledge exhibited showed students' independent inquiry and choice in all stages of their work. Hilltown teachers believe that this research project equips students with critical-thinking and communication tools necessary for high school, college, and beyond.

Hilltown's curriculum and school culture facilitate student voice and engagement, in which students own their knowledge and skill set. Beginning in kindergarten, students are encouraged to analyze and problem solve. Dan Klatz, education coordinator of Hilltown, says, students become a "product of their whole education." Students look forward to the eighth-grade project throughout their time at Hilltown. Each year, classrooms of students file upstairs to view the exhibitions. Students become familiar with the overall structure of the presentations and begin entertaining possible research topics. By the middle of eighth grade, students are introduced to the scoring rubric and focus on the project for the remainder of the year. Teachers scaffold the project to help students remain organized and on task. An eighth-grade teacher says students are "invested in a way so that most of the time [teachers] don't have to pressure them to work on their projects." The seventh/eighth-grade core teachers serve as advisors for students. Eighth graders are required to have a mentor, whom they choose themselves. The mentors, often family and community members or Hilltown faculty, give students guidance and resources throughout the process. For example, one parent, a professional animator, mentored a student whose project was on the history of animation.

This year, eighth graders dug even deeper into their explorations of topics, which teachers attributed to clearer presentation guidelines and expectations. In the past, topics had to be tied to curriculum content; however, teachers shifted their practice after realizing students could learn the research and presentation skills they needed while writing about topics they were passionate about. A Hilltown teacher explained that students demonstrate the skills they have acquired through the years, forming an "identity as researchers and as active participants in their own learning processes." Research shows that when students have voice and choice in the development and outcome of their work, their interest and motivation will increase (Toshalis & Nakkula, 2012). Questions such as "Who am I? What am I interested in? How can I pursue these interests?" are crucial to the development of youth. Klatz says that the foundation of this project is a combination of both personal and academic identities.

For teachers and students at Hilltown, the eighth-grade project is a culminating experience. They feel ownership of the work. According to Klatz, it is not just a project for eighth graders, but rather "a project of the school." Teachers from all grade levels give feedback and support to eighth graders. Students practice their presentation skills and fine-tune their ideas in front of a panel from the school. Parents and friends of Hilltown are invited to the exhibitions. One parent noted, "I was so excited to hear more about the project and see my son engaged and interested in a way that I don't get to see at home these days."

After sewing 1920's-inspired patterns, researching dams, and building a color-sorting robot, this eclectic group of eighth graders had ended their careers at Hilltown. The school also concluded their three years of professional development support as a QPA Network School, which Klatz says helped "provide structure and clarity of what makes for a balanced assessment." As Hilltown students continue to dive into topics of interest and strengthen their skills as learners, social scientists and activists, they are developing college and career readiness. Hilltown serves a model for how schools can strive to assess students in a way that is authentic and valid.

Plan and Scaffold Instruction to Reach All Students

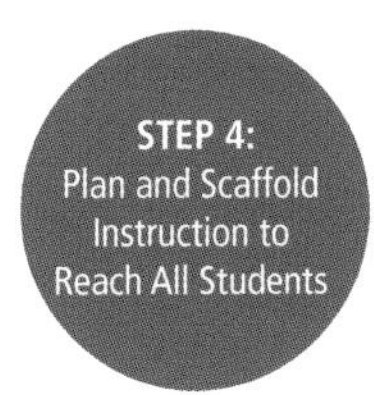

In collaboration with colleagues, teachers design classroom instruction with the essential questions, standards, and skills in mind and with clear steps and checkpoints for student feedback along the way so that all students are supported and achieve mastery.

> "The goal is to set my students up for success. I make sure my students have all of the background information before giving the assessment, and I make sure they have multiple entry points into the writing assessment. I also need to give students many chances to show mastery." —*Amy Woods, Teacher, Cape Cod Lighthouse Charter School*

At Cape Cod Lighthouse Charter School, a regional middle school of 230 students located in Orleans, Massachusetts, a small town on the beach peninsula of Cape Cod, Amy Woods and her colleagues listened to the needs of their graduates, who as a whole felt the school did not adequately prepare them for the academic style of their high school writing requirements. In planning a new English language arts performance assessment, Woods and her colleagues turned to the Common Performance Assessment Curriculum Planning Template (see Tool #8) with the goal of teaching their students academic writing. Teachers began by identifying local standards to be addressed, the Common Core objective of providing interdisciplinary opportunities, and the big ideas that students would apply to other contexts in and out of school. Next, they identified the essential questions and skills that would sustain student inquiry and stimulate thinking, and that students need to master.

In the reflection that follows, Woods describes how she responded to the call of Lighthouse graduates and inspired her students to succeed by keeping expectations clear at every step of the process of learning to write critiques of short stories.

SCAFFOLDING STUDENT LEARNING

by Amy Woods

We came up with a sort of essay "boot camp." Eighth-grade students spend the first three months of the year learning how to craft an academic, thesis-driven essay. I build background knowledge one step at a time. We begin with the basics—we use short stories to help craft thesis statements. Then we move on to finding evidence in those short stories to prove our theses. After that, students learn how to craft a first paragraph that leads into their thesis. Finally, we put it all together and write a four-paragraph essay, with two pieces of evidence (each piece is proven in paragraphs two and three, respectively), and a conclusion that usually adds one more piece of evidence.

From September to November, students write about five of these essays. Each student is working toward a December benchmark exam, where he or she must score a minimum of 4.0 on a 5.0 scale. Before that exam, students get timely feedback from me for each essay they write. As they see their numbers rise on the rubric, I can tell that they are "getting it," and more importantly, so can they.

Finally, in early December, students get the short story "Eleven," by Sandra Cisneros. They have three class periods to read the story and write a thesis essay with minimal input from me. In this essay, students must combine their creative, analytical, and practical knowledge to write an interesting, in-depth, clear piece of writing. Students are given clear expectations and criteria. I then grade the essays. Any student who does not get a 4.0 or above on the rubric does not pass the "benchmark." Those students then revise their essay with help from me, either at a study hall or after school. Once they get a 4.0 or above, I know that they have "mastered" the thesis essay. I would say about 15 percent of our eighth graders have to revise their essays every year. Also, special education students get support from a special education teacher, depending on their individualized learning plan.

In order to make this writing benchmark work, there needs to be appropriate and timely teacher feedback and scaffolding. This feedback can be written or oral. It may be question based: What are you proving in this paragraph? Where is your topic sentence? It may be directive: You need to make this clearer. Let's find a quote that helps to prove this. Students who are at a higher level in writing ability can take one of my questions and run with it. Students who have a hard time organizing one paragraph, let alone four or five, need more directive feedback to feel successful.

The key to meeting each learner at his level is to know each student. There are classes where in the span of 10 minutes, I might be working on four different essays. One child might be on his second page and have the most creative analysis I've seen, while the next is struggling with his intro paragraph or can't find a quote to back up an idea because he has trouble with comprehension.

Teachers must find the balance between scaffolding and rescuing students.

I stress improvement when I am grading. It's why I use a point-based system for the first part of the year instead of letter grade. When a student sees a 3.5 on one essay and then a 3.7 and then a 4.0, that student feels much more successful than if he would see a C, a C+, and a B-. Of course, I expect every student to shoot for the 5.0, the A+. I enjoy watching them get there at their own pace, their own path on the ladder.

Somehow, the students buy in to this. They walk into my classroom in September hating to write, especially "formal" academic writing. Yet I see their confidence build as we write essay after essay. I give lots of positive feedback, along with constructive criticism; I build their "writing self-esteem," and it's just fabulous to watch them grow.

Good writing takes practice, like piano or baseball or painting. By December, my students understand this. And I feel good that they will head to high school knowing how to write critically, and hopefully not scared of writing an analytical essay on a piece of literature.

Woods's vignette illustrates the power of consistent and goal-oriented teaching in which she relentlessly monitors the progress of her students, carefully scaffolding their learning and refusing to let a single student miss the mark. Woods facilitates her diverse group of students by recognizing and praising their efforts, being open to rethinking and customizing instructional practices, stopping to develop specific skills as needed, and guiding the class through a robust process of revision.

Terry Thompson (n.d.), in his article "Are You Scaffolding or Rescuing?" describes how, in his reading instruction, there is a fine line between *scaffolding* and *rescuing*. Scaffolding provides a framework with supports that allow every student to master a given level and learn to read independently. Rescuing happens when our scaffolds are not working and we begin to take over for the reader. This is unfair to struggling readers. "It's an easy mistake, because when you think about it, both rescuing and scaffolding stem from a foundation of collaboration and assistance (Section 3, para. 1)," Thompson writes. In true scaffolding, the teacher acts as facilitator, "supporting, modeling, and encouraging. But not taking over the reader's work at hand (Section 3, para. 2)." In performance assessment design, teachers create prompts that encompass a progression of teacher modeling, and students taking responsibility for learning.

In their planning and subsequent instruction, Woods and her colleagues must keep in mind the most effective ways to engage students. The Student Engagement Alignment Tool is designed for teachers to evaluate their performance assessments to assist them in figuring out ways to maximize student engagement (see Tool #32). Below are some of the attributes teachers look for:

- Students are introduced to the project by an activity or question that captures their attention and initiates the process of inquiry.
- Students are challenged to think deeply around a complex, open-ended question and are encouraged to generate further questions, answers, and solutions.
- A plan has been made for teacher feedback to be provided to students at key checkpoints throughout the project to ensure that all students stay on track and can make midcourse corrections to maximize their success and engagement.
- Peer feedback is used to improve student work.
- Students have opportunities to practice and develop their collaborative working skills with their peers.
- Presentation skills are taught and practiced.
- Students assess their own work using rubric criteria before submission and reflect on their performance on the assessment, identifying strengths and weaknesses and targeting areas for growth.

STUDENT PEER EDITING

Peer editing teaches students to collaborate and give feedback to another person, a fundamental aspect of readiness for life beyond high school. The Student Peer Editing Checklist (See Tool #33) gives students a protocol that sets the stage for a safe and productive dialogue. The protocol lists requirements under the section headings: format, idea development, supporting evidence, organization, and conventions. Initially, the peer editor reads the paper and places a check mark (√) next to each question the author has completed with success, and an (X) where the writing did not fulfill the requirement. Guidelines assist the peer editor in providing as clear feedback as possible. Next, the peer editor presents the feedback to the author, and the author picks at least three significant revisions to tackle for the next draft.

Supporting Students Effectively through Self-Assessment

Whether referring to an essay for English class, a science lab, or a mathematics test, teachers constantly remind their students, "Check your work. Refine your thesis." Similarly, creating common assessments requires teachers to check and revise their work before they begin teaching, as they teach, and after the unit is complete. The process is cyclical. As teachers receive feedback from student work, classroom activities, consulting with students, and conferring with colleagues, they make changes and attempt the lesson again.

An essential way teachers implementing QPA performance assessments check their own work is through scoring conversations. At John F. Kennedy Middle School in Hudson, Massachusetts, English teachers Kathleen Tobiasson, Rachel Scanlon, and Mackenzie Korhn engaged in a scoring conversation focused on visual work. The three teachers discuss how their individual approaches to an assignment to create a brochure on influenza, and the different level of scaffolding each teacher provided, led to very different outcomes. Scanlon spent more class time supporting the brochure task, directly instructing students in using technology and allowing time for collaboration and peer editing of brochures. Tobiasson and Korhn let students work more independently on the brochure and spent much more time focused on writing. As the teachers collectively grade and review the student work from the tasks, they notice differences in the quality of the work produced for each task, particularly the brochures. Based on each teacher's self-assessment and the scoring results, they intend to modify their plans for next year to provide increased scaffolding for the brochure task.

One of the issues the Kennedy teachers struggled with as they reflected on the brochure task is an issue that has challenged all QPA Network Schools: How do district leaders and teachers make time for presentations in oral and visual formats? Devoting time to this type of performance assessment is critical if students are to have multiple opportunities to develop these skills.

Teachers can use the Assessment Validation Checklist (see Tool #1) in reviewing their plans to address the elements of effective assessment design and to plan next steps. Aspects of technical quality—including clarity and focus, fairness, student engagement, universal design, and alignment to standards—need to be embedded in the curriculum. As teachers use the checklist to conduct the self-assessment, it is important to reflect on approaches to teaching and to make sure the common assessment and the accompanying instructional plan for each teacher address opportunities for all students and include instructional practices that actively engage students.

Opportunities for All Students: Universal Design for Learning

> You're at the airport, find your rental car, step in, and start it up. You check the address of your hotel and check the global positioning system (GPS). You try saying the address aloud and, miraculously, the hotel name appears on the screen. A prompt asks you if you would like to arrive in the shortest time or avoid highways. Then you change the display to make the screen brighter, decrease the volume, and switch the language to American English from British. As you head out of the parking lot, it guides you methodically through each turn and then prompts you with the next step. A few minutes later, you make a wrong turn. The GPS chimes, "Recalculating route.... Turn left at next intersection," and—offering instructive feedback—guides you back on the right track.

The GPS analogy offers a valuable lesson for teachers as they conduct self-assessment, continue their planning, and instruct their students. David Rose and Jenna Gravel (2009) draw a parallel between the GPS and the principles of *Universal Design for Learning.* Just as the GPS is set up with structures that provide options to drivers with varied needs, the Universal Design for Learning gives guidelines for how curriculum can be tailored to meet the needs of all students.

When designing performance assessments, the following Universal Design guidelines offer options to students with differing ways of demonstrating their learning. Give students the opportunity for:

- *Multiple Means of Representation,* such as:
  - o Options for perception, such as alternatives for auditory or visual information;
  - o Options for language and symbols, such as clear definitions of vocabulary and syntax and illustrations of key concepts nonlinguistically; and
  - o Options for comprehension, such as those that activate background knowledge and support memory and transfer of learning to other situations.
- *Multiple Means of Action and Expression,* such as:
  - o Options for physical action, such as accessing tools and assistive technologies;
  - o Options for expressive skills and fluency, such as varying forms of media and scaffolding for practice and performance; and
  - o Options for executive functions, such as those that guide effective goal setting and strategy development and those that facilitate managing information and resources.
- *Multiple Means of Engagement,* such as:
  - o Options for recruiting interest, such as those that increase individual choice and autonomy or enhance relevance, value, and authenticity;
  - o Options for sustaining effort and persistence, such as those that vary levels of challenge and support or foster collaboration and communication; and
  - o Options that teach coping skills and strategies and develop abilities to self-assess and reflect on work.

(From Center for Applied Special Technology [CAST], 2008)

Choice and autonomy allow for greater student engagement

As teachers check that all students have equal opportunity to master the common assessment, incorporating opportunities for student ownership and decision making will guarantee the assessment is accessible to all students. In providing choice in common assessments, the requirement for demonstrating mastery over target standards remains constant for every student, while the means of how a student demonstrates mastery may vary.

TEACH WITH ACCOMMODATIONS RATHER THAN MODIFICATIONS FOR SPECIAL EDUCATION AND ENGLISH LANGUAGE LEARNERS

Accommodations support a student's ability to achieve standards, while modifications change, lower, or reduce learning expectations (CCSSO, 2010, Application to Students with Disabilities Standard). Accommodations are used to decrease the effects of a student's disability and are categorized by how they support access to learning expectations:

- Presentation—Allow students access to information.
- Response—Allow students to complete assignments and assessments using different methods.
- Setting—Change the location or conditions of the assessment setting.
- Timing and scheduling—Increase or change the way time is organized for an assessment.

A WINDOW INTO PERFORMANCE ASSESSMENT WITH SPECIAL EDUCATION STUDENTS

by Austin Mueller

"If we had at our grasp the most elegant curriculum in the world and it missed the mark for students with learning disabilities, highly advanced learners, students with limited English proficiency, young people who lack economic support, kids who struggle to read, and a whole host of others, the curriculum would fall short of its promise (Tomlinson & McTighe, 2006, p. 3)."

Before a lunch table was half-full, the line for lollipops was at least ten students deep. "Could I have three cherry-limeade and three watermelon?" Sixth graders had first lunch and would usually buy out the best flavors from my students. "Sure, so that's (pause) six lollipops and umm...one sec." My student would stop to think about the cost, "That's three dollars." The sixth grader paid with a five-dollar bill, and my student, looking at the cash register, would say, "So, they owe me three, they gave me five." He practiced counting up from how much they owed to how much they had paid, "Here's your two dollars back. Thanks!"

Some of my students would subtract the amount owed from the amount paid, some students started to memorize that a specific number of lollipops was equivalent to a specific dollar amount and they did not need to complete the calculation each time, some students needed to talk through each step of the transaction with staff, but each had achieved or was working toward a level of proficiency.

Several months prior to the lollipop fundraiser, staff found students with severe special needs to be struggling with standards in their individualized education plans. The special education team identified understanding coin and dollar values as an initial target, with the eventual goal of proficiency using money in the community. Instruction was organized into a scaffolding progression (Thompson, n.d.):

- I Do/You Watch—Structured worksheets, coin activities, and iPad app games were used.
- I Do/You Help—Staff introduced money exchange with board games: "If something is worth $100, how many $50's is that worth? How many $20's?"
- You Do/I Help—Students estimated prices with teacher assistance.
- You Do/I Watch—Students were given real prices and practiced purchasing items from staff using real money.

Students' accommodations included calculation devices, large print, visual organizers, graphic organizers, and extended time according to needs, as well as continuing instruction. Assessments that lack accommodations set up practitioners to rescue students from curriculum rather than to aptly scaffold learning. Performance assessment's multistep process encourages teachers and aides to identify opportunities where accommodations fit scaffolding. Without steps and accommodations identified along this progression, teachers often skip from the lesson (I Do/You Watch) to homework and a test (You Do/I Grade).

On community trips to malls and restaurants, students practiced estimating and spending money. Proficiency meant that students were able to identify, request, and pay for an item, as well as check that they received the correct amount of money in return. Their final assessment was the fund raiser in which they practiced selling lollipops at lunch, which meant using multiplication skills with monetary amounts and then accurately making change for their general education peers. When faced with problems that included money, students felt empowered to use their skills and found that their skills were transferable.

Performance assessments with accommodations and scaffolding help students of all levels explore and learn strategies most appropriate for their learning styles. If the goal is to prepare students for college, careers, and ultimately life beyond school, then teachers must help students of all levels to investigate and understand how they learn. Teaching to the Common Core encourages assessing this depth of understanding and requires assessments that are highly adaptable to accommodations. Performance assessments afford this flexibility for subject teachers to collaborate with special educators to create inclusive classrooms. If we are seeking to provide an environment that allows students to demonstrate their knowledge with the greatest level of proficiency and independence, well-crafted performance assessments offer more opportunities and flexibility for scaffolding and accommodations.

Students practice math skills with fake money

Refine the Alignment and Adjust Practice through Self-Assessment

STEP 5: Refine the Alignment and Adjust Practice through Self-Assessment

Teachers understand that the work happens over time, collaboration and feedback improve practice, and constant revisions are a necessary part of the process.

> "One of the most challenging and yet powerful places to begin to improve the connections between high school and college is to align course content and student performance expectations." —*Conley, 2010, p. 55*

The rice farmers in Inakadate learned from years of making increasingly sophisticated and intricate designs that exquisite outcomes require a vision, detailed plans to carry it out, and the flexibility to refine the steps along the way. District and school leaders also must start with a vision of graduates who will move into college and/or career with knowledge and important 21st century skills such as collaboration and communication. Alignment at the school level means building a local assessment system and a map of the common assessments throughout the grade levels. Alignment at the classroom level means identifying standards and levels of cognitive complexity, and planning instruction with the goal of reaching each student. This kind of critical schoolwide alignment of instruction with assessment, pervasive throughout the building, takes time and requires periodic refinement to fit the needs of all students and to respond to change from the world outside of school.

Let's Get Started: Entry Points for Aligning Instruction and Assessment

The work of aligning instruction and performance assessments has many entry points. A teaching team or school or district leaders might decide to proceed as follows:

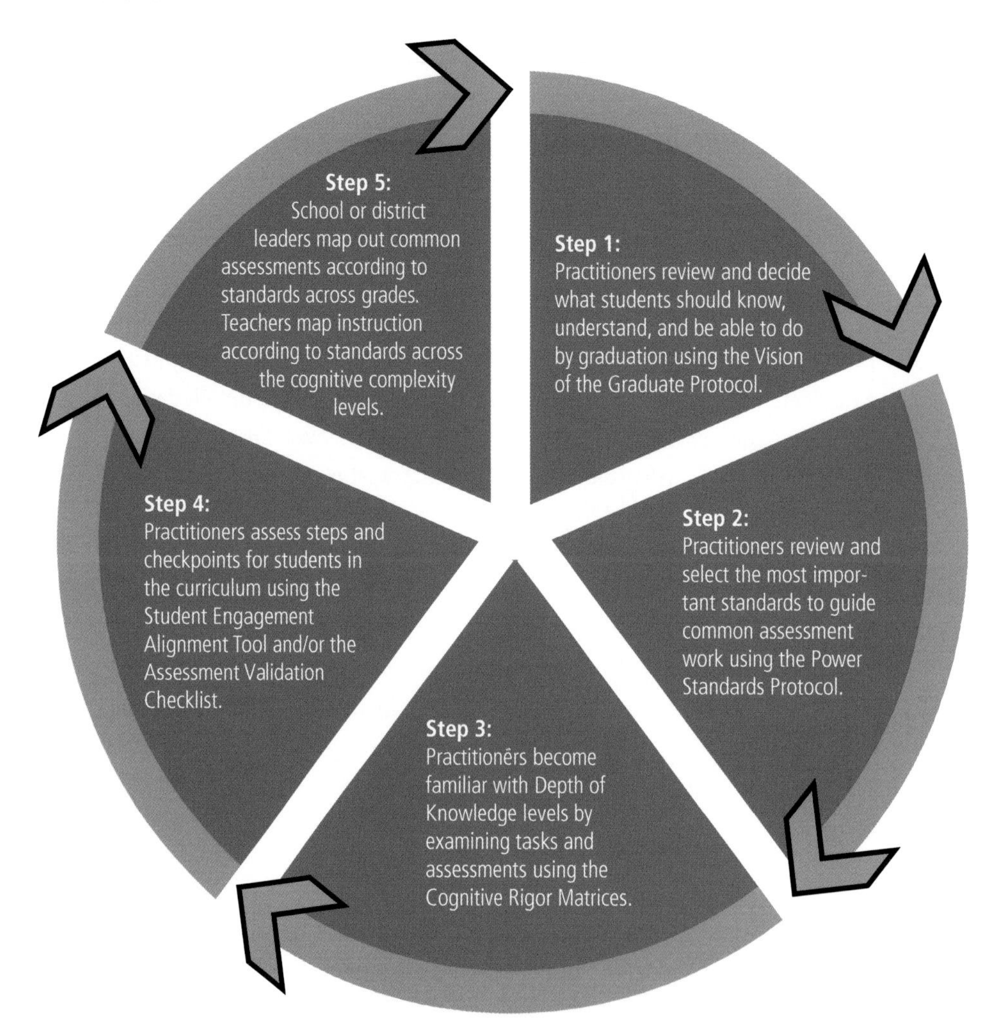

Refining Our Work through Self-Assessment

Aligning instruction, curriculum, and assessment is a cyclical process. Aligning instruction to the essential standards selected by school and district leaders, and infusing them throughout teacher practice, demand collaboration and reflection. Through the self-assessment process, practitioners constantly review and amend their own work. As they engage in this review, practitioners should ask themselves the following questions:

Quality Aligned Instruction	Are promotion and graduation requirements aligned to appropriate, agreed-upon standards that include 21st century skills?
	Are teaching and assessment practices for each course or classroom aligned to key standards?
	Is the content and cognitive complexity for each assessment aligned with established content and skills sequences and/or grade-level standards?
	Do all students have adequate time to build upon prior learning and to both practice and master complex skills and content?

TOOLS USED IN THIS CHAPTER

Tools for Aligning Instruction and Assessment

TOOL #	TOOL NAME	PAGE #
1	Assessment Validation Checklist	T3
5, 6	Cognitive Rigor Matrices (ELA/SS and Mathematics/Science)	T10, 11
8	Common Performance Assessment Curriculum Planning Template	T13
14	Looking at Assessment Work Protocol	T24
16	Power Standards Protocol	T27
32	Student Engagement Alignment Tool	T53
33	Student Peer Editing Checklist	T54
39	Vision of the Graduate Protocol	T64

CHAPTER 3

DESIGN: COMMON PERFORMANCE ASSESSMENTS

The best assessment is... "educative," not onerous. The tasks educate learners about the kinds of challenges adults actually face, and the use of feedback is built into the process. In the real world, that's how we learn and are assessed: on our ability to learn from results.

—Grant Wiggins, Healthier Testing Made Easy

Student Work: Bridge Construction

The seventh-grade English team at John F. Kennedy Middle School in Hudson, Massachusetts, a suburban middle school of 425 students, sat around a table planning a performance task at a Quality Performance Assessment (QPA) Network meeting at the beginning of the year and pondered these questions: How do we give our students opportunities to read and deeply connect with important informational text, as the Common Core requires? What can we teach that will involve our students in analysis and in use of supporting evidence in their writing? How can we do all this in a way that makes these adolescents care about what they are learning?

After considering the requisite local standards and the new emphases of the Common Core, the three teachers eventually agreed to focus on the standards of analysis, supporting evidence, and understanding informational texts. Next, they needed to choose an assessment format that would promote deep conversations among their students as well as oblige them to use supporting evidence and analysis in their writing. In the end, the model QPA Common Position Paper (see Tool #23) proved their best option because it fit well in the curriculum. It was critical to select a topic that would inspire adolescents to write. In a sixth-grade science unit

on diseases, the students had studied Typhoid Mary. Mary Mallon—a cook in New York from the late 1800s quarantined against her will for being a carrier of typhoid—was charged with spreading the disease in several establishments where she prepared and served food. Knowing the students had this prior knowledge, the team planned the curriculum for the task around the experiences of Typhoid Mary.

In reviewing the seventh-grade standards, the team double-checked that they were aligned to critical skills and content of their grade and that the subject fit well with the QPA task directions (see Tool #28). They required students in all three classes to complete the following tasks (see task description on page 61-62):

- Present an argument in letter format about Typhoid Mary from the perspective of either Mary Mallon or the health inspector ordering the quarantine. Complete multiple drafts and peer-edit at least one draft. The QPA Common Position Paper Rubric (see Tool #24), containing the *criteria*—idea development, supporting evidence, organization, and conventions and style—specifies for students how teachers will score their writing.

- Create an informational brochure about influenza, a contemporary infectious disease. This brochure will be scored using the QPA Common Visual or Media Rubric (see Tool #29 & #30).

Building the foundation of the assessment around the school's learning standards avoided the pitfall of simply planning around a "cool" idea without first giving careful thought to what students need to know and be able to do. The QPA rubrics provided scaffolding for the teachers, as they were already aligned to the Common Core and offered guidance on the skills to embed in the unit, such as citing relevant, specific, and accurate evidence. By planning backward, teachers designed the assessment plan to captivate the students and embedded it in familiar content, including choice of perspective and visual options as part of their plan. The Kennedy seventh graders immediately took ownership of the project as they took sides on the controversial social issue of forcible quarantines. During this type of instruction, students, especially adolescents, will be more deeply involved in their own learning, as they have a choice about which side to take and from which perspective to write.

Process of Common Performance Assessment Design

The plan QPA teachers follow as they design a performance assessment is outlined in the following steps:

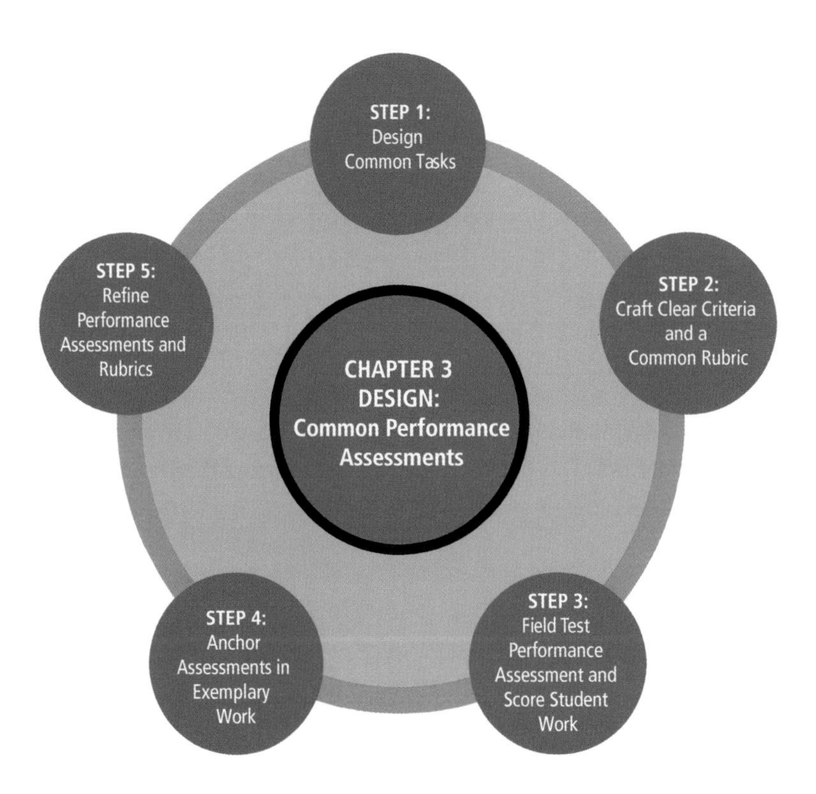

DECODING THE JARGON

Defined terms, italicized on first reference in the text, are listed in alphabetical order.

Anchor works are samples of student work that teachers use to set the standard for performance of a rubric level to promote reliable scoring and consistent interpretation of rubrics. Anchors can also be used to show students what a final product looks like at a given grade and proficiency level.

Common performance assessments consist of a carefully orchestrated learning plan composed of individual tasks in which a whole school, grade-level teams, or discipline-area teams work collaboratively to adapt, create, or implement existing tasks and rubrics, and then score student work reliably.

Common rubrics are designed and used by teachers across grade levels or subject areas to evaluate student work consistently and fairly.

Communities of practice are professionals working together effectively in a group, guided by a common goal.

Criteria stem from standards and describe student performance along a continuum that assesses the student's degree of understanding and skill.

Reliable refers to inter-rater reliability, where a group of teachers (or scorers) come to an agreement on what a rating and corresponding performance descriptors mean and score student work consistently.

A ***valid*** assessment means the assessment measures the content that it was intended to measure at the intended level of rigor.

Introduction

This chapter focuses on common performance assessment design through a collaborative, teacher-driven approach. *Common performance assessments* consist of a carefully orchestrated learning plan composed of individual tasks in which a whole school, grade-level teams, or discipline-area teams work collaboratively to adapt, create, or implement existing tasks and rubrics, and then score student work reliably. Common performance assessments can be comprised of a single task or several tasks, which could include a written task, a visual/multimedia task, and an oral task that together form the complete performance assessment and provide a more complex picture of student skills by including multiple entry points.

Taking the time to embed, design, and organize common performance assessments upfront makes the measurement of the assessment less subjective and establishes a level of clarity that removes the unknown from the assessment for the student. Developing and adapting performance assessments in teams of teachers is a powerful form of professional growth because teachers construct a collective knowledge of assessment literacy and design that they can then take back to their own classrooms. It is not necessary to start from scratch. QPA has created a bank of validated assessments designed to be adapted to a local curriculum (see QPA Common Tasks Overview text box on page 61-62).

Design Common Tasks

In planning the task(s), include evidence of aligned standards, an authentic audience, clear directions, text complexity, clear expectations, as well as written, oral, visual, and multimedia formats.

> "The overall process of implementing the performance assessment proved a challenging task. Mainly, performance assessments require careful planning...The performance task also needed to be a logical extension of the curriculum. This made the task more relevant to the students and helped them profile their learning via a more realistic lens." —*QPA Teacher*

The Kennedy seventh-grade English teachers began planning performance assessments with the same standards and tasks and corresponding rubrics in mind. Yet each teacher brought her individual interests and expertise to the curriculum in her own classroom as she developed the learning plan using a template similar to the Common Performance Assessment Curriculum Planning Template (see Tool #8). As a way to explore various perspectives on an issue, Kennedy seventh-grade teacher Kathleen Tobiasson chose the novel *Seedfolks*, by Paul Fleischman, about a vacant lot transformed into a community garden in a diverse neighborhood. Another seventh-grade teacher, Rachel Scanlon, engrossed her students by focusing on public reaction to the AIDS epidemic in the 1980s. Scanlon immersed her class in the experiences of middle school student Ryan White, a hemophiliac who was expelled from middle school for having the AIDS virus. Mackenzie Korhn, the third member of the Kennedy team, engaged students with readings about immigration as they considered the extent to which Mary Mallon's Irish immigrant status contributed to her treatment. All three teachers invited guest speakers, including the school nurse, who talked about the flu and the spread of disease, and a Peace Corps volunteer, who talked about the power of culture in shaping our perspectives.

The teachers designed unique standards-based plans around critical issues and readings in each of their classes while still completing the same common performance tasks and using the same rubrics. Performance tasks can deeply engage students in their work when they are provided with important issues, choices, and authentic tasks, such as constructing a cogent argument with a clear audience and purpose and creating brochures that allow them to visually represent their knowledge to convey a public health message. Such assessments mirror situations and tasks students will encounter in their lives outside of school, in college, and in their jobs. While Kennedy teachers designed their own tasks, some school leaders opt to build on one of the tasks that QPA has designed for educators to adapt to their school's curriculum and culture.

COMPONENTS OF A COMMON PERFORMANCE ASSESSMENT

- **Task description**—given to students for each component of the assessment.
- **Rubric**—used by students to clarify requirements of the assignment and by teachers for consistent scoring.
- **Teacher directions**—set common guidelines for students while still allowing for individuality in how tasks are embedded in curriculum (see Tool #28).
- **Anchor of proficient student work**—ensures that students and teachers interpret the rubric with an agreed-upon standard. Anchors are selected when student work is available after the first use of the task.

Designing performance assessments with a clear understanding of what students should know and be able to do is critical to planning cross-disciplinary, purposeful, and rich learning opportunities for students. The Kennedy seventh-grade team chose to focus on the Common Core writing standards listed below:

- W.7.1. Write arguments to support claims with clear reasons and relevant evidence.

- W.7.5. With some guidance and support from peers and adults, develop and strengthen writing as needed by planning, revising, editing, rewriting, or trying a new approach, focusing on how well purpose and audience have been addressed.

EXAMPLE

TYPHOID MARY POSITION PAPER

Seventh-grade student work excerpt of letter to Mary Mallon written from the perspective of the New York Board of Health:

"If you recall your past experiences with the department of health, you have completely ignored our claims and wholly disregarded our reasons to put you in quarantine. We have records that justify that, "[You were] isolated on North Brother Island, and then released with the condition [you] would not work with food. However, [you] assumed the pseudonym 'Mary Brown,' returned to cooking, and in 1915 infected 25 people while working as a cook in New York's Sloan hospital; two of those infected died (Rosenberg, 2)." These records indicate your unyielding opinion that you are not a carrier of typhoid, when in fact the tests that have been done on you have come back positive. Even when released from quarantine you defy the law and your word that you would discontinue your cooking career. It is because of your ignorance that these people are suffering. Your attitude and disrespect for the Department of Health needs to cease, and you must be able to take into account the lives you are jeopardizing by persisting in the culinary arts."

Creating rich purposeful learning through performance assessment also requires grounding plans in essential questions that engage students in inquiry and debate. The essential questions below immersed students in presenting evidence from the content they were studying:

Typhoid Mary Unit Essential Questions:

- How are primary sources and narratives shaped by perspective?
- How does culture shape the perspective of people?
- How is power determined by society?

These questions exemplify the rich connections that can be made when debate, inquiry, and evidence are connected to rich curriculum topics, as the Kennedy teachers did with Typhoid Mary. Tobiasson explains the centrality of essential questions this way:

"Essential questions need to be part of the whole unit and build connections throughout. These questions are not just for teacher plans, but for student learning. I use them to help students develop their ability to show evidence. I am always asking students to think about these questions and show how they are connecting their learning to the essential questions with specific content-related evidence."

When used consistently throughout the unit for class discussions, reflective journal writing, and as writing prompts on tests and quizzes, essential questions provide one strategy for building the critical Common Core skill of showing evidence.

Performance assessments that are based on standards help students to understand what is important to learn and allow teachers to gauge the effectiveness of their own teaching. Educators who use QPA practices shape the performance tasks in such a way that students can demonstrate that they have achieved the standards. Through the administration of a performance assessment, teachers gather evidence on how well students mastered the unit's standards, and use the information to tweak plans, gain a better understanding of individual student's learning needs, and, if necessary, revise their goals.

TEXT TYPES FROM THE COMMON CORE

Argument

- A reasoned, logical way of demonstrating that the writer's position is valid.
- An argument's purpose may be to change the reader's point of view, to bring about action on the reader's part, or to ask the reader to accept the writer's explanation of an issue.

Informational/Explanatory Writing

- Explanations convey and clarify information so that the reader gains knowledge about a topic.
- Explanations start with the assumption of truthfulness and answer questions about why or how.

Narrative Writing

- A mode to convey experience, either real or imaginary, that uses a storyline structure.
- Narrative writing's purpose may be to instruct, inform, persuade or entertain.

(Adapted from CCSSO, 2010)

Balancing Depth and Breadth

Rather than attempt to cover as much content and as many skills as possible, QPA teachers find a balance between the breadth of coverage and depth of learning, and, in turn, they design assessments pertinent to the needs, curiosities, and passions of the students. Norman Webb's Depth of Knowledge framework (1997) guides teachers as they plan to impart the thinking and skills students need as citizens of our complex, multicultural world. As they plan, teachers align assessments with Depth of Knowledge levels—which have applications in every subject area—providing a way to measure the depth of students' understanding of content.

QPA practice asks teachers to make decisions about cognitive complexity as they embed QPA Common Tasks in their schools. Ensuring that common tasks within the same school are aligned to target the same Depth of Knowledge level is part of grounding the performance assessment in the standards. It is important to discuss the expectations for cognitive complexity in terms of the students' level and the time in the school year before asking students to complete an assessment. For example, teachers might choose to focus on the *criteria* of idea development and supporting evidence according to the scale below:

Idea Development:

- Less complex: Students argue one of two or more thesis statements provided by the teacher (best for pre-assessments).
- More complex: Students write thesis statements with teacher guidance in collaborative groups or individually.
- Most complex: Students develop their own original thesis statement.

Supporting evidence:

- Less complex: Students select evidence from a set of sources provided by the teacher.
- More complex: Students find sources with teacher guidance in collaborative groups or individually.
- Most complex: Students find their own sources of evidence.

Early in the school year, teachers may choose to assess an element at a lower depth of knowledge in order to scaffold students' development of thinking and research skills. For example, the teachers at Kennedy Middle School gave the Typhoid Mary task above as their first major essay early in the fall. Teachers provided students with the supporting evidence sources as well as a choice of thesis statements. Later in the year, they increased the cognitive complexity as students improved their skills. Conversations among teachers increase their understanding of the instructional sequence and of scaffolding that maximizes student learning and achievement, and ensure that what is being assessed is comparable.

Exploring Text Complexity

> "Over time, students who are exposed to a variety of text types with increasing complexity also learn how text features differ by genre, and they gain confidence in peeling back the layers of complexity for a deeper understanding of what is read."—(Hess & Hervey, 2011, p. 1)

In the case of the Kennedy brochure task, the teachers carefully selected a variety of informational texts that would provide background knowledge and motivate students to do their own writing. Common Core standards emphasize that to prepare students for the complexity of college and career, literacy must be central in every academic discipline. As students move through their developmental reading levels, teachers scaffold their instruction using the "staircase of complexity." Along the way, students are challenged by opportunities to practice close and careful reading of a variety of texts, and school leaders provide the resources that allow teachers to make time in their curriculum to differentiate, using varied instructional strategies for the diverse classroom population.

A series of tools developed by Karin Hess and Sheena Hervey (2011) provide a structure for selecting a variety of texts that support the Common Core shifts in creating the staircase of complexity for students to climb as they progress. The Planning Worksheet: Analyzing Features of Text Complexity for Instruction & Assessment (see Tool #35) offers teachers a detailed format for examining and determining the complexity of individual texts for instructional purposes.

Rather than a sudden increase in the complexity of texts, the shift should be gradual and measured, so that students increase their understanding of texts over time. Two Gradients of Text Complexity Rubrics—one for informational texts and one for literary texts—designed by Hess and Hervey (2011), describe how to examine and select readings for scaffolding text complexity (see Tools #11 & 12). With these tools, teachers can select readings with specific, deliberate goals in mind. The rubric descriptors are: layout, purpose and meaning, structure/discourse, language features, and background knowledge. Each text can be rated for each element by level (1-4): simple, somewhat complex, complex, and very complex. Criteria are listed in each box. For example, a simple layout has "consistent placement of text, regular word and line spacing, and large plain font"; a simple purpose contains "a single or simple purpose conveying clear or factual information"; and a simple structure indicates "connections between ideas, processes or events are explicit and clear." Some texts might have a simple layout, but somewhat complex language features, such as simple and compound sentences rather than just short, simple sentences. After categorizing several books, school leaders or teaching teams can create a chart that lists the author, title, genre, grade level, and reading level along with the complexity ratings from the rubric. This is a way for a school or teaching team or a teacher to select readings appropriate to the assessment, increasing the complexity of the reading during the course of a semester or from one grade to another.

VOCABULARY IN THE COMMON CORE

Tier One Words

- The words of everyday speech usually learned in the early grades.
- They are not considered a challenge to the average native speaker, although English language learners will have to attend closely to them.

Tier Two Words

- General academic words found in written texts rather than speech.
- They represent more subtle or precise ways to say relatively simple things—*saunter*, instead of *walk*.

Tier Three Words

- Domain-specific words that are key to understanding a new topic within a field of study.
- They appear more in informational texts and are often explicitly defined by the author.

(Adapted from CCSSO, 2010. Originally from Beck, McKeown, and Kugan, 2002, p. 8)

Effective Task Format

Students learn best when teachers author their own tasks, or modify existing tasks, based on specific learning expectations. An effective performance assessment task contains a statement or question that motivates students to do their best work on a particular aspect of the course curriculum. In designing a range of performance tasks over the course of a school year, teacher teams keep in mind that the Common Core calls for a range of student writing: "Write routinely, over extended time frames (time for research, reflection, and revision) and shorter time frames (a single sitting or a day or two) for a range of discipline specific tasks, purposes, and audiences" (Standard 10, Writing Standards Grades 6–12, CCSSO, 2010, p. 42). Each task is designed to be transparent, with clear explanation of the assignment so that students will experience a consistent format for assessments across subjects. Each task includes: a teacher-written summary of the assignment, an explanation of the topic, a requirement for evidence sources, and descriptions of the audience, time frame, and writing process (see Samples of QPA Common Tasks on pages 73-78). This format is also helpful to teachers as they reflect on the requirements of Common Core as well as the elements that support the administration of an assessment that is common across classrooms.

Some students need a different approach to begin the writing process. The presentation option offers a way to capture students' interest in writing in multiple ways: kinesthetically, orally, or visually. Through this option, students develop 21st century and higher-order thinking skills as they apply their research and writing to an oral presentation or visual/multimedia format. The presentation options can be designed to tap into students' creativity and personal talents, such as art, music, drama, and technology.

The guidelines below support teachers as they create tasks:

- Spark students' imaginations and creativity. Use words or phrases that invite a variety of interpretations and responses and connect to an essential question.
- Involve an authentic audience, such as parents, other students, community members, other teachers. Make sure students understand the audience's familiarity with the topic and the level of formality in writing style appropriate to the audience.
- Provide clear directions and expectations for genre, length, sources, and format, and familiarize students with elements of the rubric for the assessment.
- Offer succinct directions that will not stifle originality in students' work.
- Include expectations about how students find, use, and cite evidence sources. Distinguish summarizing, synthesizing, and quoting source material from plagiarism.
- Ensure the task is appropriate in content and form to the grade level of the students.
- Design the task for both the student and the scorer, so they can clearly interpret the rubric.

Teachers must ensure the task is appropriate in content and form to the grade level of the students.

QPA COMMON TASKS OVERVIEW

QPA has worked with QPA Network Schools to create and field-test four common tasks that are aligned to the Common Core for ELA and literacy across disciplines. The tasks have been administered in grades 7 through 12 using QPA Common Task rubrics across the grade span (see Tools #17-30). The tasks are designed to be administered across the disciplines and have been administered in English, humanities, history, and science classes.[1] The tasks are designed to allow for maximum flexibility for embedding of tasks in the curriculum of the school and promoting 21st century skills while providing opportunities for student engagement.[2]

Position Paper Task

Students take a stand on a controversial issue and construct an argument to convince the audience of their position.

Literary Analysis Task

Students choose one or more pieces of fiction and compare and contrast one or more character(s), literary device(s), theme(s), or historical context(s) of the works.

Analysis of Media Task

Students compare and contrast how multiple types of media portray one event or story from literature, current events, or history.

Research Task

Students conduct research on a topic using a variety of sources.

THE PRODUCTS

Each task has two components: a written product and a presentation. For the presentation, students may either do an oral presentation or create a visual/multimedia product. QPA strongly recommends that task administration include both written and presentation products to deepen content knowledge, promote 21st century skills, and increase student engagement.

---

[1] The literary task is the only task that is ELA focused.

[2] QPA Common Tasks provide maximum flexibility for teachers and students. As readers consider the stakes and level of comparability needed, it is important to take into account that higher stakes will require more reliability in scoring, which will impact the design of the performance assessment.

WRITTEN PRODUCT

Students present their work in the written format that is appropriate to the task, audience, and purpose.

Examples of written tasks:
- o Research paper
- o Essay
- o Lab report
- o Literary analysis
- o Media analysis
- o Play
- o Historical character study
- o Proposal

ORAL COMMUNICATION PRODUCT

Students present their work orally, using their choice or the teacher's choice of format.

Examples of oral tasks:
- o Exhibition
- o Oral presentation
- o Speech
- o Debate
- o Simulation
- o Panel discussion
- o Group presentation
- o Song or short play
- o Radio broadcast or podcast

VISUAL/MULTIMEDIA PRODUCT

Students present their work in a visual or multimedia product and complete an artistic statement.

Examples of visual/multimedia tasks:
- o Booklet or pamphlet
- o Poster
- o Webpage or blog
- o PowerPoint presentation
- o TV show or movie
- o Webcast
- o Public service announcement
- o Graphic comic
- o Picture book

Tuning the Task

Once the task is written, a group of teachers convene to fine-tune it using the Tuning Protocol for Tasks. Engaging in this protocol is particularly important, as common tasks are used across classrooms. The process of tuning increases task effectiveness and teacher ownership (see Tool #38). Using either the same or an adapted protocol, teachers sometimes involve students in tuning a task in order to get their perspective on how best to revise their practice.

EXAMPLE

KENNEDY MIDDLE SCHOOL POSITION PAPER TASK SUMMARY

- **Topic:** The quarantine of Mary Mallon during the typhoid epidemic in New York City. Please choose one of the perspectives below:
  - Take on **Mary Mallon's** point of view. Write a letter to New York City public health officials convincing them that you should be released from quarantine and allowed to lead a normal life outside the confines of North Brother Island.
  - Take on the **New York City Board of Public Health's** point of view. Write a letter explaining to Mary why she must stay in quarantine on North Brother Island.
- **Genre:** Argument writing: The goal of your paper is to provide compelling evidence for the reader that your argument is correct. The essay must be research based.
- **Evidence sources:**
  - Text: *Typhoid Mary: Captive to the Public's Health*, by Judith Walzer Leavitt, Beacon Press, 1997.
  - Video: NOVA—"The Most Dangerous Woman in America," written and directed by Nancy Porter, 2004.
  - Additional sources are encouraged but not required.
- **Audience:** The audience will be either the New York City Board of Health, if writing from the perspective of Mary Mallon, or Mary Mallon, if writing from the perspective of the New York City Board of Health.
- **Time frame:** Two weeks, including research, reflection, and revision through multiple drafts as well as peer and teacher edits.

EXAMPLE

KENNEDY MIDDLE SCHOOL VISUAL TASK SUMMARY

- **Topic:** Influenza is a common disease in contemporary America. For this assessment, you will explore the resource packet about the disease and then create a brochure to show your ability to comprehend informational texts.
- **Genre:** Brochure. The brochure must be research based. The brochure's design must incorporate evidence from your research to convince the viewer to handle influenza appropriately.
- **Evidence sources:**
  - o Texts: CDC brochures and other information provided by teacher in resource packet.
  - o Speaker: School nurse.
- **Audience:** Kennedy Middle School students and teachers.
- **Time frame:** One week, including research, reflection, and revision through two drafts as well as peer and teacher edits.

STEP 2

Craft Clear Criteria and a Common Rubric

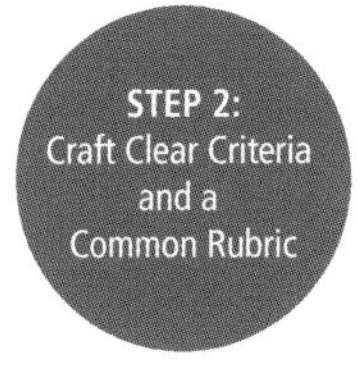

Teachers develop clear criteria and expectations for a proficient student performance and then collaborate to build a rubric that includes performance levels, novice to expert, based on the identified standards.

> "I learned that it is extremely important to note in the text evidence of each criteria (or lack there of). It helped to refer back to the notations when scoring and justifying our thoughts. I typically do this, but not as thoroughly as I did today." —*QPA Network Teacher*

Without sufficient planning, performance assessments might easily be measured subjectively, based on the teacher's own judgment. For this reason, fair assessment of performance tasks is steered by clear and appropriate criteria. Criteria specify aspects of assessments that teachers should concentrate on to determine students' understanding of the assignment and to provide a consistent and fair evaluation of student work. Such well-defined criteria also give students direction in their learning. Students gain a better understanding of what is expected in terms of the quality of their work and how it will be evaluated. With this understanding, expectations are no longer a mystery to students.

The most effective criteria are derived from the standards and emphasize the "most revealing and important aspects of the work," according to McTighe and Wiggins (2005, p. 173). In a science lab, for example, the most important aspects of the work should be a close following of the lab's procedures so as to arrive at accurate findings, followed by the quality of analysis of the results.

The QPA Common Tasks are models for teachers to adapt to their school's curriculum. Teams of teachers can design their own common assessments in every subject area tailored to what they want their students to know and be able to do. When designing a common assessment, QPA teachers look at exemplars of student work and extract from those models criteria based on the purpose of the assessment work. Teachers use the selected criteria to create a *common rubric* to assess the proficiency of student work. The rubric describes the degree of quality, proficiency, and understanding along a continuum.

> "Thus, a rubric for understanding must provide concrete answers to our key assessment questions: What does understanding look like? What differentiates a sophisticated understanding from a naïve understanding, in practice? What does a range of explanations look like, from the most naïve or simplistic to the most complex and sophisticated? (Wiggins & McTighe, 2005, p. 175)"

In order to truly evaluate the student's degree of understanding, the rubric assesses each trait separately. Two position papers, for example, could be rated not proficient for very different reasons: one paper might have well-developed thoughts, but many grammatical errors that distract from the paper's thesis; another paper might have perfect grammar and little development of ideas. If the teacher chose not to rate the traits separately, the two students could potentially score identically and not realize why or how to improve their writing,

QPA introduces faculties to developing a common rubric with a light-hearted activity called Cookie Monster (see Tool #9), a powerful activity for teachers. After experiencing this approach, teachers often realize the value of soliciting a multitude of views as they move on to create a common rubric for a performance assessment.

COOKIE MONSTER ACTIVITY

Chocolate chip cookies are a staple in the pantries of most U.S. kitchens. In fact, six billion chocolate chip cookies are consumed in the United States each year, representing 30 percent of the cookie market. In 1997, Massachusetts even designated them the Official State Cookie. Yet, consider this: Are all chocolate chip cookies created equal? Obviously not. Some people like store bought, others insist on homemade. Some prefer chewy, others want them crispy. There is no common standard for a "proficient" chocolate chip cookie.

Cookie samples used at a QPA Summer Institute

In the Cookie Monster activity, a team of teachers brainstorms to identify the most important qualities of a chocolate chip cookie and then creates performance levels for those criteria on a four-point scale. From there, the group tests several cookies, ranging from homemade to packaged, store-bought cookies, against their scale.

For example, in one professional development session, teachers created the categories below:

Flavor | Texture | Shape/Size | Source

The group broke the "source" criterion into the following descriptors:

Level	4	3	2	1
Criterion descriptor: Source	Homemade with love as you know the person who made it	Homemade	Mass produced	Expiration date is in the next decade

The taste test enables the group to explore the difference between a rubric that works well for an individual and a rubric that works well as a *common rubric* for a group of people who need to use it consistently and reliably. The groups share their criteria and their scores. The facilitator ranks the cookies to see if the cookies came out in the same order of quality despite the differences in the rubrics, and reveals the source of each cookie. Adjustments to the rubric are made based on the taste testing.

Teacher from QPA Summer Institute shares cookie rubric brainstorming ideas

The facilitator then leads the group through a discussion in which they apply the "chocolate chip cookie mindset" and the learning from this activity to the creation of common rubrics. The group debates the questions below:

- Are all criteria equally important?
- What are the essential characteristics seen across all rubrics?
- What if a cookie has a high score in number of chips or size, but a low score in taste? Does that matter?
- What if one cookie is warm? How does that influence the score? What factors in student work throw scoring off?
- What are the implications for rubrics we use in our classes/courses?

In the final step, the facilitator leads the group through a discussion of the five different types of criteria used in rubrics. When creating a rubric, it is important to keep these criteria types in mind and to consider whether some are more essential than others:

- **Process criteria**—Did you follow the right steps (e.g., science investigation; data collection; developing an outline; following a routine)?
- **Form criteria**—Did you apply correct formats and rules (e.g., correct citation format; correctly labeled; organized properly)?
- **Accuracy of content criteria**—Is the answer correct; is the right relationship explained; is the concept understood or accurately applied?
- **New knowledge criteria**—Did the student go beyond the accurate solution and correct process to gain new insights, raise new questions?
- **Impact criteria**—Did the final product achieve its intended purpose (e.g., solve a problem; persuade the audience; synthesize information)?

Through this process, teachers realize how a common rubric resulting from teamwork differs from one developed individually.

A rubric is best tested by scoring student work, or in the case of a cookie rubric, tasting and scoring cookies. Measuring the quality of the student work with the rubric confirms that it is aligned to the standards and that the levels of performance effectively allow scorers to distinguish one level from another. A well-designed rubric assesses what is most essential in the performance. This is not necessarily the easiest aspect to assess. For example, it is easy to determine whether students have completed five paragraphs or used correct citations. It is much more difficult to assess whether students have written a compelling argument or provided the reader with a new perspective. Typically, a rubric consists of four or five criteria, such as idea development or organization, and each of those elements has performance descriptors or subcriteria that describe work at a certain level of proficiency, from novice to expert. Common rubrics must be tested collaboratively so that teachers create a common language and shared expectations to achieve technical quality. Once teachers internalize the diverse voices of their colleagues heard while creating the common rubric, they may transfer that knowledge to their own classroom-based rubrics as well (Wiggins & McTighe, 2005).

Rubrics are indispensable for teachers in creating performance assessment plans and in evaluating student work with fairness, accuracy, and reliability. They are indispensable for students in self-assessment of drafts and peer editing. Rubrics can be self-created or adapted; or existing rubrics with strong technical quality can be used if they have been tested with student work using the Calibration Protocol (see Tool #4). When rubrics are used effectively, they guide students and provide them motivating feedback as they undertake and complete formative as well as summative assessments. Rubrics can direct teachers as they give constructive feedback on drafts of student work, and inform students as they revise those drafts. A rubric serves as a vehicle for helping students to understand expectations.

STEP 3

Field-Test Performance Assessment and Score Student Work

STEP 3: Field Test Performance Assessment and Score Student Work

Colleagues field-test the performance assessment with students; as a team, they practice scoring student work to assess effectiveness and revise the rubric.

> "The word *interpretation* was used eight times during the Calibration Protocol. We don't have shared interpretation, language, and meaning. We are still relying on personal interpretations of the rubric. We need to move toward a shared interpretation to get to reliable scoring." —*Teacher at QPA professional development debrief session*

After constructing a common rubric to assess mastery of the standards in question, teachers return to their classrooms and administer the task to students. The rubric becomes an integral part of teaching as the class uses it to help guide their learning. Students familiarize themselves with the rubric, keeping it on hand to guide their performance, and teachers refer to it when examining student work. Yet, just as students conduct peer edits and revise their writing, there is a revision process built into creating a common rubric. A first draft of the common rubric is not a finished product. In essence, teachers now conduct a peer edit of the rubric to check for problems with language or missing elements; refinement is part of the cycle of developing a rubric. Teachers ask students to be open to the revision process, and similarly, teachers must be ready to scrutinize their own work and be open to constructive critique from colleagues in the interest of improving instructional practice.

The process of editing and revising rubrics promotes consistent scoring of student work among colleagues and is the next step in designing a *valid* and *reliable* performance task. Teachers calibrate their own scoring methods with the Calibration Protocol (see Tool #4). The 35-minute exercise gives a group of teachers the opportunity to score a piece of student work. First, the teachers score the work individually using the rubric. Next, they share their scores and then examine ways in which reviewers' scores vary for each area of the rubric, seeking to understand the varying perspectives and discussing whether there are aspects of the rubric that hinder coming to consensus on scoring. Finally, the team debriefs the discussion itself. As part of this process, teachers specifically examine the rubric and come to an agreement on the number of subcriteria students need to master for a piece of writing to be rated "proficient." Without that calibration, scoring is not reliable. In QPA-developed rubrics, all of the subcriteria are required to be met for a "proficient" score. For example, in the QPA Common Position Paper Rubric (see Tool #24), under the criterion "Idea Development," a student must accomplish the following subcriteria:

a. My thesis (claim) is important, clear, and defensible.

b. My argument demonstrates my understanding of the topic. I explain and show the reason for each idea used to support my thesis.

c. I explain the significance of my thesis/argument (the "so-what?" of my paper).

To attain an "advanced" level, a student must achieve all of the above subcriteria as well as two or three more complex requirements from the advanced column, such as "I use my own voice and perspective in presenting my argument." Scoring guidelines clarify such scoring decisions and support the consistent interpretation of the QPA Common Task rubrics across teachers. The QPA Common Task Scoring Guide (see Tool #27) serves as a reference tool to establish a common understanding and reliable scoring across diverse schools during QPA Network scoring sessions. Providing guidance to common scorers, based on practice with the rubric, is an important step on the road to technical quality as scorers move beyond personal interpretation to a common interpretation of the rubric.

QPA COMMON TASK SCORING GUIDE

Following is an excerpt from the QPA Common Task Scoring Guide for QPA-written rubrics. The guide serves as a model for the level of detail that is necessary for scoring across schools in a network or district in order to achieve reliability.

When scoring with the rubric:

- Start with the proficient (3) column and go to the left to the advanced (4) column if the paper is stronger than the proficient descriptors, or to the right to the developing (2) column if the paper is weaker than the proficient descriptors.
- For the proficient level (3), an essay must have every bullet present. For all other levels (1, 2, and 4), the essay must have most of the bullets in the level to earn that score.
  - o If a paper has a single bullet in multiple categories, default to the middle score.
  - o The advanced level requires all criteria in level 3 plus two of the three criteria in advanced (4).
- Scorers must select a score point; 2.5 or 1.5 is not an acceptable score.
- Scorers must keep each criterion separate in their minds to avoid double-counting mistakes.
- The score reports and annotations represent the "consensus scores" for essays and should be looked to when interpreting the meaning of any wording in the rubric.

Anchor Assessments in Exemplary Work

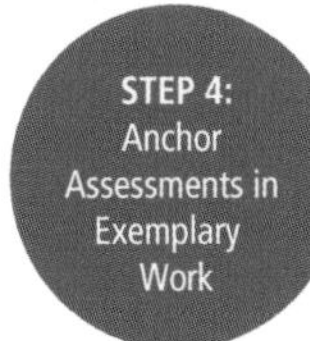

Anchor works illustrate what student work looks like at each performance level for a given task to support reliable scoring across grade levels and subject areas.

> "I want my students to carry around pictures in their head of quality work. It's not enough to make a list or rubric of what makes a good essay or a good science experiment. This is an important step, but it doesn't leave a picture, a vision, an inspiration. It's not even enough to read a great piece of literature together and analyze the writing, or to look at the work of a great scientist. If I want my students specifically to write a strong essay, to design a strong experiment, I need to show them what a great essay or experiment looks like." —Berger, 2003, p. 83

The power of having a clear picture of what quality work looks like is significant for students and essential for teachers implementing common performance assessments. QPA Network teachers understand the importance of *anchor works* as they meet in network meetings to score common performance assessments across schools. Anchor work is carefully selected by QPA Network teachers and the QPA team in advance of the scoring session to clarify for all teachers what a final product looks like at a given grade level and proficiency level. The anchor work brings the rubric to life and supports teachers not only in interpreting the rubric consistently but in aligning their instruction to the rubric. As teachers discuss the instructional steps that support students in the creation of proficient student work, they unpack key aspects of the rubric and take with them an image of the final product.

Teachers working in *communities of practice* can use anchor work to train themselves on how to score student work reliably and accurately in cross-school scoring sessions. One new teacher commented in a QPA professional development session, "As a new teacher in the building, I didn't know what fifth-grade work looked like. It would have helped me to have anchors to look at." In a group of between five and eight colleagues, teachers follow the Training with Anchors Protocol (see Tool #37). They read the model task and student work and score it with the rubric individually, checking for evidence of criteria. After briefly sharing scores, the group compares score differences, being careful to give only evidence-based comments. The group then reaches consensus about the score for each element of the rubric and the reasons for the score determination. After recording the consensus

score and the reasoning behind the score, the colleagues discuss what they can learn from the process to increase reliability and improve student performance, and identify implications for instructional practice. The process is repeated for other anchor papers. As one QPA teacher wrote about the anchor-training process, "These (scoring) conversations are very important, because they help us all consider how we make judgments about student work, what consistency means, and how we define what we teach and what we expect of students."

Anchors can represent a variety of student work types, such as papers, media, and videos of oral communication. These anchors can be used with students of all teachers administering the common assessment. When the assignment is an open-ended task, students can carefully analyze these anchors against the rubric to further elucidate how to emulate this level of work. In this way, anchors create pictures in students' minds of the level of work they are trying to attain.

At Fenway High School in Boston, Massachusetts, teachers identified anchors that correspond with each level of the rubric to exemplify the distinct levels for students writing their Senior Position Papers. These anchor papers serve as exemplars for students as they research and write their papers, so that they have a clear understanding of their target and can revise their writing until it meets the graduation benchmark. Anchor papers demystify performance standards for both teachers and students. Use of anchors is integral to an effective assessment design because it gives students more opportunities to attain their goals when they know what the end product should look like, and it leads to more equitable outcomes.

STEP 5

Refine Performance Assessments and Rubrics

STEP 5: Refine Performance Assessments and Rubrics

The school/teacher teams continue to revisit common performance assessments over time, as this is an iterative process.

> Engineers at NASA spend years in a cycle of design, test, and panel reviews before any Mars Rover can be launched. Each successive probe is built on the experience of the successes and failures of the last model. By contrast, historically teachers have been isolated in classrooms and not exposed to this process of collaborative and active continuous improvement. Receiving constructive feedback from colleagues relieves teachers' isolation and improves their instructional practices. Similar to the NASA process, designing performance tasks is an iterative and collaborative process and normally reaches fruition through several cycles of design, test, and review.

Samples of QPA Common Tasks from QPA Network Schools

QPA Common Tasks are designed to allow for maximum flexibility in embedding tasks in the curriculum of the school, promoting 21st century skills, providing opportunities for student engagement, and modeling alignment to the Common Core State Standards for ELA and literacy across disciplines. The task samples provided in this section are real examples from the QPA Network Schools. Included with the tasks are pedagogical decisions made by teachers as they implemented the tasks, as well as examples of student work scored at the proficient level.* The task summaries are designed to provide a consistent format that includes details for students on audience, task, purpose, and other key information. However, summaries do not address the full curriculum, expectations, or teaching context in which the task is embedded.

* All documents necessary to implement the QPA Common Tasks are included in the Tools section of the guide. Additional task examples and student work samples with annotations are available on the QPA website: www.qualityperformanceassessment.org.

EXPLORING THE POWER OF CULTURAL RELEVANCE IN A QPA COMMON TASK EXAMPLE

Codman Academy is a small charter high school of 150 students in Boston, Massachusetts. 96% of its students are African American or Latino; 22% speak a first language other than English; and 69% are low-income. In the 10th-grade humanities course Power, Equality, and Freedom in America, all students are expected to identify, visit, research, and conduct oral histories on a "people's history site" that highlights the accomplishments of those people not traditionally emphasized in U.S. history. Each student is expected to write a position paper on why their site should receive greater publicity in Boston. The curriculum in which this performance assessment is embedded is an example of curriculum that is culturally relevant. Culturally relevant curriculum "empowers students intellectually, socially, emotionally, and politically by using cultural referents to impart knowledge, skills, and attitudes" (Ladson-Billings, 2009, p. 20). As students at Codman explore the history of the Freedom Trail, they are inspired to see the roles of people of color and the working class through a new lens. The task is powerful for students, as it places American history in the context of the students' hometown through the power of fieldwork and having an authentic audience.

CODMAN ACADEMY POSITION PAPER TASK SUMMARY

- **Topic:** After finishing a field study of Boston's traditional historical sites, you will argue that the landmarks can better represent the "people's history" by recognizing traditional histories while also focusing on the experiences and contributions of groups like African Americans, Native Americans, women, and poor people.
- **Genre:** Argument writing: The goal of your paper is to provide compelling evidence for the reader that your argument is correct. The essay must be research based and include evidence from fieldwork on Boston's Freedom Trail.
- **Evidence sources:**
  - Text: *A Young People's History of the United States* by Howard Zinn.
  - Articles discussed in class relating to American history.
  - Personal records: Students visit historical sites on Boston's Freedom Trail and record their observations through writing, photos, and video.
- **Audience:** The National Park Service and visitors to Boston's Freedom Trail.
- **Time frame:** Fieldwork: two to three weeks; writing: two to three weeks.

THE BOSTON FREEDOM TRAIL POSITION PAPER TENTH-GRADE STUDENT WORK SAMPLE

"People walk along the Freedom Trail and admire the beautiful statues and history, but they overlook a huge part of Boston's past and present: the working class. More people's history based on the working class citizens of the 1700s should be publicized in the Boston Common, where riots against raised bread prices, the Stamp Act, and tea tax took place. The working class people's action and dedication were influential in these riots, proving that they have earned more recognition than the current representation on the Boston Common. The Park Service should include landmarks that show how working class citizens fought for their rights and bravely demonstrated to improve the quality of their lives, building Boston into the city it is today."

EXPLORING THE POWER OF INTERDISCIPLINARY PERFORMANCE TASKS IN A QPA COMMON TASK EXAMPLE

At the Francis W. Parker Charter Essential School all students take a humanities class in grades 7–12, in which English, history, and the arts are fully integrated and taught using an interdisciplinary model. Parker approached the QPA Common Tasks with attention to how the arts can play a role in supporting student understanding of historical content as students build literacy skills. Parker embedded the research paper task in a unit on 18th-century American society focused on portraiture of the time period. The skills of art observation and critique were as important to the task as the skills of research and writing. This pedagogical approach is stated in Parker's mission: "To move the child to the center of the education process and to interrelate the several subjects of the curriculum in such a way as to enhance their meaning for the child."

FRANCIS W. PARKER CHARTER ESSENTIAL SCHOOL RESEARCH PAPER TASK SUMMARY

- **Topic:** What can we learn about 18th-century American society based on portraits from that colonial period?
- **Genre:** Informational writing: The goal of the research paper is to use evidence to educate the reader about 18th-century American society through the art of the time.
- **Evidence sources:**
    - o 3 primary sources—paintings.
    - o 1 or more reference sources—the artist and three subjects.
    - o 2 book sources—artifacts and/or painting analyses.
    - o 2 database sources—artifacts and/or painting analyses.
- **Audience:** Classmates and teacher—to inform their understanding of how images can be used by people to portray their lives.
- **Time frame:** Three weeks, including research and revision through multiple drafts as well as peer and teacher conferencing.

COLONIAL PORTRAITURE RESEARCH PAPER TENTH-GRADE STUDENT WORK SAMPLE

"In this portrait of John Nelson, Smibert also shows how educated Nelson is by the large wig. In Colonial times wigs were also part of everyday clothing for men. Wearing a large wig that covered your head and ears was traditionally worn to keep all one's knowledge within one's self. The other element of clothing that becomes the focal point of the portrait is his large red cape. Nelson returned to Boston after being imprisoned in Quebec and France to become a very successful fur trader (Saunders 175). His clothing often reflected his wealth and wearing lush fabrics shows how important clothing and personal wellbeing were to Nelson. Later he was painted by a different artist along with his wife and children and the same attention to detail and clothing was included (Saunders 175). Using clothing and details was one of the ways Smibert was able to show a well-educated, wealthy, Colonial American."

EXPLORING THE POWER OF MEDIA LITERACY IN A QPA COMMON TASK EXAMPLE

The QPA Common Analysis of Media Task is designed to develop the skill of media awareness and analysis in students, as media literacy is a critical 21st century skill. The Common Core states that "just as media and technology are integrated in school and life in the twenty-first century, skills related to media use (both critical analysis and production of media) are integrated throughout the standards" (Key Points in English Language Arts, CCSSO, 2010, para. 12). This performance assessment can be used in any content area to look deeply at a topic through a variety of media forms and to develop media literacy. Francis W. Parker Charter Essential School chose to look at film techniques in two very different film adaptations of the play *Macbeth*. In their written work and a collaborative oral presentation, students had to choose who the director depicted as responsible for the tragedy through their analysis of the two films. Students had to deeply understand the play to analyze and critique the films and use complex cinematic vocabulary to justify their analysis.

FRANCIS W. PARKER CHARTER ESSENTIAL SCHOOL ANALYSIS OF MEDIA TASK SUMMARY

- **Topic:** How do films interpret which character is responsible for the tragedy of *Macbeth?* You will select various scenes and compare the two versions based on various film techniques, choices in setting, props, and the actors' blocking and delivery of lines.
- **Genre:** Informational writing: provide analysis and textual evidence that demonstrate understanding of both the literary text and the film adaptations, and the creative decisions of the director in bringing the text to the screen.
- **Evidence sources:**
  - o Video: Rupert Goold's version of *Macbeth*.
  - o Video: Roman Polanski's version of *Macbeth*.
  - o Text: *Macbeth* by William Shakespeare.
- **Audience:** Humanities students and teachers in this class—to inform their understanding of the text and movie selections in future classes.
- **Time frame:** Three weeks, including reading Macbeth, viewing movies, and the writing process, including multiple drafts.

Student Reflection

"I learned how to watch films (or it could be anything like read an article, look at a visual) and take out the most important information. Also by watching the 2 films that were both based on the same story, I learned how to find the similarities and differences, then take this information and write a paper or take the same information but change it to an [oral presentation] script."

ANALYSIS OF MEDIA TENTH-GRADE STUDENT WORK SAMPLE

"Another use of props is during the most pivotal scene involving the witches when they tell Macbeth his prophecy. In this scene, they are all wielding gruesome surgeon's tools. However, it is not so much the tools themselves that are wrong, but the misuse of good things. The use of life-saving tools for a supposed evil purpose adds a malevolent mood to the scene, making the witches appear prone to murder. Since the witches are shown as ones who could murder, and it is shown in at least one instance they did murder, it causes the audience to think of them whenever a death happens."

EXPLORING THE POWER OF VISUAL PERFORMANCE TASKS IN A QPA COMMON TASK EXAMPLE

Students need opportunities to learn and present their work visually. Visual or multimedia tasks allow some students to go deeper and better understand the content, and for other students they are more engaging. The English teacher at Cape Cod Lighthouse Charter School asked students to complete a written comparative literary analysis. Students also chose how they would represent the theme from their paper visually and wrote an artistic statement explaining the evidence behind their artistic choices. The artistic statement is an important part of the performance assessment process for students presenting their ideas visually. It provides a window into the students' thinking and separates a "pretty" project from one that is based on evidence and a meaningful understanding of the content. QPA Network teachers reported that the artistic statement made grading visual projects much easier, more reliable and kept students focused on making purposeful artistic decisions in their projects. This type of purposeful creation for visual elements, in which students can explain the evidence and rationale for their artistic decisions, is required of students in college and career.

CAPE COD LIGHTHOUSE CHARTER SCHOOL VISUAL/MULTIMEDIA PRESENTATION TASK SUMMARY

- **Topic:** Draw or paint a scene based on the book *The Pigman* and the short story "The Treasure of Lemon Brown" that represents the theme of loneliness. Then give a one-minute speech as to how this scene connects to the points made in your paper.
- **Genre:** Visual representation of literary analysis: The goal of your visual image is to inform the viewer about the themes presented by the literary authors.
- **Evidence sources:**
  - o Text: *The Pigman,* by Paul Zindel.
  - o Text: "The Treasure of Lemon Brown," by Walter Dean Myers.
- **Audience:** Classmates and teacher.
- **Time frame:** Three weeks to read texts and complete multiple drafts of literary essay and visual multimedia piece, including artistic statement.

Visual/Multimedia Presentation Eighth-Grade Student Drawing

VISUAL/MULTIMEDIA PRESENTATION EIGHTH-GRADE STUDENT ARTISTIC STATEMENT

"Both Angelo Pignati, from *The Pigman,* and Lemon Brown are very lonesome because of something that happened to them earlier in life. Mr. Pignati's wife Conchetta died about three months before John and Lorraine found him, and Lemon Brown lost his son Jesse in a war. This loneliness also had a huge impact on both of their lives and I tried to show this in my drawing. Lemon Brown is wrapped in rags and has a long dirty beard and long hair. When his son died, Brown lost his will to succeed in life and was reduced to living on the streets and picking through trash. On Pignati's side, I demonstrated how loneliness affected the character's life by drawing all of his electrical equipment strewn across behind him, showing he hasn't cleaned up his house since his wife died. The mess illustrates he is so miserable about her death that he refuses to even admit it happened. Both illustrations depict how loneliness changed the characters' outlooks on their lives."

EXPLORING THE POWER OF ORAL COMMUNICATION IN A QPA COMMON TASK EXAMPLE

Pentucket Regional High School in Massachusetts has committed to assessing students on five Habits of Learning as a graduation requirement (see page 25). The Habit of Communication is one that is assessed by its inclusion in student portfolios. In the eleventh grade students are required to present a portfolio defense. To prepare for the eleventh-grade defense, the tenth-grade team has developed a time-efficient way to provide multiple opportunities for student presentations. Students present in small groups of classmates and one teacher. Teachers and other staff members volunteer to be scorers during their planning period so that all presentations can be completed during one class period in groups of five. All students score each other's presentations, and in a discussion held after the presentation, scores are shared and calibrated so that the group's teacher can submit the final score to be used for the course grade. This time-efficient process allows oral presentations to be completed for all students in one period, even in class sizes as large as 30. College and career readiness requires that school leaders and teachers find creative solutions such as this to ensure that all students practice communication skills multiple times each school year.

PENTUCKET HIGH SCHOOL POSITION PRESENTATION TASK SUMMARY

- **Topic:** Convince your audience to take your position on an issue that matters to people living in American society. You can choose your issue.
- **Genre:** Argument: The goal of your presentation is to provide compelling evidence for the audience that your argument is correct. The presentation must be research based.
- **Evidence sources:** Independent research based on position paper.
- **Audience:** About five classmates and one teacher.
- **Time frame:** The presentation should last between 5 and 7 minutes. Preparation for this presentation builds on research done during development of position paper. Students should spend 3–5 days preparing for and practicing presentation before presenting to the group.

Excerpt from Question & Answer after presentation:

Teacher: I liked how you talked about hurting the whole ecosystem. Could you explain more about that?

Student: Well, if you take the bass away, the bigger fish will go away. And if you take away the bigger fish, the predatory birds of the area will also migrate away. So the feeding systems that happen underwater affect what happens overhead. It is a circle of life.

ISSUE IN AMERICA POSITION PRESENTATION TENTH-GRADE STUDENT WORK TRANSCRIPT

"*Excerpt from presentation:* Bass fishing during the spawn should be illegal because it is very easy for fisherman to take advantage of the bass when they are on their spawning bed, leading to decreased bass populations and harmful effects on the whole ecosystem. During spawning time, the bass have increased hormone levels and will attack anything that comes close to their nest. I have a quote from Don Gassaway, who is a fisherman, explaining "males will aggressively defend the nest site from anything they perceive as a threat." I have personally experienced this. My dad and I fished on Lake Winnipesaukee and we could basically choose which fish we were going to catch because they were so aggressive and attacked our hooks. Even when fishermen return the bass, the increased stress of getting caught will kill the fish, leaving their nests and eggs open to predators and endangering the bass population."

Let's Get Started: Entry Points for Designing Common Performance Assessments

While the steps to designing common performance assessments are numbered, one through five, the work of designing performance assessments is not linear in nature. Just as school or district leaders might opt to begin their QPA performance assessment work with quality aligned instruction or by analyzing data, there are options even within each chapter of this guide. The process unfolds as the work is initiated and continuously refined.

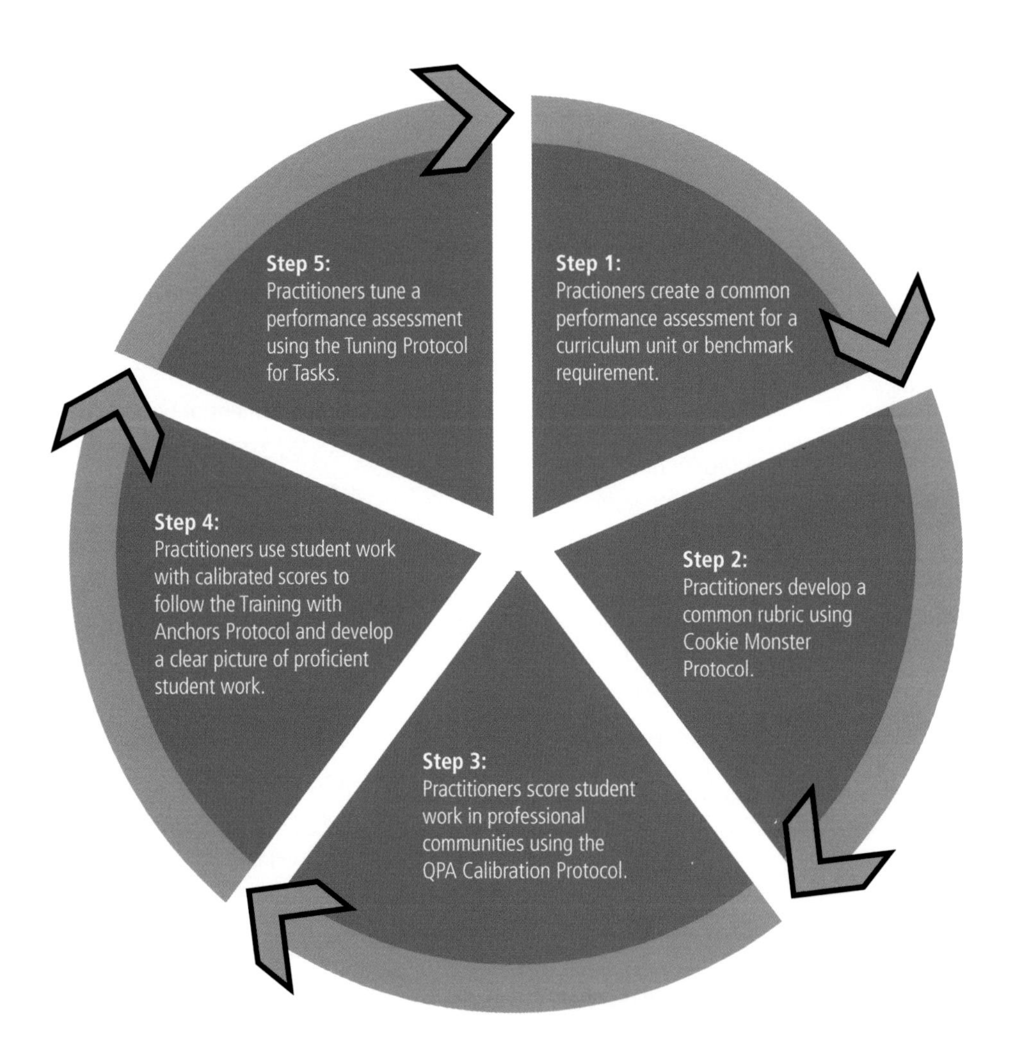

Refining Our Work through Self-Assessment

Developing common performance assessments is a cyclical process. Teachers convene to design and plan the common elements, and apply their individual expertise to the curriculum in their own classrooms. After students undertake the assessments, the rubric, scoring of student work, and assessment design are carefully reviewed and tested for consistency. The self-assessment process also ensures that teachers are constantly reviewing and amending their own work. Teams of teachers must ask themselves the following questions:

Quality Task Design	Do the assessments provide opportunities for students to demonstrate the standards through multiple modes and to exercise ownership and decision making in real-world settings?
	Do the rubrics used by teachers and students have clear criteria and descriptions of performance at each level?
	For each common performance task, have teachers identified anchors of student work to provide examples of proficient work?
	Has a team of teachers examined and revised the common tasks and rubrics using student work?

TOOLS USED IN THIS CHAPTER

Tools for Common Performance Assessment Design

TOOL #	TOOL NAME	PAGE #
4	Calibration Protocol	T9
8	Common Performance Assessment Curriculum Planning Template	T13
9	Cookie Monster Protocol	T17
11	Gradients in Complexity: Text Complexity Rubric for Informational Texts	T21
12	Gradients in Complexity: Text Complexity Rubric for Literary Texts	T22
17	QPA Common Analysis of Media Task	T28
18	QPA Common Analysis of Media Rubric	T29
19	QPA Common Literary Analysis Task	T31
20	QPA Common Literary Analysis Rubric	T32
21	QPA Common Oral Communication Task	T34
22	QPA Common Oral Communication Rubric	T35
23	QPA Common Position Paper Task	T37
24	QPA Common Position Paper Rubric	T38
25	QPA Common Research Task	T40
26	QPA Common Research Rubric	T41
27	QPA Common Task Scoring Guide	T43
28	QPA Common Task Teacher Directions	T45
29	QPA Common Visual or Media Task	T49
30	QPA Common Visual or Media Rubric	T50
35	Planning Worksheet: Analyzing Features of Text Complexity for Instruction & Assessment	T59
37	Training with Anchors Protocol	T61
38	Tuning Protocol for Tasks	T62

Students peruse booths at Youth Conference

Teachers present results from discussion about power standards

CHAPTER 4

ANALYZE: DATA ANALYSIS FOR PERFORMANCE ASSESSMENT

We, as designers of widespread alternative assessments, must make every effort to create an assessment that will provide us with accurate results and truly show what students know.

—QPA Network Teacher Reflection

Student Work Sample: Student presents research findings on the impact of cigarettes on lung capacity

In a seventh-grade physical science class, students at Cape Cod Lighthouse Charter School in Orleans, Massachusetts, built balloon-powered cars designed to demonstrate concepts related to the forces of motion, and then, in an exhibition of their work, gave individual presentations on their cars and staged races against each other's cars. After the completion of these exhilarating presentations, the Lighthouse science teacher met with the validation team for approval of the task. Validation would mean the assessment measured its intended standard—in this case, knowledge of Newton's third law of motion.

The team referred to the Assessment Validation Protocol (see Tool #3) to arrive at its conclusions. On review, they found the task actively engaged the students, provided an authentic learning opportunity, and adhered to principles of fairness and universal design. And, as one person commented, "Sounds like a fun project!" On the other hand, others observed that the expectations on the data-recording sheet did not fully align to the intended standards.

The Assessment Validation Protocol is adapted from the work of Karin Hess (2009).

The questions on the data-recording sheet, which the science teacher provided for student work samples, did not seem to elicit profound reflections about physical laws of motion. Rather, the questions prompted students to think more about how to make their cars go faster. For example, the teacher asked students: "What changes did you make? After you made changes, did you see an improvement?" One student wrote: "I straightened the axle to make the car run straight and I made the front of my car a triangle to build more momentum." In the next question, the teacher asked: "Which run of all six was the best? Why do you think so?" The student responded: "The third run was the best. On the first run, my car curved, which made it slower. On the second, run the straw was bent slightly, which slowed it down. The third run, my car was the best it could be." Students had the observational data to make connections to laws of motion, but the questions did not push students to take this step.

During the task validation, teachers gave the task positive marks for the intended rigor of alignment to the content standards, but in the category of "assesses what is intended to be assessed," they commented: "Students don't seem to really work with the formulas…they see it, but may not fully develop and understand it."

In the final recommendation, while the task met many of the criteria in the Assessment Validation Protocol, the team felt that the task needed improvement in the areas of alignment and clarity and focus. Among other comments, the validation team advised the teacher to deepen questioning so that students would be forced to explain why changes made a difference in relation to the laws of motion. They also noted that the students could receive a good grade by "completing all required sections of the rubric, but not fully understand it." The team did not validate the task and requested that the teacher revise it and return for another review. This is not, however, regarded as a failure, considering the cyclical nature of the work. With valuable feedback, practice improves, and as a result, students benefit.

In the past, performance assessments often did not adequately address critical content or skills of content areas in disciplines such as science or mathematics. This science teacher, aided by the validation team, strove to reach beyond simply providing a compelling and fun activity for his students to creating a rigorous physics assessment aligned to specific content standards.

PROCESS

Process of Quality Data Analysis

The method school leaders and teachers use as they collect and analyze data is outlined in the following steps:

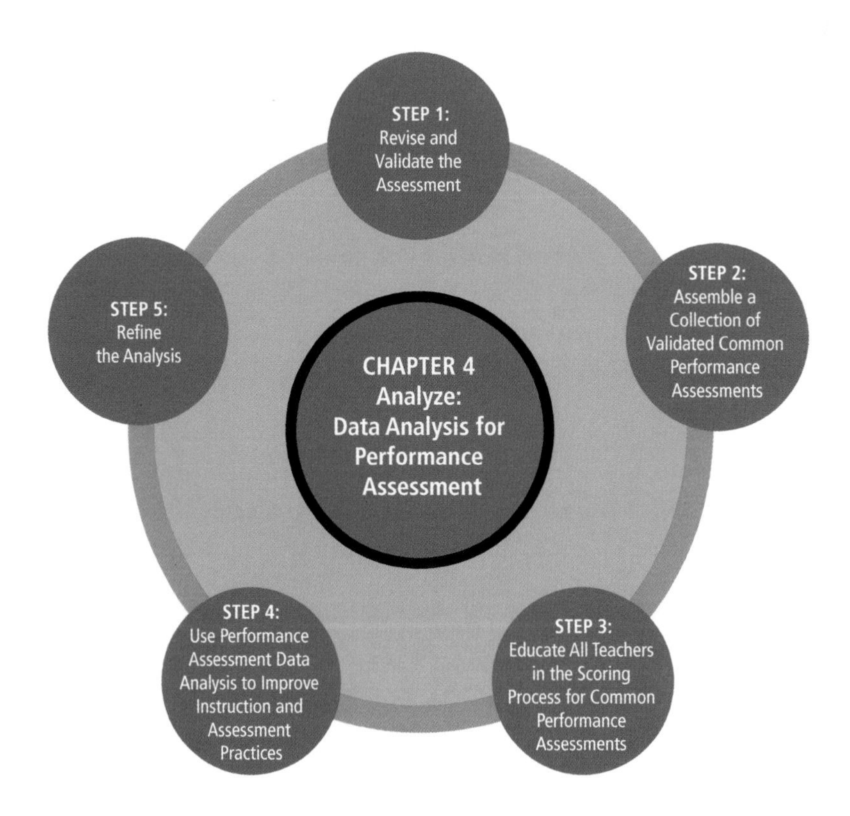

DECODING THE JARGON

Defined terms, italicized on first reference in the text, are listed in alphabetical order.

Calibration is the process of assuring that teachers have a common understanding of the work quality that corresponds to different score points (or performance levels) in a common rubric.

Proficiency is the degree to which students meet expectations for essential skills and knowledge.

Local assessment systems are collections of multiple types of assessments that go beyond individual classrooms to measure the academic performance of all students and create a coherent K–12 education.

Sufficiency describes a combination of related, validated assessments that provide enough assessment evidence to accurately infer the level of proficiency of a student on a standard.

Technical quality describes an assessment that is valid, reliable, sufficient, and free of bias.

A validation team is an interdisciplinary group of teachers who meet to review and analyze performance assessments to ensure they are clearly aligned to standards and measure what they are intended to measure.

Validity ensures that learning assessments are clearly aligned to standards and that they measure student performance on the intended standards.

Introduction

This chapter describes the steps school and district leaders take to collect and analyze data to help set schoolwide, team, and individual classroom goals and priorities for change, with a particular focus on equity and excellence. Education leaders begin the process by revising and validating performance assessments; developing a collection of validated assessments as models; collaborating among colleagues to learn the scoring process; and using the performance assessment data to improve the work.

Revise and Validate the Assessment

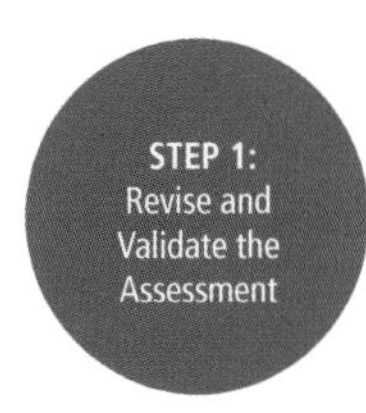

A team of teachers formally reviews and analyzes performance assessments for their alignment to standards and to ensure they meet criteria for validation, with the goal of providing constructive advice for improving practice.

> "After I did the Assessment Validation Protocol, I thought about all the rubrics I've written in the past years and realized the many changes I needed to make." —*QPA Summer Institute Teacher Participant*

- Does the assessment provide the information about mastery of standards/content for which it was designed?
- Do student work samples demonstrate *proficiency* for the subject and grade level?
- Do teachers and other school faculty use data from performance assessments, in addition to other assessment data, to inform curriculum planning, instruction, and (re)design of assessments?

These essential questions focused the faculty's work at the Cape Cod Lighthouse Charter School in the selection of *technical quality* as an entry into performance assessment. As the faculty produced their common performance assessments, they wanted to make sure that a given assessment elicited the intended information about student learning.

An important step in determining *validity* is ensuring that learning assessments are clearly aligned to standards and that they measure student performance on the intended standards. To meet validity requirements, assessments must be appropriate for the standards being measured. For example, to obtain a valid measure of a student's ability to write a cohesive, well-organized argument, teachers could ask students to write an essay or a letter addressed to a particular audience. To measure students' ability to express and defend ideas orally, teachers might require them to give a presentation on a specific topic before an audience.

Cape Cod Lighthouse Charter School started the validation process in January 2011. The teachers used the Assessment Validation Protocol (see Tool #3), which allowed them to share and critique assessment tasks in a formal setting. Several teachers, including the seventh-grade science teacher, prepared and presented an assessment they wished to validate. The assessments ranged from an independent reading project to a foreign language assessment to a social studies museum artifact project. In preparation for the validation session, teachers gathered all documents related to their assessments—including prompts, standards maps, rubrics, and scaffolding materials—to share with their colleagues.

Teams met three times before the end of the school year and reviewed 12 assessments that included tasks in every subject and all three grade levels. Once teachers or teaching teams completed a common task, they completed the Assessment Validation Cover Sheet (see tool #2) for submission to the school's *validation team*. Interdisciplinary validation teams reviewed these assessments, but they did not validate a single one on the first round.

Why was this lack of validated assessments considered a success? A lack of initial validation meant the process was successful in uncovering the assessment creators' blind spots and assumptions so that the assessments could be refined for future use. For example, one question in the validation protocol asks if the scoring guide is clear. Of the 12 assessments presented at Lighthouse Charter, only three validation teams felt the rubric was clear on the first review. Presenting teachers could then take their colleagues' precise feedback and revise the rubric before giving it to students again. Once revisions were made, teachers could resubmit the task to the validation team. Lighthouse resumed this process in the fall of 2011 to validate the first 12 assessments.

One teacher commented that the process is helpful because it supports teachers in "getting at the essence of where problems lie in our assessments and tweaking them so the quality of the assessment is improved." Lighthouse has created a community of practice where teachers collaborate and provide valuable feedback to each other to improve the *validity* of their assessments.

It takes time and deliberate effort to establish a collaborative process where teachers can comfortably give each other constructive critique and feel at ease with the revision process. The 50- to 60-minute process helps the team of at least four people ascertain whether the assessment presented has achieved technical quality. After choosing roles, the facilitator reviews the norms.

Briefly, the presenter walks the team through the materials and explains the context of the assessment. Then, the members examine the assessment materials silently and ask clarifying questions about the materials or the process. Next, as the presenter takes notes silently, the facilitator leads groups through each section of the Assessment Validation Checklist (see Tool #1). The main sections of the checklist are:

- Alignment
- Clarity and Focus
- Student Engagement
- Criteria and Levels

- Fairness
- Adherence to Principles of Universal Design
- Student Work Analysis

Each of the seven sections lists a series of criteria, such as "Is clearly aligned to specific content standards," "Is linked to ongoing instruction," and "All students have access to resources." The team seeks consensus on each section, one item at a time. Next, the team reads the presenter the feedback from each section. The presenter takes time to ask clarifying questions and to provide further information and other reflections, but must resist the tendency to justify his or her work. Finally, the facilitator leads a debrief session, always concluding with a conversation about the implications of the information learned for instruction.

EXAMPLE

SAMPLE FEEDBACK FROM THE VALIDATION SESSIONS INCLUDED THE FOLLOWING COMMENTS:

- **Alignment**—Students learn about one system in depth, but the standard calls for them to master all the body systems. Can you create a test or way they learn from other students to ensure they understand all systems?
- **Clarity and Focus**—More detail about the process and intent would be beneficial to students. What is the essential question and how is this communicated to students?
- **Student Engagement**—Structure a time and protocol for students to compare cars (See Forces of Motion performance assessment at the beginning of the chapter) to see why one performed better than the other based on the laws of motion.
- **Criteria and Levels**—The rubric needs work. It needs to be easier to read. It is missing a few categories such as display and presentation, and quality of writing.

Technical quality, one of the three essentials of the QPA performance assessment system, is at the heart of the validation sessions. Rather than relying on basic intuition or chance to ensure that tasks are valid, Lighthouse teachers systematically determine whether assessments meet the validation criteria. The validation process assures teachers that tasks are fair and aligned with standards and teaching. By undertaking this process, school leaders and teachers are well on their way to improving practice through careful analysis. The process can thereby ensure that measures of student learning provide students, parents, teachers, and administrators with relevant, meaningful information about what students know and can do.

The validation process helps the school maintain a consistent high level of instructional practice. As a teacher commented in a QPA professional development session debrief of the validation protocol, “Even when professionals teach the same grade, they can have different interpretations of the same rubrics. How do we build consistency across content areas? How do we make expectations clear? I think this validation conversation can really support that process and lead to clearer expectations and increased consistency in our district.”

During a validation session, a teacher and a QPA coach review a performance assessment using the validation protocol

Another validation session participant noted its potential to transform practice, stating, “Looking at assessments with a critical eye was extremely beneficial and will not only help me become a better teacher, but will also certainly enhance my students’ learning and improve their depth of knowledge.” As teachers and leaders build fluency with performance assessments, they also build their school or district’s capacity to develop and implement professional development activities that facilitate this work.

The validation team functions like a building inspector. The house is not ready for a final walk-through until after the building inspection team has put their stamp of approval on it. Sometimes the inspector requires minor revisions to the building. Similarly, a performance assessment is not considered complete until fully validated.

QPA Assessment Validation Protocol

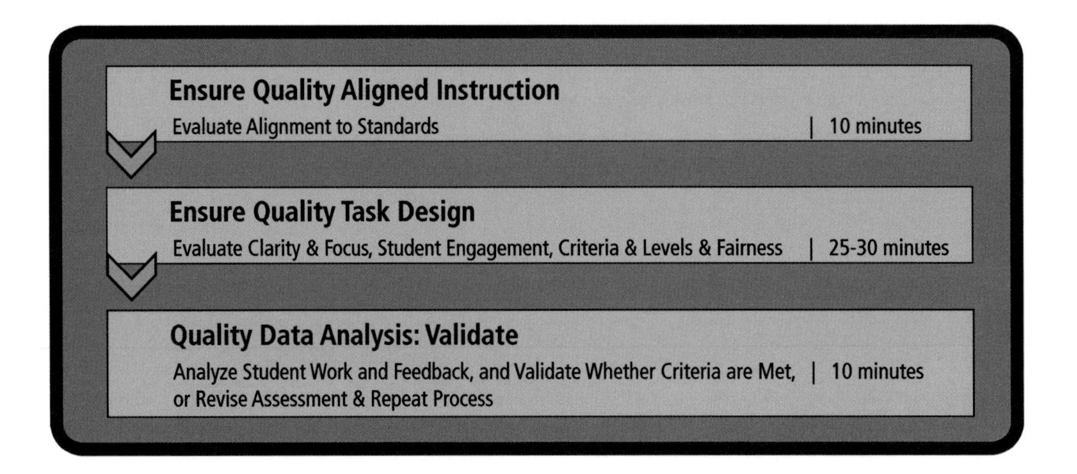

STEP 2

Assemble a Collection of Validated Common Performance Assessments

STEP 2: Assemble a Collection of Validated Common Performance Assessments

As common performance assessments achieve validation, school leaders create a binder or electronic file of samples of agreed-upon proficient student work.

> "Both educators and the students need to be involved in authentic learning in order to create change. Engaging in assessment validations is authentic learning for educators." —*QPA Summer Institute Teacher Participant*

All common assessments in a school—including graduation portfolios, presentations, and exhibitions—should eventually be validated through the validation process similar to the one outlined above. This level of technical quality means that all teachers have a clear vision of what effective assessment looks like and an understanding of what proficient work looks like in a given grade and subject. Validated assessments, with proficient work samples, can serve as key documents for teachers new to the building or teachers who change assignments within the building. In electronic or binder form, validated assessments serve as exemplars or prototypes so that all scorers know what *proficiency* looks like by reviewing the collective work of an assessment-literate community of practice. This investment of time pays huge dividends. In a school whose leaders plan backwards, validated common performance assessments become the foundation of the school's curriculum. These validated assessments and accompanying rubrics represent the proficiency levels that all students in the school are expected to meet. As a result, the school has a transparent set of documents that outline its expectations and standards for student achievement.

At Marblehead Community Charter Public School, a QPA Network School, exhibitions of student work are available for the school's parents and students to review online. In one example, the fifth-grade teachers posted the complete unit plan for their Medieval Faire, beginning with the essential question "Who had power in medieval society?" and ending with a description of all the major assessments. Visitors to the website can see several different lessons that students completed during the course of the assessment, the websites students used in their research, and the art, music, and writing standards addressed in the unit.

Student exhibition at Boston Arts Academy

Exhibitions are powerful summative assessments that guide school leaders and teachers in analyzing the school's assessment system. Teachers can learn from seeing individual students present their work and then returning to the exhibition to look at the work of the whole school. By the time students graduate from Marblehead in eighth grade, they have experienced 15 whole-school exhibitions. These exhibitions, held three times annually, are aligned with the school's mission statement:

> ...to create a partnership among community members, teachers, parents, and students that will provide our early adolescents with the support necessary to reach their highest individual potential intellectually, socially, emotionally, and physically, so they are highly contributing members of our democratic society; and to provide a laboratory for examining, developing and fostering the interrelatedness of the school as a learning community and the community as a learning environment.

In June 2012, every student in fourth through eighth grade participated in an exhibition of student work entitled "Character and Identity." The exhibition focused largely on historical figures and their contributions to a subject or field as well as several interdisciplinary projects. Eighth graders, for example, dressed in costumes of famous mathematicians or scientists and delivered "hooks" to the audience to entice them to listen to their reports: "I am widely regarded as the first computer programmer and respected as one of the most important women in mathematics.... My name is Augusta Ada Byron, Countess of Lovelace, and I created the first calculator."

Sixth-grade students invited their parents to a carnival of games they had invented. The students wrote reports on the games, in which they included the theoretical and experimental probabilities of scoring certain point values. "This project helped me learn probability a lot better, because we got to calculate probability in real-life instances instead of a textbook," one student said.

At the opening assembly of the exhibition, Nina Cullen-Hamzeh, Marblehead's head of school, emphasized that these exhibitions teach "students how to be reflective in their work." Younger students observe the process and learn from the older students' work, presentation style, and interaction with their audience. All students are challenged to explain their work to their peers, parents, and community members. This authentic audience creates a real-world setting that inspires students to do their best work and prepares them to be members of the community beyond school. Teachers also learn from the experience as they watch their students perform or present what they have learned. The teachers then reflect on the process with their colleagues after the exhibition.

QPA recommends school or district leaders build similar *local assessment systems* with common performance assessments such as exhibitions and graduation portfolios. A local assessment system could be a set of performance assessments over a single subject area, such as science labs using a common rubric in grades 9 through 12 and culminating in a juried science lab for seniors. Alternatively, it could consist of a progression of carefully designed assessments in sixth, seventh, and eighth grade that focus on a key skill such as oral communication or solving word problems. On a larger scale, district and school leaders can create a districtwide or schoolwide performance assessment system such as producing and defending a graduation portfolio, as was done in Pentucket. In the process, mapping assessments is a way to determine whether the selected assessment is the best match for the standards being assessed. It also gives school and district leaders a visual of all the assessments conducted across the district, and can be used to reveal any disparities in the teaching of content or skills to different groups of students.

Once they have a collection of validated tasks, the faculty can determine whether there is *sufficiency* in their local assessment system. Sufficiency ensures that there is enough evidence from the assessment system to make a valid and reliable decision about a student's overall proficiency. When students walk across the stage at graduation, teachers want to feel confident that students are prepared for what they will face next in their education, their careers, as citizens, and in life. At Vergennes Union High School in Vergennes, Vermont, the school community has committed to creating a system of performance-based graduation requirements with opportunities for both teacher- and student-designed assessments. Vergennes wants graduation to be based on what students can actually *do*, not on how many classes they have sat through. In the system, common tasks are aligned to nine performance-based graduation requirement competencies that have basic student-centered definitions and address Habits of Mind, content knowledge across disciplines, and 21st century skills.

An Example of Sufficiency in a Graduation Portfolio

Performance-Based Graduation Requirements (PBGR)

Vergennes Union High School Performance-Based Graduation Requirements from the VUHS Learner Profile of the 2012-2013 Course of Studies:

Self-efficacy

1. I understand personal wellness and my own strengths and weaknesses and use this knowledge in identifying goals, setting priorities, managing progress, and planning for my future.
2. I am an active and contributing member of my local, state, national and global communities, in which I am working to develop a multi-faceted understanding of myself, of others, and of the natural world.

Critical Thinking

3. I use inquiry and research to acquire, analyze, synthesize and evaluate information and ideas. I use these skills to solve problems, justify conclusions and connect to enduring learning.
4. I solve problems and/or conduct investigations using appropriate methodology in math and science.
5. I read, comprehend, and can respond to a variety of texts, and I am an active member of a literate community.
6. I experience and convey ideas, thoughts and feelings through the Fine Arts.

Communication

7. I use written communication and appropriate technical language for a variety of audiences and purposes.
8. I use oral communication for a variety of audiences and purposes.
9. I use technology effectively to find, organize, and communicate information for a variety of purposes.

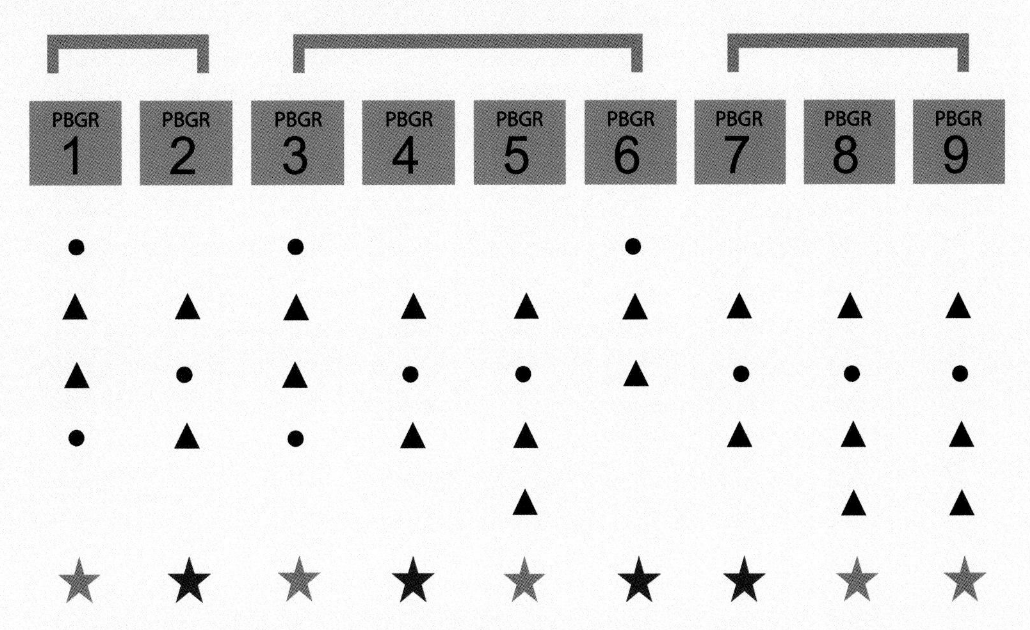

Each of the following represents the variety of assessments a student might complete and select for a portfolio during high school. From this body of work, a student would choose culminating graduation portfolio pieces for his or her final presentation and portfolio defense in senior year.

● = Formative Assessment

▲ = Summative Assessment

★ = Teacher-Designed Performance Assessment used in Graduation Portfolio

☆ = Student-Designed Performance Assessment used in Graduation Portfolio

Educate All Teachers in the Scoring Process for Common Performance Assessments

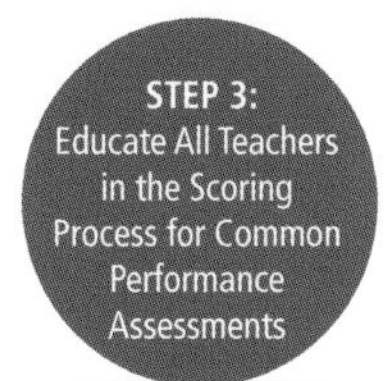

Increase the consistency of expectations and quality of student work by calibrating work samples for each administration of a scoring session and by educating teachers new to scoring with anchor papers.

> "If we are pushing for a comprehensive system of common performance assessments, there is no room for inconsistencies in our scoring, even at the level of a single-school community." —*Reflection of a QPA Network Teacher*

At Souhegan High School, located in the suburban community of Amherst, New Hampshire, students take the state standardized tests once, in eleventh grade. The faculty sought an approach to measure student progress in a more regular and meaningful way so that they could stand by their reports on student growth to parents, community members, and the school board. They determined to set up a system of common performance assessments. With this decision, the entire faculty agreed to take the energy and time necessary to step back and analyze their data as a team, and committed to improving the technical quality of their growth measures. In selecting performance assessments as their focus, they transitioned from using only standardized tests as their performance measure to including formative, authentic tasks rooted in a purposeful context that reflect the real work of a given discipline. Such purposeful learning, they reasoned, would engage students by developing and assessing important and relevant skills and knowledge. The data would also provide teachers across all grades and disciplines with data to improve their practice and thereby increase student learning.

The ongoing schoolwide process focuses on credible and reliable scoring of common performance assessments against a common rubric. Each time individual teachers administer a common performance assessment, subject-area teams convene to score several pieces of student work together to make sure that they approach the undertaking with consistency. As they undertake a process of calibrating and validating the task, it informs their practice, and teachers keep making revisions. At the culmination of this process, Souhegan will have a system of calibrated proficient anchor works. In the summer of 2012, Souhegan was still in the middle of this process, which takes many rounds of the cycle of examining the work and returning to the classroom. Souhegan set a goal for the 2011–2012 school year of increasing by 5 percent the number of students in grades 9–12 who are proficient as effective communicators and, in actuality, increased the proficiency rate by 10 percent between fall and spring.

In the course of the year, teachers discovered that the work is messy, cyclical, and ongoing. One teacher commented on revising and agreeing on a common rubric:

> "[Rubric revision] is not just about an obsession with technical quality; rather, it's a feedback loop that impacts curriculum, instruction, and assessment. When we agree on standards that we are aligning and how we assess them in a rubric, we are also setting our expectations for mastery of student work and considering the instruction that gets to mastery. It is an iterative process that touches on all aspects of teaching and learning."
> —*Souhegan Teacher*

Calibrating Our Scoring

After revising the rubric, the team begins to look at student work with the goal of instituting reliable scoring across subject areas and/or grade levels. Common performance assessments will not be effective at increasing student achievement and equitable outcomes unless they are reliable. Reliable means a group of teachers (or scorers) comes to an agreement on what a rating means and scores student work the same way. This consistency of agreement can only come from teachers scoring together and engaging in conversations where they score student work, explore why their scores differ, and come to consensus about what the score for a particular piece of work should be for a given grade and subject.

QPA envisions scoring student work as "umpire school" for teachers. In baseball, the fairness of the league depends on a team of umpires trained to reliably call balls and strikes as the pitches cross the plate. To effectively referee the game, the umpires train and practice until their calls agree consistently, and until they all agree on a strike zone.

QPA teacher scoring session

Like umpires, teachers need to agree on the strike zone as well as what proficient work looks like when it crosses the plate. Like umpires, teachers need to allow for student individuality in assessment while still being clear on the strike zone. The umpire must consider the batter's height and position at the plate, but within those parameters the strike zone must be constant. The strike zone should not, and cannot, expand for students with challenging lives outside of school, for students who are members of certain racial or class groups, or for students who are trying their best, but are not there yet. The standard is fixed, and teachers must function as umpires when scoring work but as coaches when supporting students in reaching the benchmark set by the common assessment.

It is critical that teacher expectations for student work be consistent. The task's scorers must agree on a rating system and then score each assessment with that system. The process of reaching this agreement is not always easy. It forces teachers to work collaboratively and to come to terms about what proficient work looks like and adopt a common language that defines it. In some schools, teachers have elected to share their scores in the age-old rock-paper-scissors style by having everyone put the number of fingers out for the score at the same time. This allows teachers to score without the social pressure of recalculating their personal score to fit the group score. This is an important step in building the level of transparency and honesty needed to create a powerful and reliable community of practice focused on common assessments. The time invested in achieving reliability in communities of practice pays huge dividends as individual teachers begin applying the standard when scoring in their own classrooms.

The *Calibration* Protocol (see Tool #4), which is also used for rubric revision, permits a group of three to six teachers to calibrate scoring of student work in a 45-minute session. This protocol allows teachers both to score without the social pressure of being worried about differences in scores and to come to a consensus on the scores An optimal goal for teams and school leaders to set for scoring reliability is 80 percent agreement on scoring student work. That is, of the total pieces of student work that are scored, multiple scorers arrive at the same rating for at least 80 percent of the work.

With this type of collaborative process, QPA believes that it is possible to design performance assessments that are reliable and attain a high standard of technical quality. When teachers share their plans and then score student work together, they are able to see which plans elicited the best work and then refine their own plans accordingly. Professional development in assessment literacy empowers teachers to:

- Design performance tasks and rubrics aligned to standards;
- Maintain a consistent scoring process, using anchor work and accompanying annotations to guide and support their interpretation of their common rubrics; and
- Monitor and analyze student achievement.

When collaborative scoring is part of professional development and teacher practice, it is possible to develop reliable common performance assessments across schools, grades, and content areas to meet state requirements, while honoring local teachers and school curriculum.

As the Souhegan teachers discovered, creating a solid, consistent reporting system for common performance assessments requires teachers to learn to score reliably. Training teachers to score increases the efficacy of the assessments in every classroom and for every student. The Calibration Protocol provides a tool to score student work against a common rubric as a team. Through repetition of the process, teachers begin to understand what proficient looks like.

Each time a grade-level or subject-area team administers a common performance assessment, they need time to meet to score at least two pieces of student work together. This helps teachers learn to score consistently. The team also must make time to look at the anchor works together to keep in mind what a proficient sample looks like. With calibration among grade levels or subject areas, expectations for students are understood and fixed at the right level. Calibrating scores of common performance assessments provides fair and equitable results for teachers and students. When teachers return to their classrooms and evaluate their own students' work, rather than basing their scoring on their own system or relying on an educated guess, they recall the deliberative conversation experienced during the Calibration Protocol.

STEP 4

Use Performance Assessment Data Analysis to Improve Instruction and Assessment Practices

STEP 4:
Use Performance Assessment Data Analysis to Improve Instruction and Assessment Practices

Performance assessment data informs curriculum planning, instruction, design, and redesign of assessments, ensuring there is a continuous feedback loop that focuses on the next step, helping all students to achieve while improving assessments.

"The school/teacher teams must continue to revisit common performance assessment data over time as teams work to improve instruction." —*QPA Summer Institute Leader Participant*

The Souhegan High School faculty opted to analyze performance assessment data as its entry point into QPA, identifying areas of need and making appropriate instructional changes to strengthen student learning. A traditional data-based inquiry cycle begins by looking at the data, a key driver for school and district transformation. The QPA Framework—no matter which starting point is chosen—is a version of an inquiry cycle with QPA as the focal point.

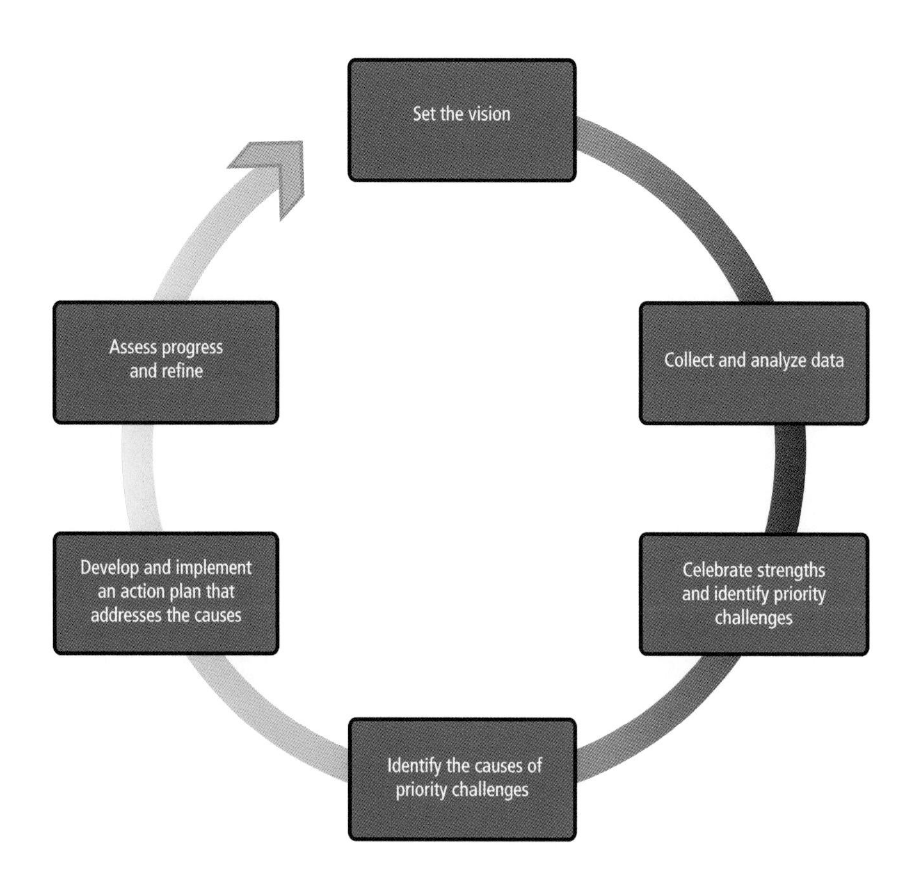

Data-Based Inquiry Cycle

This model for data-based inquiry includes a deliberative process in which teachers and administrators examine and analyze a range of data, identify challenges, and develop action plans to address them. Data-based inquiry is not a quick-fix solution to challenges that district and school leaders face. It requires a reallocation of the use of time. The process can lead to improving instruction and assessment and, in turn, result in higher student achievement. Research indicates that data-based inquiry—using data from a variety of sources, including standardized, formative, and summative assessments—correlates with school effectiveness (Marzano, 2003; The Education Trust, 2005).

As in the Souhegan example, the faculty participates in the data-based inquiry cycle and divides into multiple inquiry groups that each take on a different challenge identified by a review of school data. Faculties might split into interdisciplinary academic teams pursuing a challenge identified within a grade, discipline teams investigating a learning gap within a subject area, or a schoolwide data team. At Souhegan, the whole staff pursued effective communication and collaboration, breaking up into disciplinary teams for the calibration process. At a district level, an inquiry cycle might assess the strengths and challenges in providing the structures and supports for implementing performance assessments. The process works similarly for any inquiry group:

1. **Set the vision:** In a QPA school, student-centered learning is the vision.

2. **Collect and analyze data:** Gather a variety of data sources, including formative assessments, standardized tests, student work, surveys, and interviews, and analyze to reflect on student learning. In QPA, the focus is on student performance assessment data.

3. **Celebrate strengths and identify priority challenges:** Examine the data to identify areas in which the school is doing well and areas where there are challenges. Prioritize the challenges that will most directly lead to improved student learning and achievement.

4. **Identify the causes of priority challenges:** Hypothesize causes for each challenge identified and collect additional data to research further.

5. **Develop and implement an action plan that addresses the causes:** Develop an action plan that addresses the identified causes of the challenges.

6. **Assess progress and refine:** Determine whether the action plan is improving student learning by collecting and analyzing the data. Make midcourse corrections (Center for Collaborative Education, 2005).

Often when schools begin data analysis, they immediately turn to standardized test scores. While standardized tests are one source of valuable information, QPA shifts the focus closer to the classroom, to student and teacher work created in performance assessments. The Student Work Analysis Tool (see Tool #34) guides teachers to focus on the evidence in student work that informs next steps for instruction. Gathering samples of student work is one of the most powerful ways of understanding students' learning and allows teachers to collect evidence of students' progress over time and to refine their own instructional practice. Schoolwide common assessments are important to include because they happen regularly during the year and are reflective of the teaching and learning happening in the classroom. Also, teachers learn to assess them using a common rubric, which results in more consistent, less subjective scoring. Disaggregating data, whether performance based or from standardized tests, helps reveal the relative performance of subgroups of students and differences in performance for different ethnic groups and gender.

DEVELOPING A CULTURE OF INQUIRY FOR EQUITY: ONE SCHOOL'S STORY

by Tanya Friedman

In every classroom at our school—the San Francisco Community School, a K–8 school in San Francisco, California—we discovered a clear pattern of African American and Latino students not meeting our school standards. In every classroom, white students were the only students who achieved the highest level on the writing rubric. We were devastated. While each of us could name reasons why our own students hadn't achieved the standards, there was no way to talk our way around the whole-school picture.

Over the past seven years, our partnership with the Bay Area Coalition for Equitable Schools has helped us to face the equity gap in new ways. In the first year of our partnership, a team participated in the coalition's weeklong summer institute, where we examined results of our writing assessments and uncovered disturbing achievement patterns.

Uncovering that pattern of inequity, as we were learning how to conduct data-based inquiry, inextricably linked inquiry and equity for me. Out of that weeklong experience, our professional development team developed a whole-school data-based inquiry about writing instruction. We planned whole-school strategies—common use of rubrics and frequent opportunities to write and revise—to help students meet standards. As a faculty, we spent two full days a year (one in the fall and one in the spring) calibrating our writing standards from kindergarten through eighth grade and scoring writing by every student. We analyzed data from these whole-school scores to adjust our instruction.

To make this whole-school inquiry feel present and alive in our classrooms, we also devised "minicycles," which framed the whole-school inquiry at the classroom level. We asked teachers to choose students from our underserved groups whose writing had not met the standards and to design strategies aimed at strengthening their skills. To help us think strategically and systematically about why students weren't achieving, we each picked one focus student and conducted an inquiry about that student. We devised a research question, planned out strategies and data-collection procedures, and recorded our hunches and challenges. By sharing strategies, seeking information from the students' previous teachers, and asking each other questions, we began to take collective responsibility for the students who were not meeting the standards. Our classroom inquiries, along with our whole-school work, improved students' writing performance and allowed us to trace which strategies worked most effectively with which students. For five years in a row we closed the equity gap in writing achievement on school and district assessments.

This first schoolwide inquiry impacted our school culture in at least two important ways. First, it established that our purpose for inquiry is to create equity. Second, it initiated our practice of collecting and disaggregating data, no matter how small the numbers. For me, equitable achievement began to seem possible, even just around the corner.

Despite the benefits of this inquiry, our ongoing work has revealed the complexity and difficulty of creating equity in achievement and school experience. While we still have more questions than answers, we've found three elements to be especially important in developing and sustaining a culture that supports inquiry for equity:

- Create structures and support for teachers to reflect on how issues of race, class, and culture play out in their own lives, in the school, and in the classroom.
- Offer a variety of structures and entry points for equity-driven inquiry.
- Dedicate time, space, and support for both formal and informal inquiry.

Administrators use data to ensure equity in school improvement efforts

---

More information about the Bay Area Coalition for Equitable Schools (BayCES) can be found at www.bayces.org. BayCES is one of the four partner organizations that form the Teacher Research Collaborative.

Friedman, T. (2006). Developing a culture of inquiry for equity: One school's story. In L. Friedrich, C. Tateishi, T. Malarkey, E. R. Simons, & M. Williams (Eds.), Working toward equity: Writings and resources from the Teacher Research Collaborative. Berkeley, CA: National Writing Project.

School leaders and teachers can use the Data Analysis Protocol (See tool #10) to analyze trends in performance by rubric criteria, class section, or grade or to examine student work from the performance assessment task. Instead of simply keeping an overall score of an essay, a project, or a presentation, for example, recording student scores on each rubric criterion gives teachers information about the individual student's progress in developing specific content or skills. In planning for the analysis, select student work to look at and questions to guide the analysis. Select samples of student work that are proficient, just below proficient, and far below proficient, and chart the common characteristics of the student work at each level. To begin the protocol, choose a facilitator, timekeeper, and recorder. Second, examine the data with a particular focus. Pose a set of questions as focus areas of the examination. For example:

- Does the data reveal strengths or weaknesses in specific rubric criteria (e.g., Idea Development, Supporting Evidence, etc.)? In which criteria are students strongest? Weakest?
- If you have data from assessments that use different modalities (e.g., writing and presentation), does the data reveal any patterns about student communication of their understanding in different modalities?
- If you have data from different courses or class sections, does the data reveal any patterns between classes?
- Are there differences in student subgroup scores by race/ethnicity, language, special education status, income, or gender?

In the third step of the protocol, draw inferences from the data, asking the questions: Are you surprised by anything you saw in the score data (or student work data, if used)? What factors might contribute to the patterns you noticed? What might account for any differences between groups of students? Finally, use the analysis to inform instruction and plan next steps for targeting the needs of the students.

Analysis of Supporting Evidence Criteria in Performance Assessment Results

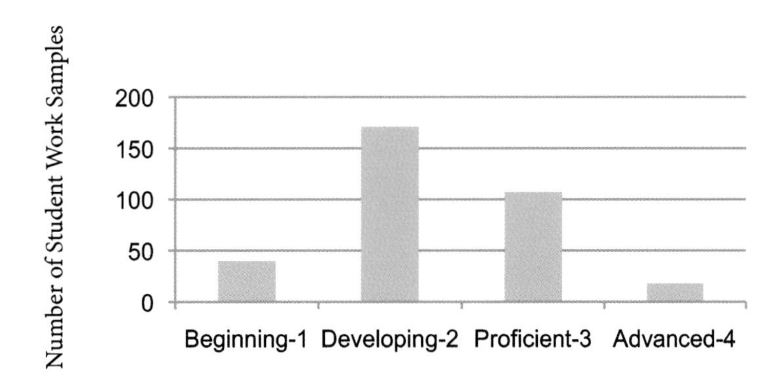

Understanding Scores Versus Grades

In the process of collecting and analyzing data, it is important to differentiate between scores and grades. Grading is at least in part subjective; therefore expectations might differ from one classroom to the next, resulting in a wide disparity in students' grades across the school. Grades often take into account class participation, timeliness, behavior, attendance, and extra credit. A proficient score should be the same no matter what. Even if grades focused only on cognitive performance, the same quality work could earn different grades depending on the time of the school year. For example, a particular essay should earn the same score no matter when it was written, but that score could correspond to a different grade in a teacher's grade book at the beginning of the year versus the end of the year. Grades reflect performance relative to expectations at the time.

When teachers use a rubric to score projects, they are looking for certain aspects of student work within different categories (e.g., idea development, supporting evidence, organization, and conventions & styles). The explanatory bullets in each category position students along the rubric, showing what elements they have mastered and areas where they have room to improve. When teachers give students specific guidelines on an assignment along with a rubric with specific criteria, students write and edit their papers to fit the standards. According to one teacher, scoring with the rubric "points out what areas [students] need to work on and breaks it out nicely."

Refine the Analysis

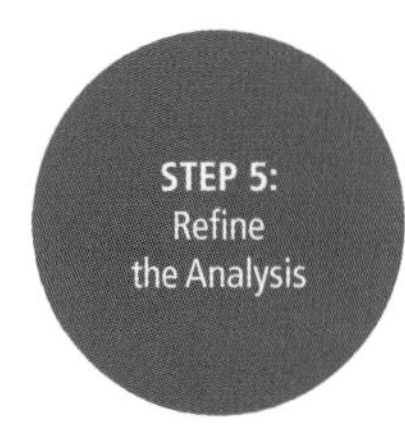

The school/teacher teams continue to revise the data analysis process over time, as this is an iterative process.

> "In performance assessment work, there is always an opportunity to revise. Our work is never done, and the QPA Framework and tools gave us a great way to see in which direction we should focus our improvements." —*QPA Summer Institute Leader Participant*

It is the culmination of the senior class's high school career, and they have completed all the requirements for graduation and arrive at the graduation ceremony with their extended families. As each student takes the final walk across the stage, the school leader should be able to look each student squarely in the eye, shake hands, and present the diploma with the knowledge that for each student the document is trustworthy and credible. The implementation of the Common Core requires that at least part of the credibility of the diploma will be based on a student's readiness for college and career. All school and district leaders must analyze the quality and rigor of the work students produce to ensure students are prepared. College and career readiness cannot be summarized in one number on a test, but is to be found in the skills, knowledge and dispositions demonstrated by each student that walks across the stage. Teachers and school leaders must do the difficult job of establishing common standards, designing performance assessments that are valid and reliable, and engaging in common scoring of student work to arrive at a common understanding of what constitutes proficiency, so that all students are ready for the future.

Entry Points for Analyzing Performance Assessments

Just as school leaders and teachers might opt to begin their QPA performance assessment work with quality aligned instruction or understanding by design, there are options even within each larger framework. A grade-level team starting data analysis might decide to:

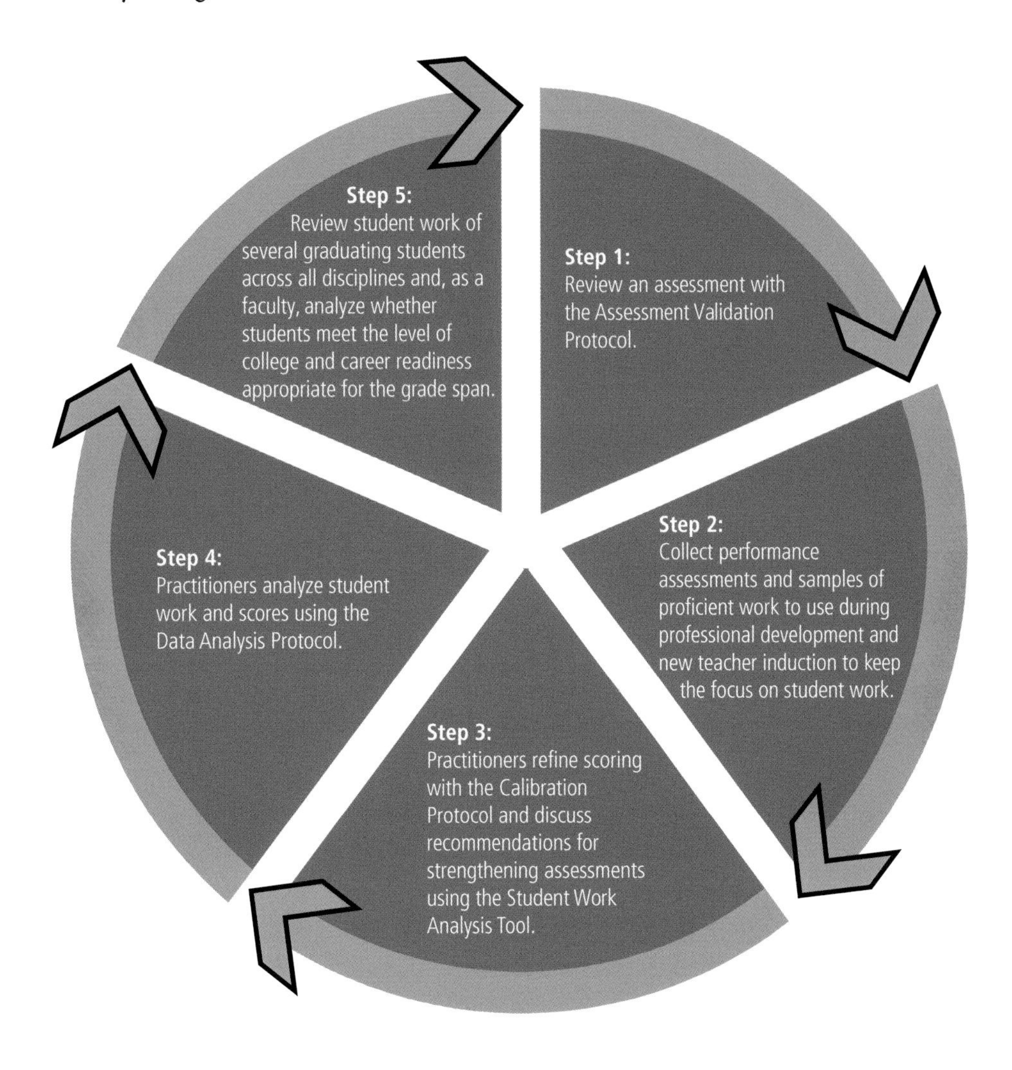

Refining Our Work through Self-Assessment

The self-assessment process ensures that teachers are constantly reviewing and amending their own work. School and district leaders must ask themselves the following questions:

Quality Data Analysis	Do assessments provide the information about mastery of standards/content for which they were designed?
	Have a sufficient number of common performance assessments been validated to make promotion and graduation decisions?
	Is there a process for collecting scoring data and auditing the scoring process to ensure scores are consistent across administrations and raters?
	Is there professional development for scorers that uses scoring guidelines and anchor student work samples?
	Is there a systematic process for teams of teachers, other faculty, and leaders to analyze scoring data for student subgroups and to use performance assessment data to inform curriculum planning, instruction, and assessment?

TOOLS USED IN THIS CHAPTER

Tools for Performance Assessment Data Analysis

TOOL #	TOOL NAME	PAGE #
1	Assessment Validation Checklist	T3
2	Assessment Validation Cover Sheet	T6
3	Assessment Validation Protocol	T8
4	Calibration Protocol	T9
10	Data Analysis Protocol	T19
34	Student Work Analysis Tool	T57

Students work together on performance assessment for science class

CHAPTER 5

COLLABORATE AND LEAD: COMMUNITIES OF ASSESSMENT PRACTICE

I was able to craft an assessment with my colleague, think about its impact on our students, work through its implication, consider the usefulness of the rubric, and work with other communities to see how this could serve to close the achievement gap.

—QPA Network Teacher Reflection

Student Work Sample: Macbeth Diorama

At Hudson High School, in Hudson, Massachusetts, teachers set a goal to create an online portfolio system across all English and social studies classes. Students chose artifacts from each course that demonstrated progress toward mastering six learning expectations—collaboration, critical thinking, creativity, making connections, communication, and initiative—and went through a process for selecting and reflecting on the work. For teachers, their focus on student work inspired them. One Hudson teacher commented, "Seeing more student work is really helpful, so we can share ideas and see what kids are doing and how they are learning best."

Specific, *measurable goals*—such as Hudson's ambitious decision to make online portfolios for each social studies and English student—lead a community of practice toward accomplishing its purpose and making an impact on classroom practice. Too often in schools, committees continue to meet and plan, but fail to achieve measurable results. Often, by the end of the school year or when the community of practice loses its momentum, little or no action has taken place. Clear, measurable goals prevent this frustration by focusing discussion on action and how to achieve the desired outcomes.

At Hudson, a two-year, collaborative venture in performance assessments revealed that teachers needed additional training in technology, as well as professional development in the school's learning expectations, to improve consistency across classrooms. Teachers are also planning to develop grade-specific benchmarks for each learning expectation so students demonstrate appropriate proficiency at each grade level. "Teachers have become more reflective regarding their instruction as they move toward this unified approach. The department understands it is imperative that students are provided with ample opportunity to develop the academic skills identified in learning expectations," a Hudson report concluded. Without school leaders and teachers making the time and commitment to work collaboratively in communities of practice at many levels, this online portfolio system would not have been possible.

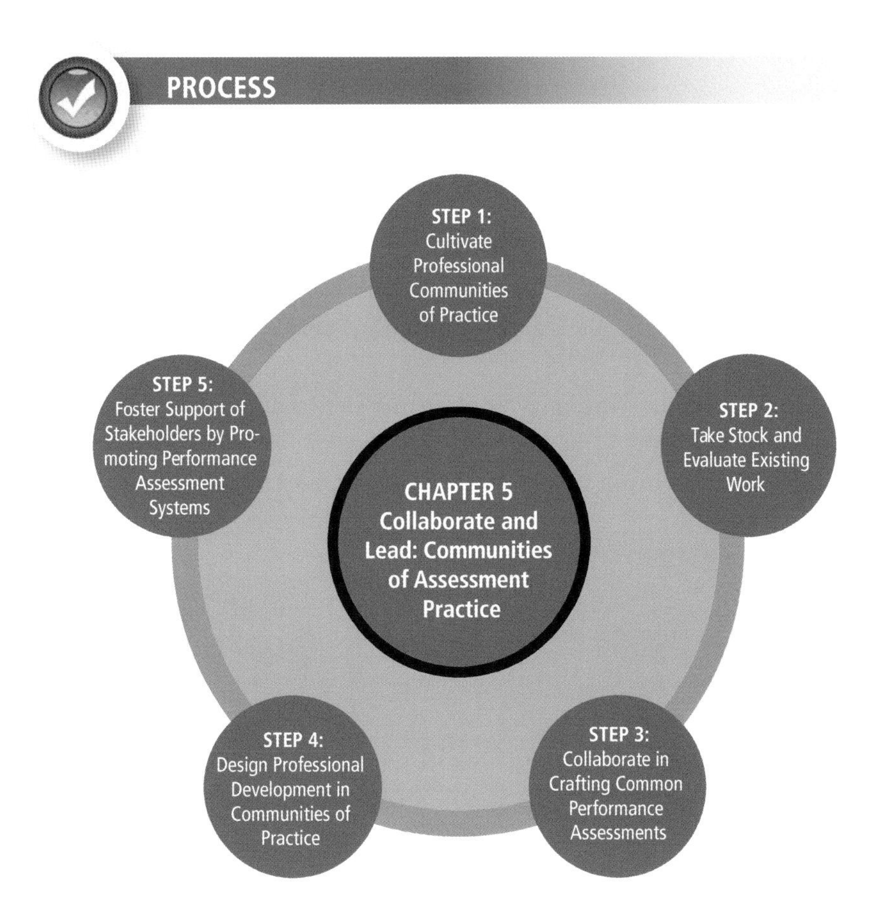

Process of Collaboration

Fostering collaborative practices in school communities is delineated in the following steps:

1. **Cultivate Professional Communities of Practice**
   School communities devote common planning time and staff meetings to professional communities of practice concentrated on implementing performance assessment with QPA *protocols.*

2. **Take Stock and Evaluate Existing Work**
   Communities of practice initially collect and evaluate the work they have undertaken for engagement and real-world contexts, adherence to the Common Core, and depth of performance assessment.
3. **Collaborate in Crafting Common Performance Assessments**
   Teachers engage in all steps of the QPA Framework collaboratively as they work with common performance assessments: school communities score student work, validate assessments, and partake in text-based discussions with protocols to create common language and expectations, and to develop assessment literacy.

Process of Leadership

The role of school and district leaders in supporting schools that are dedicated to performance assessment systems is outlined below:

4. **Design Professional Development in Communities of Practice**
   With teacher input, administrators plan professional development in communities of practice that supports the ability of all teachers to implement common performance assessments and develop assessment literacy.
5. **Foster Support of Stakeholders by Promoting Performance Assessment Systems**
   Assessment policies - including those that integrate state student assessment systems with local performance assessment- are developed and promoted through a process that builds political will and support from all stakeholders.

DECODING THE JARGON

Defined terms, italicized on first reference in the text, are listed in alphabetical order.

Culture of discourse describes the professional environment of team members who converse deeply about critical issues related to the improvement of teaching, learning, and assessment practices.

Measurable goals have a specific intention or result that is quantifiable.

Norms are ways of working together that can help groups be more thoughtful and productive. Norms exist in every learning community, whether or not they are named or agreed upon.

Protocols give communities of practice a specific procedure to follow during the course of a meeting in order to provide a respectful and productive focus to important conversations about teacher practice and student learning.

Introduction

Nurturing collaboration among teachers is a critical step in the entire Quality Performance Assessment (QPA) process. Specific professional development in how to share ideas and deprivatize practice gives teachers the skills they need to step out of their individual classrooms and work with teammates to design performance assessments, look at student work, or calibrate a common rubric. Teachers with targeted practice in collaboration share best practices and align their assessment designs across disciplines and grade levels.

When district and school administrators are literate in assessment practices, model collegiality and collaboration, and participate in professional development, teachers feel supported in their efforts to design and implement performance assessment.

STEP 1

Cultivate Professional Communities of Practice

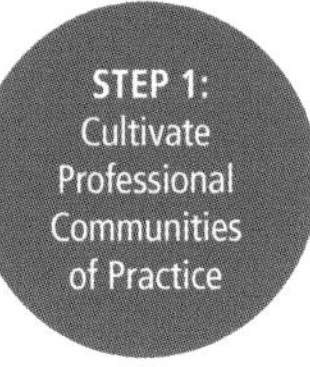

School communities devote common planning time and staff meetings to professional communities of practice concentrated on implementing performance assessment with QPA protocols.

> "Keeping student work at the center and using protocols is the only way to stay aligned to the Common Core." —*QPA Network Teacher*

For the QPA approach to permeate the practice and culture of the school across grades and disciplines, school leaders and teachers must commit to developing a culture of decency and trust where reflective, collaborative work is key. In professional communities of practice, members of the school community work together effectively and are guided by a common purpose, such as aligning instruction with habits and standards across grade levels. All members of the community—teachers, administrators, students and their families—collaborate, grapple with important issues, and play a significant role in the school's decision-making process. All school members share a common vision of what the school should be like and create goals that lead them toward this vision.

Establishing effective communities of practice that are committed to improving student, team, and school performance is a complex and challenging undertaking. First and foremost, school and district leaders must take the initiative to revise schedules to include daily planning time, significant common planning time, professional development days, summer institutes, and retreats.

The most successful communities of practice accomplish QPA work and make use of common planning time, staff meetings, and professional meetings productively. A clearly defined purpose energizes the community of practice because all members understand exactly why they are together. The common purpose serves to keep the community of practice focused at all times. All actions and decisions are made relative to this purpose so that time can be used as efficiently as possible and participants can remain focused on student achievement.

Community of Practice circle

CHARACTERISTICS OF EFFECTIVE TEAMS

In schools, effective teams:

- Have a *culture of discourse* at their center.
- Have a clearly defined purpose that guides their work and specific, *measurable goals* that they achieve.
- Are committed to *norms* that guide how the team operates.
- Are disciplined in maintaining their focus.
- Communicate effectively within the team and with those outside of the team.
- Improve the ability of team members to function as a team in the future (Center for Collaborative Education, 2005).

Culture of Discourse

In a culture of discourse, team members discuss and think about significant issues related to improving teaching, learning, and assessment. Team members demonstrate respect for each other by valuing differences of opinion and being open minded in regard to others' ideas. Disagreements and challenges are welcome in team discussions, as they often push collective thinking to a deeper level. Ultimately, many of these conversations result in improved student learning and growth.

It takes time and discipline to raise the quality of teacher discourse—to focus on ideas and application rather than on the housekeeping details that often take up so much of teachers' time. Teams may use text-based discussions, case studies, and *protocols* for looking at student work to deepen their conversations and get them focused on the substantial issues surrounding teaching and learning. When a culture of discourse is at the center of a team's operations, the work of the team is better informed by the expertise of its members and more likely to effect lasting change.

At the beginning of the QPA process, or as issues arise, the QPA tool Collaborative Cultures Survey (see Tool #7) gives teams a vehicle to assess their level of collaboration and to figure out areas where they need to improve. The tool also helps faculties prioritize where they would like to improve their professional culture, with the understanding that progress happens one step at a time.

While it is important that a team reach its goals, how it reaches them is equally important. Dynamic teams show evidence of growth over time. For example, in the first year, members may become familiar with the team format and protocols used to guide discussions. In subsequent years, teams may make individual refinements and changes according to their needs. Improving each member's ability for teamwork not only helps the existing team, but also moves the whole school forward. These team skills may include developing trust among group members, being open and honest with feedback and praise, creating agendas, developing communication methods, and facilitating meetings.

FINDING TIME FOR COLLABORATIVE WORK

- Negotiate with the district for early-release time.
- Release students early one day a week.
- Use teaching assistants to release teachers for team meetings.
- Begin school 30 minutes later one day a week and ask teachers to come in 30 minutes early for a one-hour block of meeting time.
- Limit full faculty meetings to once monthly.
- Create regular common planning time for academic team meetings or study groups by sending all students in a cluster or grade level to specialists during a designated period (Center for Collaborative Education, 2005).

Norms and Protocols Guide Team Collaboration

As groups of teachers work together, the variety of approaches they represent may lead to unproductive conflict and disagreement if there are no ground rules for conversation and planning. Setting *norms* of mutual respect and equal participation, for example, can help groups deal with the common disagreements and conflicts that often stall or derail effective group work. In an environment structured by norms, members question, support, disagree, and take risks while working together respectfully and purposefully toward shared goals.

The Setting Norms Protocol (see Tool #31) guides groups through a process of establishing norms to improve teamwork, enabling teachers to tackle challenging work such as assessment validation. When a school's validation team meets to validate their peers' performance assessments, for example, invariably some submitted assessment tasks are not validated the first time. Giving your colleagues a failing grade on their prized work is difficult, but honest feedback improves practice. Norms train teachers to give constructive criticism in a safe environment.

Even after setting norms as a team or faculty, maintaining a cooperative environment requires a concerted, ongoing effort. In professional communities of practice, colleagues use protocols to look at student and teacher work, offering support and feedback. Failure, mistakes, and uncertainty are openly shared and discussed, often leading to greater risk taking and experimentation in instructional practice. The Guidelines for Effective Meetings protocol (see Tool #13) gives teams a constructive approach for conducting meetings. These guidelines are adaptable to the needs of individual teams and kept on hand to revisit as necessary. With these types of protocols, all members of a team can voice their opinions without interruptions, and one or two people cannot dominate the conversation. One QPA Network teacher recognized that once teachers in a community of practice acknowledge their differences, more can be accomplished: "It's great to surface disagreements. Even if we can't resolve our differences, we can note important questions that we want to solve together in the future."

TOOL 15

The Microlab Discussion Protocol (see Tool #15) addresses a specific sequence of questions in a structured format with small groups, using active listening skills. The Microlab is useful for team building and democratizing participation because it asks participants to give everyone a chance to speak, while the participants withhold judgment. The Microlab asks groups to discuss concrete examples of previously administered performance assessments that effectively assessed student learning. It asks teachers to review the skills and content knowledge assessed as well as the types of evidence that demonstrated those skills and knowledge. The Microlab builds a common vision around effective performance assessments and serves as a useful starting point for an in-depth discussion of future work in performance assessments.

Another useful starting point for a conversation around performance assessment is the Text-Based Discussion Protocol (see Tool #36). This discussion-based protocol encourages participants to read and discuss a short article or excerpt from a book that will have direct implications for performance assessment and student learning. The structure of the protocol is set up so that all participants have an opportunity either to read aloud a sentence or two of particular significance to them or to address a discussion question posed by the facilitator. Clear guidelines encourage a respectful conversation in which each participant's voice is heard.

When teachers first begin using protocols as a way of looking at their students' work, teacher assignments, and instructional practices, the process may feel formal or stiff. Because teachers are not used to sharing work publicly with peers, the process can feel intimidating. However, with time and practice, the protocols create a safe, nurturing environment for teachers to make public their students' and their own work. As teachers gain experience, their comfort level rises, as do the benefits.

GENERAL GUIDELINES FOR ALL PROTOCOLS

Before a group uses protocols to look at student and teacher work, it is helpful to review the following guidelines with all participants.

Norms for participants:

- **Be respectful of teacher-presenters.** By making their work more public, teachers are taking a risk. As colleagues expose themselves and their work to peer review, remember to be thoughtful in how you word your responses.
- **Contribute to the substance of the discussion.** Thoughtful, probing questions and comments are beneficial. "Cool" questions enable participants to take the work to a deeper level.
- **Be aware of airtime.** Protocols sometimes run on a tight schedule. Try to keep your comments succinct and relevant to the discussion.
- **Be respectful of the facilitator's role.** Do this especially in regard to keeping time and following protocol guidelines.

Guidelines for facilitators:

- **Be assertive about keeping time.** Each part of a protocol is crucial to the success of the exercise. Make sure you allow time for all parts of the protocol.
- **Be protective of teacher-presenters.** Many teachers may not be used to colleagues' critiquing their work. Try to determine just how "tough" your presenter wants the feedback to be. Inappropriate comments or questions should be recast or withdrawn.
- **Be provocative of substantive discourse.** While "warm" feedback is supportive, it often doesn't push a presenter's thinking. Encourage probing, "cool" questions and comments for a more beneficial protocol experience (Center for Collaborative Education, 2001, 2005).

Take Stock and Evaluate Existing Work

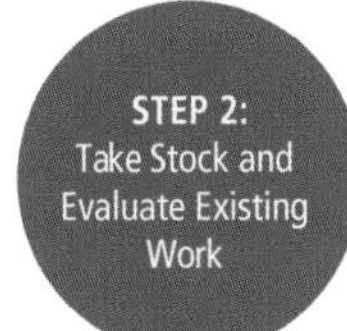

Communities of practice initially collect and evaluate the work they have undertaken for engagement and real-world contexts, adherence to the Common Core, and depth of performance assessment.

> "Everyone can gain something from looking at student work. It's a great way of moving teacher practice forward and overall a very powerful tool."
> —*QPA Network Teacher*

Once a school community has immersed itself in the language of protocols and norms and feels at ease voicing their opinions in a safe environment, it is time to use those tools to evaluate and improve student and teacher work. When teachers look collaboratively at student and teacher work, they inevitably refine instruction, curriculum, and assessment with the goal of improving student learning. School leaders and teachers collect data to document how close students are to meeting their learning goals. Since student work is one of the most authentic data sources teachers have to gauge student progress, teachers follow a structured process to analyze and discuss this work. QPA protocols provide structure and guidelines for these discussions to keep the focus of each conversation on improving student learning.

The school schedule reflects this commitment to improving student learning by allowing for regularly scheduled, significant amounts of common planning time for protocols. Looking collaboratively at student work requires more teacher time than does individual grading of the work. Finding time for this in-depth process can be a challenge. However, the benefits to the school community are worth creating the time and space.

LOOKING AT ASSESSMENT WORK PROTOCOL

This protocol (see Tool #14) allows a group of teachers to consider student assessments in light of a focusing question, the Common Core, and Webb's Depth of Knowledge framework (1997). There are seven steps in this 40- to 50-minute protocol involving a group of 4–8 people. First, the presenter silently shares the focusing question, student work, and supporting documents with the group. The group observes or reads the work in silence and make notes. The facilitator then asks each member of the group, "What do you see?" Group members provide answers without making judgments about the work. If the facilitator interprets a statement as a judgment, he or she asks, "Where is the evidence?" Next, the facilitator asks each member of the group, "What questions does this work raise for you?" As group members list their questions, the presenter takes notes. Subsequently, the facilitator asks, "What standards do you think the student is working on, and how are they reflected in the assessment?" Group members use the Depth of Knowledge framework (Level 1—Recall; Level 2—Basic Application of Skill/Concept; Level 3—Strategic Thinking; Level 4—Extended Thinking) to reflect on the level of rigor of the standards addressed by the student work. The presenting teacher then provides his or her perspective on the assessment, responding to questions, commenting on any unexpected comments by the teachers, and, finally, reminding the group of the focusing question. The facilitator invites the group and presenting teacher to discuss the teacher's focusing question and implications for increasing the level of rigor of the assessment and addressing the Common Core. The facilitator leads a debrief session about the group's experience and reactions to the conference.

STUDENT WORK ANALYSIS TOOL

Teachers can build understanding and agreement about consistent use and interpretation of a rubric as they analyze samples of student work with the Student Work Analysis Tool (see Tool #34). This exercise allows the faculty to figure out the level of each work sample, determine possible causes of the students' performances, and discuss recommendations for adjusting and strengthening the assessment task. This tool allows teachers to further refine performance assessments and, over time, integrate learning from this collaborative work into their instructional practices. As one QPA teacher explained about the power of analyzing student work, "The protocol gave us time to work together; it helped us dig deeply into areas we usually spend minutes on."

CALIBRATION PROTOCOL

Setting up scoring sessions with the Calibration Protocol (see Tool #4)—a tool to score student work using a common rubric— is another collaborative approach to looking at student work. At Marblehead Community Charter Public School in Marblehead, Massachusetts, teachers began their work with performance assessment by scoring student writing as a whole school. The entire staff used a teacher-developed rubric to score several sixth-grade Roman character essays written in a history class. The staff then discussed what student writing should look like across all content areas. The next whole-school calibration focused on scoring a seventh-grade mathematics project. Students had worked in teams and calculated the slope of handicap ramps in the town to assess whether the ramps were up to code. Teams then drew scale drawings of the ramp, and authored business letters to the ramp property owners to share their findings. Students also presented the project on a display board. Teachers scored this work with the project rubric. Teachers discussed problem solving, quality writing, and how to embed mathematics content into projects across the curriculum. These two calibration conversations generated schoolwide interdisciplinary writing samples for anchors of writing at each grade level and led to conversations about how to encourage problem solving in all subject areas.

GALLERY WALK

Another entry point for looking at existing student work for rigor and depth is the Gallery Walk, in which teachers exhibit and assess the work. Teachers present their student work and supporting documents on panels, and display the work as though presenting it at a gallery or museum. Individually, in pairs or groups, participants roam the gallery and silently examine the work and place sticky notes with comments on the work. School teams may choose to use a focusing question for the Gallery Walk—for example, asking teachers to exhibit written work in which students are required to provide textual evidence, and asking the question "How does this collection of work reflect the level of rigor and common expectation at our school?" Finally, teachers review the comments and reconvene to discuss implications for future work.

QPA teachers share samples of student and teacher work during a gallery walk

Collaborate in Crafting Common Performance Assessments

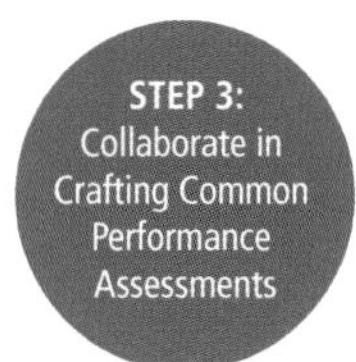

Teachers engage in all steps of the QPA Framework collaboratively as they work with common performance assessments: school communities score student work, validate assessments, and partake in text-based discussions with protocols to create common language and expectations, and to develop assessment literacy.

"Once you get a project people value, then you need to make the time to collaborate. Collaboration is critical. You need to make the time to collaborate and the time to reflect. Give yourself the time to do this, or make sure your administrators give you the time." —*QPA Network Teacher*

As school communities have text-based discussions, score work, and validate assessments as a team, their ability to work collaboratively evolves and is reflected in their instructional practice. The vocabulary of work rigor, Common Core, and technical quality becomes part of their everyday as the school community structures conversations around improving student work and informing practice as they refine assessments and return to their classrooms armed with new ideas.

Collaborating for Quality

In a closing discussion with some 20 teachers, teacher leaders, and district administrators, one participant reflected: "We never could have understood this process without doing an assessment and trying it. . . . If we don't try it and make the mistakes, we won't get to valid and reliable." This "fishbowl observer" had for the first time witnessed a session using the Assessment Validation Protocol (see Tool #3), in which her colleagues presented their second-grade Pennies for Peace Storybook performance assessment.

Student work from Pennies to Peace performance assessment

The Maine School Administrative District 15 of Gray–New Gloucester, known as MSAD 15, made a commitment to transition from a traditional model to a proficiency-based model in which students advance at their own pace upon demonstrating proficiency on the standards. The new performance-based, student-centered model would require staff, administration, and students to take the time and effort to think about school differently.

MSAD 15 contacted QPA for technical assistance in creating a plan for developing a comprehensive, prekindergarten-to-diploma local assessment system that is performance assessment-based, aligned to the Common Core, and includes common grade-level assessments with an assessment validation process. In a one-day meeting for the administrative leadership team and teacher leaders, participants developed a common understanding and definition of a local assessment system and an action plan for dedicated professional development days for the entire staff.

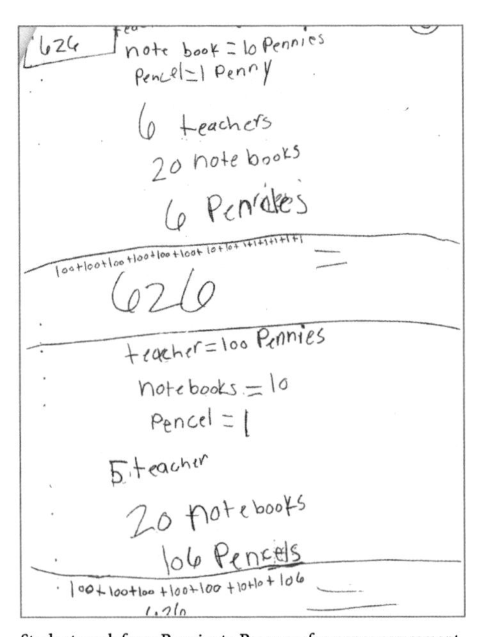

Student work from Pennies to Peace performance assessment

For two days in November, the full faculty gathered to craft a common language and a set of tools for building a local performance assessment system. The district set the expectation that by spring each teacher would implement either an individual or a common performance assessment aligned to power standards or to essential content and skills standards. By the end of the two days, the teachers had all designed posters for their performance assessment plans. As everyone browsed a gallery of the posters, the preview of a prekindergarten-to-diploma, performance-based assessment system was physically laid out in the hallway.

The second grade team created the Pennies for Peace performance assessment to address standards in math, ELA, and social studies. The assessment uses a shortened version of Greg Mortenson's *Three Cups of Tea*, in which Mortenson travels to Pakistan where he volunteers and raises funds for school improvement projects. After reading the short story to first grade reading buddies, students held their own Pennies for Peace campaign. Students then put together books, which included drawings, a comparison between the school in Pakistan and their own school, and mathematical explanations of their penny campaigns.

Several months later, the second grade team was one of three grade-level teams that jumped into the "fishbowl" with leaders and teachers from other teams observing. Each group began by scoring one piece of proficient work selected by a teacher, using the teacher's rubric or scoring guide and the Calibration Protocol (see Tool #4). Next, the group looked more deeply at teacher plans and student tasks, using the Assessment Validation Protocol (see Tool #3). In the Pennies for Peace discussion, participants raised questions about the amount of scaffolding around place value and decimals. The team recommended changing the student directions to include additional demonstrations of the mathematical concepts.

The discussion led to questions about the performance expectations for student work at the different levels, with a focus on levels: 4–Proficient with Distinction, 3–Proficient, and 2–Partially Proficient. One participant commented: "Even when professionals teach the same grade, they can have different interpretations of the same rubrics. How do we build consistency across content areas? How do we make expectations clear?" Another participant added, "Even if teachers are scoring consistently, is it at the right level of expectation?" In collaborating, the teams acknowledged where disagreements existed and reaffirmed their common goals.

Without gathering everyone at the table, individuals might be doing great work, but the experience for students would not be coherent or consistent. Teachers and leaders in MSAD 15 are working together to understand what success for all students looks like and how they will continue the iterative process of aligning, designing, and analyzing work until tasks are validated and form a system.

STEP 4

Design Professional Development in Communities of Practice

STEP 4:
Design Professional Development in Communities of Practice

With teacher input, administrators plan professional development in communities of practice that supports the ability of all teachers to implement common performance assessments and develop assessment literacy.

> "The students of Pentucket Regional School District will be passionate learners prepared for an ever-changing world." —*Pentucket Regional School District Vision Statement*

Pentucket Regional School District teachers and administrators turned to this powerful vision statement as they began the meticulous work of building an assessment system centered on Habits of Learning. Knowing that this document would be a cornerstone of their assessment policy, officials devoted ample time, thought, and effort to the process of developing the habits, rubrics, and, finally, performance assessments.

Teachers first met in April 2008 to determine the key habits, standards, and essential skills students need to master for success in college and life. Then, teachers and administrators devoted several days of summer professional development to draft the habits designed to stimulate profound learning and to help students extend their knowledge to new situations. Every school in the district circulated this draft and teachers had the opportunity to give their input. Based on that feedback, district administrators revised the habits. In the summer of 2009, more than one year after the initial meeting, teachers and administrators dedicated their Pentucket Teacher Leader Summer Institute to developing an initial version of a rubric designed to assess the habits. The district built professional development time into the following semester for Pentucket teachers to construct common rubrics for the grade-level habits.

In 2010–2011, Pentucket High School administrators designated early-release days for professional development to support the implementation of the habits performance assessment system. For example, during one session, middle school teachers went to the high school to share their examples. "This time [was] invaluable to share ideas, motivate teachers to improve their practice, and allow teachers time to continue to explore the use of performance assessments and how the Habits of Learning rubrics can work to improve our classroom instruction and outcomes," said a Pentucket High School teacher.

QPA LEADERSHIP ROLES

District leaders, school leaders, instructional coaches, and teacher leaders take on new roles, which focus on five interconnected areas:

Sharing real decision-making power with staff and faculty

The district and school leaders share authority by providing meaningful opportunities for teachers to participate in significant decision making. In each school, they cooperate with the faculty to establish academic teams, discipline-based teams, study groups, and the Leadership Team. The leaders communicate that every team's success is of paramount importance and that they will help them achieve their goals.

Providing support for effective functioning of communities of practice

School leaders ensure that teachers have the skills and understanding to participate effectively in communities of practice. These skills include defining a purpose, setting measurable goals, creating norms for operating, setting agendas, and assigning tasks. The leaders also give ongoing feedback to the various communities of practice, supporting and encouraging their work. Giving compliments and recognizing their progress goes a long way in supporting their work (see Tool #7).

Administrators discuss practice with QPA staff

Becoming an instructional leader who prompts others to continuously learn and improve their practice

School leaders visit classrooms to work with teachers and students, or attend academic team meetings to assist teachers with their analysis of performance assessment data. In this role, school leaders also offer instructional resources and professional development opportunities that move along the work of performance assessment and help teachers refine and revise their instructional practice.

Developing collaborative accountability

The principal works with the Leadership Team to hold individuals and teams accountable for reaching their goals. By asking teacher teams to document their progress in implementing common performance assessments, the principal and Leadership Team make it clear that when one team reaches its goals, the whole school moves forward.

Managing and monitoring the change process to make sure it is always moving forward

School leaders and the Leadership Team ensure that all members of the school community clearly understand all parts of the change process and are committed to the vision (Center for Collaborative Education, 2005).

Foster Support of Stakeholders by Promoting Performance Assessment Systems

STEP 5:
Foster Support of Stakeholders by Promoting Performance Assessment Systems

Assessment policies – including those that integrate state student assessment systems with local performance assessment – are developed and promoted through a process that builds political will and support from all stakeholders.

"I'm a lot like my daughter, who has a tough time learning through reading, and being able to see and hear what she does in class helps me as a parent to support her." —*Pentucket parent*

The Pentucket Habits of Learning assessment system has evolved to the point where the Pentucket parent quoted above can truly understand her daughter's learning style, and as a consequence, she is supportive of the district's efforts to integrate performance assessment into every classroom. Cultivating support from parents and community members by keeping them informed and knowledgeable about the process and the ramifications of the changes is critical when school or district leaders are attempting to create a performance assessment system. Lack of community support can overturn the most positive attempts at reform. To harness this support, school and district leaders must undertake a well-thought-out approach over time to engage parents and the community.

The Pentucket process of building a districtwide performance assessment system required committed leaders and careful planning, both of which contributed to the high level of community buy-in. The development of the habits, rubrics, and performance criteria reflected "months of exceptional work from teachers representing every school and every grade in the district," and has been a "deliberate, thoughtful, and inclusive process," noted Dr. William Hart, assistant superintendent and architect of the Pentucket assessment system. At the 2010 summer institute, teachers looked at student work against the habits rubric, and during the 2011–2012 school year students prepared their presentations, completing two assignments for each habit over the course of the year. These assessments provide meaningful, relevant information to students, parents, teachers, school leaders, and district policymakers—information that may indicate whether or not students are prepared to meet college-level expectations.

At the district level, Dr. Hart and the District Professional Development Leadership Council have supported this work. At the school level, Pentucket principals have provided teachers with the time and resources needed for professional development in assessment literacy. According to Dr. Hart, this support includes a Habits Demonstration of Mastery Task Force to guide the process at each school. There is also support for students at each building level through an advisory program that guides them through their presentation and portfolio process. By attending the presentations, parents witness the power of the process.

> "The project (HOL presentation) allowed [my son] to articulate what was meaningful to him as a learner. It was one of those light bulb moments we parents love—when your child figures out that he is responsible for his own education—and he is actually excited by that idea." *—PRHS parent letter to the PRSD School Committee*

The Pentucket school district devoted time and resources to integrate the habits of learning into the fabric of each school by setting up a task force structure. Each school had its own task force, and participants committed to spend 24 hours during the course of five months. Each task force held six two-hour meetings and two six-hour release days. Each local task force sent a representative to the District Habits of Learning Task Force monthly meetings. In an effort to promote shared leadership, the local task forces sent different representatives each month. The district charged the task forces with:

- Calendar, schedule, and timelines;
- Communication and data collection for school, district, and community;
- Collaboration systems for school and district;
- Creation of curriculum work and documentation.

After the task forces completed their work, the district required that each school set up a Habits of Learning Implementation Committee, which adhered to a strict timeline and accomplished specific goals set by district leaders. In September and October, the committees took responsibility for disseminating the accomplishments of the work, promoting best practices in a Habits of Learning curriculum, and documenting learning and student progress. Then, from November through April, each school implemented the Habits of Learning curriculum with instructional strategies, evaluated Habits of Learning student progress in student portfolios, and extended invitations to students, families, and community to participate in public presentations. Finally, in May and June, the committees took care of final logistics for presentations, created structures for students to practice for public presentations, and held public celebrations of the Pentucket Regional School System Habits of Learning.

DISTRICT ACTIONS THAT PROMOTE A PERFORMANCE ASSESSMENT SYSTEM:

District leaders should review the district's current assessment policy and consider how it could be changed to support a performance assessment system. For example:

- o Include performance assessments as a graduation requirement at all grade spans (elementary, middle, high).
- o Restructure the senior year of all district high schools to be Senior Institutes focused on research projects, internships and apprenticeships, college-readiness activities, and seminars.
- o Design (through summer performance assessment committees in each core academic discipline) and implement common performance assessments at every grade level in order to build a culture of performance assessments districtwide.
- o Align all district curriculum to the Common Core.
- o Provide districtwide professional development in backward design as the primary vehicle for designing standards-based curriculum.
- o Develop a district web-based bank of validated locally developed performance assessments that teachers can access.
- o Organize districtwide, cross-school performance task validation sessions and calibration scoring sessions.
- o Organize cross-grade-span network sessions for teachers to share and align performance assessments.

Teachers evaluate brainstorm ideas from a faculty meeting

RETHINKING STATE ASSESSMENT POLICIES

by Dan French

How can quality performance assessment take on a greater role in student assessment and accountability systems? How can quality performance assessment leverage changes in district, state, and federal policy, in classroom instruction, and ultimately in student learning? With the advent of the Common Core, there is an unprecedented opportunity to influence state departments of education to think about student assessment in new ways.

Increasingly, state departments of education are rethinking their student assessment policies in order to meet the demands of educating students for the 21st century. For example, in 2003 the Rhode Island Board of Regents adopted changes to the state's policy on high school graduation that for the first time included requirements that students demonstrate proficiency (The Rhode Island Department of Education & The Education Alliance at Brown University, 2005). The policy originated from the regents' stated beliefs that there are inequitable learning opportunities for high school students and a wide disparity in preparation students receive for future learning, career, and civic engagement.

The new policy requires students to "complete assessments that are authentic and demonstrate deep content knowledge and mastery.... Schools must offer students opportunities to complete 'diploma assessments' that will allow them to demonstrate their proficiency"(The Rhode Island Department of Education & The Education Alliance at Brown University, 2005). Further, the 2008 regulations call for performance-based diploma assessments in which students must exhibit proficiency in the core curriculum "through multiple sources of evidence gathered over time in a valid and reliable local assessment system" through a combination of portfolios, exhibitions, and course assessments (Rhode Island Board of Regents for Elementary and Secondary Education, 2008). These assessments must assess for 21st century skills, including "communication, problem solving, critical thinking, research, and reflection/evaluation across all content areas." (Rhode Island Board of Regents for Elementary and Secondary Education, 2008, p.8). In fact, the state's student assessment test counts as only one-third of a district's total assessment of student proficiency for graduation in designated areas of study.

Similarly, in 2008 the New Hampshire State Board of Education adopted a policy requiring all high school courses to be aligned to course-level competencies to foster new practices of assessment that promote and assess deeper levels of understanding. The state is now exploring ways to include a more prominent role for performance assessment in their state student assessment and accountability systems.

Rhode Island's and New Hampshire's state policies represent the leading edge of states' efforts to rethink their student assessment and accountability systems to include performance assessment as a central component of measuring student progress and promoting deeper learning. In considering new state policies that promote a more prominent role for performance assessment in student assessment systems, QPA offers the following set of foundational principles and components that assist in building a strong system of valid and reliable performance assessments.

FOUNDATIONAL PRINCIPLES

1. State student assessment systems should promote and measure the knowledge, skills, and dispositions that lead students to graduate from high school college- and career-ready.
2. State student assessment systems should promote and measure deeper learning.
3. State student assessment systems should build the capacity of educators to lead best practices in performance assessment at the local level.

COMPONENTS OF A STATE STUDENT ASSESSMENT SYSTEM BASED ON PERFORMANCE ASSESSMENTS

A state student assessment system that is based on performance assessment should include the following components:

1. A common definition of what constitutes "performance assessments."
2. A set of common performance assessments that have high technical quality.
3. Promotion of locally designed assessments with guidelines for ensuring high technical quality.
4. Regional professional development and network sessions and modules on task design and validation, as well as calibration scoring to ensure reliability.
5. A web-based bank of local and common performance assessments, as well as technology to undertake virtual scoring and validation sessions.
6. Local district peer review audits to ensure sound accountability systems and high inter-rater reliability.

Conclusion

QPA believes the development of performance assessments with high technical quality at the school, district, and state levels will prepare the diverse population of students in K–12 public schools for the complex thinking and understanding necessary to thrive in the 21st century global society. To create valid and reliable performance assessments, the process must begin by setting up professional communities of practice with deliberate training in collaboration among teachers. District and school administrators participate in this work and become assessment literate alongside teachers to support the work of creating and putting performance assessments into practice. At the classroom level, students become more assessment literate, actively participating and taking responsibility to learn the 21st century skills that will provide lifelong opportunities for continued learning. At the state level, QPA's goal is to replicate the process, graduating students statewide who are able to transfer their knowledge to their lives in college, career, and civic life as a result of deeper and more student-centered learning experiences in their K–12 education.

Student work sample: house building at Cape Cod Charter Lighthouse School

Let's Get Started: Entry Points for Communities of Practice

The work of creating communities of practice might take on many forms. A district, school, or grade-level team might decide to:

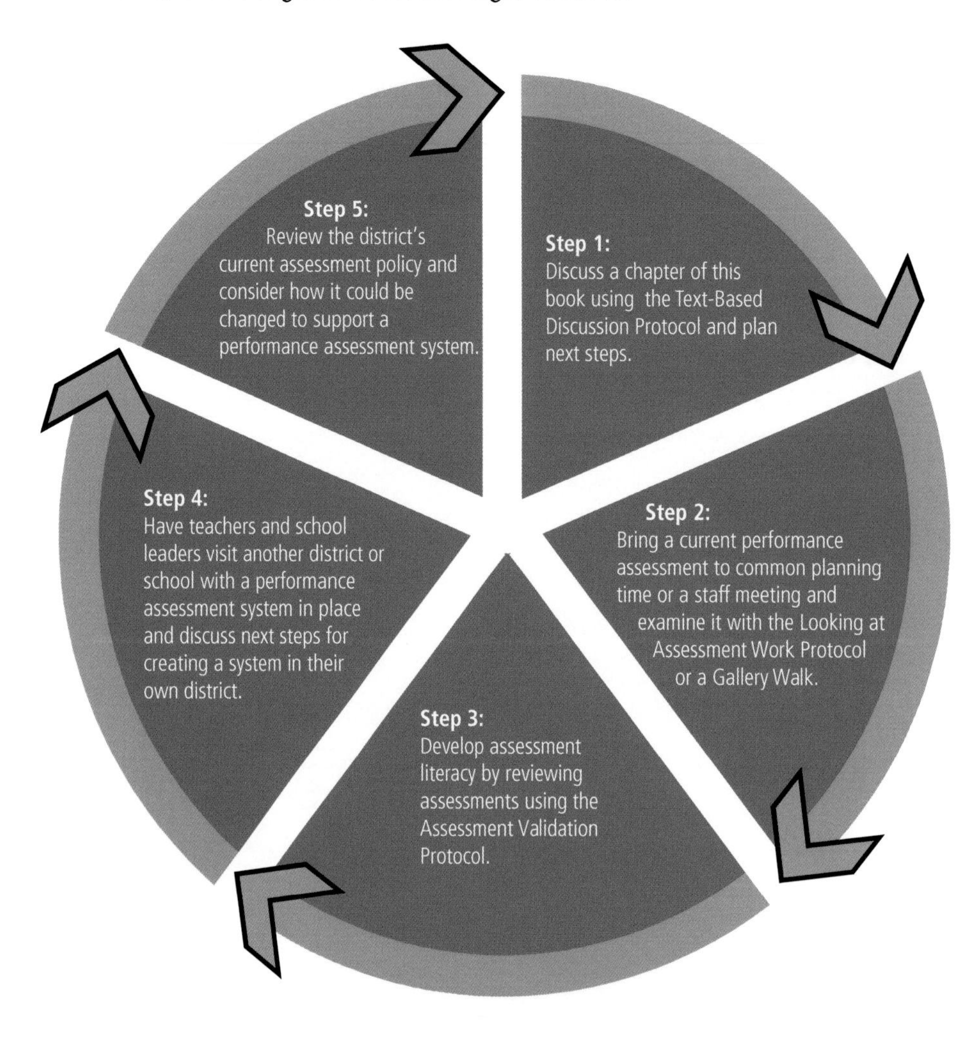

Refining Our Work through Self-Assessment

The self-assessment process also ensures that teachers are constantly reviewing and amending their own work. School leaders and teams of teachers must ask themselves the following questions:

Teacher Learning in Professional Communities of Practice	Are there opportunities to cooperate across departments and grade levels to share best practice and create vertical and horizontal coherence?
	Is the emphasis of our teams on looking at student work with defined protocols and harnessing the results of these discussions to take steps to improve learning, teaching, and assessment?
	Is the focus on creating professional communities of practice that work collaboratively to implement performance assessment?
	Are teachers demonstrating respect and improving the quality of teacher discourse with structured dialogues using protocols?
Leadership and Policy Support	Do school and district leaders cultivate assessment literacy among themselves and faculty by designing professional development in communities of practice that gives teachers what they need to implement performance assessment?
	Does shared decision making keep teachers invested in the process?
	Are school and district leaders building the support of stakeholders by making public a detailed record of assessment policies?

TOOLS USED IN THIS CHAPTER

Tools for Leadership and Collaboration

TOOL #	TOOL NAME	PAGE #
3	Assessment Validation Protocol	T8
4	Calibration Protocol	T9
7	Collaborative Cultures Survey	T12
13	Guidelines for Effective Meetings	T23
14	Looking at Assessment Work Protocol	T24
15	Microlab Discussion Protocol	T26
31	Setting Norms Protocol	T51
34	Student Work Analysis Tool	T57
36	Text-Based Discussion Protocol	T60

APPENDIX A: The QPA Framework and Self-Assessment

The Quality Performance Assessment (QPA) Framework guides teachers and administrators on how to design and implement performance assessment systems with technical quality. The QPA approach focuses on performance assessment because performance assessment allows us to see whether students are able to apply their knowledge and skills. The QPA Framework addresses three factors of success for developing and sustaining performance assessment systems: (1) the technical quality of the assessments; (2) a robust professional development model to train district and school educators; and (3) leadership support (Tung & Stazesky, 2010).

QPA DEFINITION OF PERFORMANCE ASSESSMENT:

Performance assessments are multistep assignments with clear criteria, expectations, and processes that measure how well a student transfers knowledge and applies complex skills to create or refine an original product.

The QPA Framework elements include both the content and process for designing and evaluating performance assessments. The set of processes described in the framework is designed for development over time and is cyclical in nature. Many aspects of the QPA Framework can be integrated into an existing student assessment system without a comprehensive overhaul. The graphic illustrates how the elements form a cycle of teaching and learning, with student learning at the center.

QPA Framework

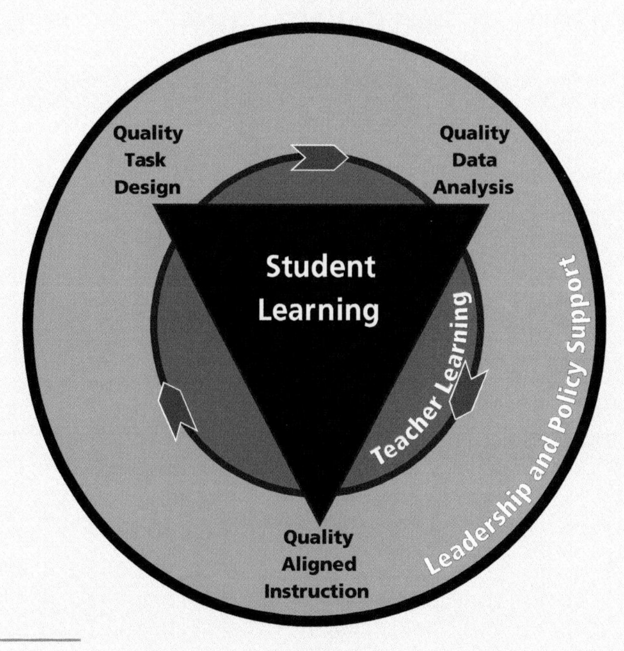

The idea of using a triangle to arrange the criteria for technical quality was inspired by the three vertices of the National Research Council Assessment Triangle, which connects Cognition, Observation, and Interpretation (National Research Council, 2001).

Student learning, at the center of the framework graphic, is the goal of this iterative cycle. QPA focuses on meaningful, student-centered learning, incorporating complex skills and content that are transferable to new situations. Learning is assessed in multiple modes and engages students through opportunities for ownership and decision making in real-world situations. The learning process supports college and career readiness by embedding 21st century skills.

Students using light board to create visual for a performance assessment

The three elements at the vertices of the triangle combine to create performance assessments with technical quality. As assessment-literate practitioners cycle through the framework, assessments become aligned to standards, reflect high-level instruction in the classroom, and produce meaningful evidence of student learning resulting in the following aspects of technical quality:

- *Validity* ensures that learning assessments are clearly aligned to standards and that they measure student performance on the intended standards.
- *Reliable* refers to inter-rater reliability, where a group of teachers (or scorers) come to an agreement on how to interpret a rating and corresponding performance descriptors and score student work consistently.
- *Free of bias* means the assessment does not disadvantage the performance of certain groups of students.
- *Sufficiency* describes a combination of related, validated assessments that provide enough assessment evidence to accurately infer the level of proficiency of a student on a standard.

Quality aligned instruction means instruction and assessment practices are interwoven and aligned to each other and to standards. All students need instruction that is accessible to their diverse learning strengths and needs based on a common vision for student success articulated clearly in standards and practice. This set of standards is based on appropriate national, state, district, and school standards that prepare students to be college and career ready. Effective instructional practice provides students with the opportunity to master these standards, and aligned assessments allow them to demonstrate what they know and are able to do.

Quality task design begins with clarity about what students at each grade level should know and be able to do. A common understanding among faculty about appropriate content and cognitive complexity in the grades they teach and in adjacent grades guides the design of prompts and scoring tools. Documentation of the assessment design and a validation process build awareness of expectations, allow appropriate performance levels to be set at each grade level, and help make the assessment accessible to all students.

Quality data analysis involves working in teams to examine teacher and student assessment work and score data to ensure that assessments are valid, reliable, free of bias, and provide sufficient evidence of learning. Conclusions from the data analysis provide information to practitioners about whether or not they are in fact teaching what is being assessed and whether patterns of student demonstration of mastery are equitable. Incorporating what they learn into practice enables teachers to plan future instruction and assessment accordingly.

Teacher learning in professional communities of practice, as represented in the cycle of teacher learning in the framework graphic, occurs when teachers engage in professional dialogue about aligned instruction, task design, and analysis of student work. Collaboration creates a synergy and provides the level of quality required for teacher and student learning through performance assessment. This process fosters ongoing conversations focused on expectations, requirements for proficiency, and practices teachers must implement to assist all students to demonstrate mastery. As it deepens professional knowledge and skills, this collaborative work requires a cultural shift that takes time and trust. Over time, teachers speak openly about their formerly private practice and reap the rewards of sharing their own teaching and their students' learning.

Leadership and policy support are represented by the outer circle of the framework. Support from teachers, families, community members, and school district officials is essential for successful adoption of performance assessments. The more all stakeholders participate in building the foundation of a QPA system, the more school leaders will be able to draw upon this base of support in the future. The need for such support makes it especially important to field test, fine tune, and scale up the performance assessment system slowly, particularly if there are high stakes outcomes such as linking student performance to graduation and promotion or to teacher evaluation. District and school leadership can build support and sustainability for performance assessments through embedding them in graduation requirements, building performance assessments into the district's formative assessment system, and developing a web-based bank of validated common performance tasks that schools and teachers can access. Leaders also support the work by cultivating a collaborative school culture that establishes a comfortable and safe environment and teacher leadership that builds buy-in for the work.

Teachers evaluate student work samples

Self-Assessment Questions

The following self-assessment questions address each element of the QPA Framework to support practitioners in evaluating the technical quality of their performance assessments. If, upon review, there is evidence to support a Yes, the performance assessment likely has strong technical quality. If the answer to any question is No, QPA provides tools, professional development modules, and coaching to support schools in achieving technical quality. Without technical quality there will be no guarantee that an assessment system has evaluated student learning fairly and completely.

Framework Element	Self-Assessment Questions	Answer
Quality Aligned Instruction	Are promotion and graduation requirements aligned to appropriate, agreed-upon standards that include 21st century skills?	
	Are teaching and assessment practices for each course or classroom aligned to key standards?	
	Is the content and cognitive complexity for each assessment aligned with established content and skills sequences and/or grade-level standards?	
	Do all students have adequate time to build upon prior learning and to both practice and master complex skills and content?	
Quality Task Design	Do the assessments provide opportunities for students to demonstrate the standards through multiple modes and to exercise ownership and decision making in real-world settings?	
	Do rubrics that are used by teachers and students have clear criteria and descriptions of performance at each level?	
	For each common performance task, have teachers identified anchors of student work to provide examples of proficient work?	
	Has a team of teachers examined and revised the common tasks and rubrics using student work?	
Quality Data Analysis	Do assessments provide the information about mastery of standards/ content for which they were designed?	
	Have a sufficient number of common performance assessments been validated to make promotion and graduation decisions?	
	Is there a process for collecting scoring data and auditing the scoring process to ensure scores are consistent across administrations and raters?	
	Is there professional development for scorers that uses scoring guidelines and anchor student work samples?	
	Is there a systematic process for teams of teachers, other faculty, and leaders to analyze scoring data for student subgroups and to use performance assessment data to inform curriculum planning, instruction, and assessment?	
Teacher Learning in Professional Communities of Practice	Are there opportunities to cooperate across departments and grade levels to share best practice and create vertical and horizontal coherence?	
	Is the emphasis of our teams on looking at student work with defined protocols and harnessing the results of these discussions to take steps to improve learning, teaching, and assessment?	
	Is the focus on creating professional communities of practice that work collaboratively to implement performance assessment?	
	Are teachers demonstrating respect and improving the quality of teacher discourse with structured dialogues using protocols?	
Leadership and Policy Support	Do school and district leaders cultivate assessment literacy among themselves and faculty by designing professional development in communities of practice that gives teachers what they need to implement performance assessment?	
	Does shared decision making keep teachers invested in the process?	
	Are school and district leaders building the support of stakeholders by making public a detailed record of assessment policies?	

APPENDIX B: QPA Network Schools and Districts Whose Work Informed This Guide

School	Grade	Location
Ashland Middle School	6–8	Ashland, MA
Boston Arts Academy	9–12	Boston, MA
Burrillville High School	9–12	Harrisville, RI
Cape Cod Lighthouse Charter School	6–8	Orleans, MA
Chelsea High School	9–12	Chelsea, MA
Codman Academy Charter Public School	9–12	Boston, MA
Fenway High School	9–12	Boston, MA
Hilltown Cooperative Charter Public School	6–8	Haydenville, MA
Hudson High School	8–12	Hudson, MA
John F. Kennedy Middle School	6–7	Hudson, MA
Lee Middle and High School	7–12	Lee, MA
Marblehead Community Charter Public School	4–8	Marblehead, MA
Mission Hill School	K–8	Boston, MA
Murdock Middle/High School	6–12	Winchendon, MA
MSAD 15	K–12	Gray/New Gloucester, ME
Parker Charter Essential School	7–12	Devens, MA
Pentucket Regional School District	K–12	West Newbury, MA
Phoenix Charter Academy	9–12	Chelsea, MA
Springfield Renaissance School	6–12	Springfield, MA
Souhegan High School	9–12	Amherst, NH
Vergennes Union High School	9–12	Vergennes, Vermont
Young Achievers Science and Math Pilot School	K–8	Mattapan, MA

Glossary

Anchor works are samples of student work that teachers use to set the standard for performance of a rubric level to promote reliable scoring and consistent interpretation of rubrics. Anchors can also be used to show students what a final product looks like at a given grade and proficiency level.

Assessment literacy consist of understanding types and purposes of assessments and having the ability to apply one's technical knowledge about assessments in practice.

Backward design is a way to plan curriculum with the end in mind, taking into consideration performance assessments, standards, level of rigor, and learning goals. In backward design, teachers identify the desired standards, skills, and habits they want students to master; create the assessment that will best measure whether students have reached proficiency; and then plan the instruction and curriculum that will help students optimally achieve the target standards (Wiggins & McTighe, 2005).

Calibration is a process of assuring that teachers have a common understanding of the work quality that corresponds to different score points (or performance levels) in a common rubric.

Common performance assessments consist of a carefully orchestrated learning plan composed of individual tasks in which a whole school, grade-level teams, or discipline-area teams work collaboratively to adapt, create or implement existing tasks and rubrics, and then score student work reliably.

Common rubrics are designed and used by teachers across grade levels or subject areas to evaluate student work consistently and fairly.

Communities of practice are a group of professionals working together effectively and guided by a common goal.

Criteria stem from standards and describe student performance along a continuum that assesses the student's degree of understanding and skill.

Culture of discourse describes the professional environment of team members who converse deeply about critical issues related to the improvement of teaching, learning, and assessment practices.

Depth of Knowledge (DOK) framework, is a model that allows educators to analyze the cognitive level, or depth of content understanding and complexity of thinking, implied by a learning goal or required to complete an assessment task (Webb, 1997).

Enduring understandings are important ideas that have lasting value beyond the classroom and are central to a discipline. As learners make deeper meaning of these enduring understandings they also become equipped to apply the learning to new contexts (Wiggins & McTighe, 2005).

Essential questions are overarching, inquiry-based questions that are used to frame the central understandings and content of a unit of study or performance assessment. Essential questions allow students to reflect and debate larger issues and themes and to thoughtfully uncover deeper meaning through exploration of the diversity of possible answers.

Formative assessments are assessments for learning that continuously track each student's ongoing learning and mastery of target standards. Formative assessments provide the teacher with information on which students are making progress, which students need additional instruction, and which concepts are not clearly understood.

Free of bias means the assessment does not disadvantage the performance of certain groups of students.

Habits are the critical skills, knowledge, and dispositions (i.e., the learner's feelings, attitudes, values, and interests) that give teachers information about how students approach learning. Schools refer to these habits in a variety of ways, for example: Habits of Mind, Habits of the Graduate, or Habits of Learning.

Learning competencies encompass the school's habits, standards, and essential skills that students are expected to demonstrate in order to graduate or move to the next grade level.

Local assessment systems are collections of multiple types of assessments that go beyond individual classrooms to measure the academic performance of all students and create a coherent K–12 education.

Measurable goals have a specific intention or result that is quantifiable.

Norms are ways of working together that can help groups be more thoughtful and productive. Norms exist in every learning community whether or not they are named or agreed upon.

Performance assessments are multistep assignments with clear criteria, expectations, and processes that measure how well a student transfers knowledge and applies complex skills to create or refine an original product.

Power standards are the most essential standards selected to guide assessment work (Ainsworth, 2003).

Proficiency is the degree to which students meet expectations for essential skills and knowledge.

Protocols give communities of practice a specific procedure to follow during the course of a meeting in order to provide a respectful and productive focus to important conversations about teacher practice and student learning

Quality Performance Assessment (QPA) is a set of practices and principles for implementing performance assessments with technical quality that requires educators to work together to align, design, and analyze performance assessments to increase student achievement and equity of outcomes.

Reliable refers to inter-rater reliability, where a group of teachers (or scorers) come to an agreement on how to interpret a rating and corresponding performance descriptors and score student work consistently.

Rubrics apply criteria to different levels of performance and can be used on a variety of different products/performances (e.g., a writing rubric or mathematics problem-solving rubric).

Sufficiency describes a combination of related, validated assessments that provide enough assessment evidence to accurately infer the level of proficiency of a student on a standard.

Summative assessments determine whether or not students have mastered the standards in question, either at a classroom level, in the case of a performance assessment or exam at the end of a unit, or at the district or state level, in the case of standardized tests or performance assessments administered to measure the progress of students in an entire grade, school, or district.

Technical quality describes an assessment that is valid, reliable, sufficient, and free of bias.

21st century skills are skills that take into account the global economy, technology, and changing workforce requirements. These skills include complex thinking, analytical skills, collaboration, computer skills, creativity, media literacy, and cross-cultural skills.

Understanding by Design, developed by Grant Wiggins and Jay McTighe, is a three-stage structure designed to lead teachers through a process that focuses on designing curriculum beginning with the student learning goals in mind (Wiggins, 1989; Wiggins & McTighe, 2005).

Universal Design for Learning, developed by David Rose and Jenna Gravel (2010), is a set of guidelines for tailoring curriculum to meet the needs of all students, including those with special needs, and to give them opportunities to demonstrate their learning in a variety of ways.

A valid assessment means the assessment measures the content and skills that it was intended to measure at the intended level of rigor.

A validation team is an interdisciplinary group of teachers who meet to review and analyze performance assessments to ensure they are clearly aligned to standards and measure what they are intended to measure.

Validity ensures that learning assessments are clearly aligned to standards and that they measure student performance on the intended standards.

References

Ainsworth, L. (2003). *Power standards: Identifying the standards that matter the most.* Englewood, CO: Advanced Learning Press.

Alliance for Excellent Education. (May 2011). *A time for deeper learning: Preparing students for a changing world.* Retrieved from Alliance for Excellent Education website: http://www.all4ed.org/files/DeeperLearning.pdf

Beck, I., McKeown, M., & Kucan, L. (2002). *Bringing words to life: Robust vocabulary instruction* (1st ed.). New York: The Guilford Press.

Berger, R. (2003). *An ethic of excellence: Building a culture of craftsmanship with students.* Portsmouth, NH: Heinemann.

Bloom, B. S. (Ed.). (1956). *Taxonomy of educational objectives: the classification of educational goals.* New York: McKay.

Brown, C. and Mevs, P. (2012). *Quality performance assessment: Harnessing the power of teacher and student learning.* Boston, MA: Center for Collaborative Education.

Bransford, J., Brown, A. L., & Cocking, R. R. (1999). *How people learn: brain, mind, experience, and school.* Washington, DC: National Academy Press.

Campbell, W. (2010). Rice field art: Inakadate, Japan. Retrieved from the Daily Art Fixx website: http://www.dailyartfixx.com/?s=rice+field+art

Center for Applied Special Technology CAST (2008). Universal design for learning guidelines version 1.0. Wakefield, MA: CAST. Retrieved from http://www.cast.org/library/UDLguidelines/version1.html.

Center for Collaborative Education. (2001). *Turning Points guide to collaborative culture and shared leadership.* Boston: Center for Collaborative Education.

Center for Collaborative Education. (2005). *Equity and high achievement: CCE small schools planning guide.* Boston: Center for Collaborative Education.

Conley, D. T. (2007). *Toward a more comprehensive conception of college readiness.* Eugene, OR: Educational Policy Improvement Center.

Conley, D. T. (2008). *Educational Leadership* "What Makes Student College Ready?," 66(2).

Conley, D. T. (2010). *College and career ready: Helping all students succeed beyond high school.* San Francisco: Jossey-Bass.

Darling-Hammond, L., & Rustique-Forrester, E. (2005). The consequences of student testing for teaching and teacher quality. *Yearbook of the*

National Society for the Study of Education, 104, 289-319. doi: 10.1111/j.1744-7984.2005.00034.x

Friedman, T. (2006). Developing a culture of inquiry for equity: One school's story. In L. Friedrich, C. Tateishi, T. Malarkey, E. R. Simons, & M. Williams (Eds.), Working toward equity: *Writings and resources from the teacher research collaborative.* Berkeley, CA: National Writing Project.

Gagnon, L. (2010). *Ready for the future: The role of performance assessments in shaping graduates' academic, professional, and personal lives.* Boston: Center for Collaborative Education.

Gallagher, C. W. (2011). BQ *interview report.* Boston, MA: Northeastern University.

Goldschmidt, P., Martinez, J. F., Niemi, D., & Baker, E. L. (2007). Relationships among measures as empirical evidence of validity: Incorporating multiple indicators of achievement and school context. *Educational Assessment,* 12(3), 239-266. doi: 10.1080/10627190701578297

Hess, K. (2009). *Local assessment toolkit: Assessment task validation tools—Criteria for high quality performance assessment.* Retrieved from www.nciea.org/publications

Hess, K. (2011). Tools for Examining Text Complexity. Retrieved from http://www.nciea.org/publications/Updated%20toolkit-text%20complexity_KH12.pdf

Hess, K., Carlock, D., Jones, B., & Walkup, J. (2009). *What exactly do "fewer, clearer, and higher standards" really look like in the classroom? Using a cognitive rigor matrix to analyze curriculum, plan lessons, and implement assessments.* Paper presented at the Council of Chief State School Officers, Detroit. Retrieved from http://www.nciea.org/beta-site/publication_PDFs/cognitiverigorpaper_KH11.pdf

Hess, K., & Hervey, S. (2011). *Local assessment toolkit: Tools for examining text complexity.* Retrieved online at http://www.nciea.org/publication_PDFs/Updated%20toolkit-text%20complexity_KH12.pdf

Kiker, J. (2007). Move beyond "seat-time" and narrowly defined knowledge and skills. *Techniques,* 82(5), 38–40.

Ladson-Billings, G. (2009). *The dreamkeepers: Successful teachers of African American Children* (2nd ed.). San Francisco: Jossey-Bass.

Lundell, D. B., Higbee, J. L., Hipp, S., & Copeland, R. (Eds.). (2005). *Building bridges for access and success from high school to college: Proceedings of the Metropolitan Higher Education Consortium's Developmental Education Initiative.* Minneapolis: General College and the Center for Research on Developmental Education and Urban Literacy.

Marzano, R. J. (2003). *What works in schools: Translating research into action.* Alexandria, VA: Association for Supervision and Curriculum Development.

McTighe, J., & Wiggins, G. P. (2004). *Understanding by design: professional development workbook.* Alexandria, VA: Association for Supervision and Curriculum Development, 2004.

National Governors Association Center for Best Practices, Council of Chief State School Officers. (2010). *The Common Core Standards in English Language Arts & Literacy in History/Social Studies, Science, and Technical Subjects.* Washington D.C.: National Governors Association Center for Best Practices, Council of Chief State School Officers, Washington D.C. Retrieved from http://www.corestandards.org/assets/CCSSI_ELA%20Standards.pdf

New Hampshire Department of Education. (2013). *NH College and Career Ready Competencies aligned with Common Core State Standards.* Retrieved from http://www.education.nh.gov/competencies/

National Research Council (Ed.). (2001). *Knowing What Students Know: The science and design of educational assessment.* Washington, DC: National Academy Press.

Newmann, F. M., Bryk, A. S., Nagaoka, J. K. (2001). *Authentic intellectual work and standardized tests: Conflict or coexistence?* Retrieved from Consortium Chicago School Research website: http://ccsr.uchicago.edu/sites/default/files/publications/p0a02.pdf

Pellegrino, J. W., Chudowsky, N., & Glaser, R. (Eds.). (2001). *Knowing what students know: The science and design of educational assessments.* Washington, DC: National Academy Press.

Rhode Island Department of Education, & The Education Alliance at Brown University. (2005). Rhode Island diploma system: Local assessment toolkits Retrieved August 31, 2012, from http://www.ride.ri.gov/highschoolreform/dslat/system/sys_ovr.shtml

Rose, D. H., & Gravel, J. W. (2009). Getting from Here to There: UDL, global positioning systems, and Lessons for Improving Education. In Gordon, D.T., Gravel, J.W., & Schifter, L.A. (Eds.) *A policy reader in universal design for learning,* 5-18. Cambridge, MA: Harvard Education Press.

Schmoker, M. J. (2011). *Focus: Elevating the essentials to radically improve student learning.* Alexandria, VA: Association for Supervision and Curriculum Development.

Stemler, S. E., Sternberg, R. J., Grigorenko, E. L., Jarvin, L., & Sharpes, K. (2009). Using the theory of successful intelligence as a framework for developing assessments in AP physics. *Contemporary Educational Psychology,* 34(3) 195–209.

Stiggins, R. J. (1999). Teams. *Journal of Staff Development,* 20(3), 17–21.

Stiggins, R. J., & DuFour, R. (2009). Maximizing the power of formative assessments. *Phi Delta Kappan,* 90(9) 640–644.

Stuart, L. F. (2003). *Assessment in practice, a view from the school: Creating a school culture of learning and assessment.* Wellesley, MA: Teachers21.

The Education Trust. (2005). *Gaining traction, gaining ground: How some high schools accelerate learning for struggling students.* Washington, DC: The Education Trust.

Thompson, T. (n.d.). *Are you scaffolding or rescuing?* Retrieved from Choice Literacy website: www.choiceliteracy.com

Tomlinson, C. A., & McTighe, J. (2006). *Integrating differentiated instruction & understanding by design.* Alexandria, VA: Association for Supervision and Curriculum Development.

Toshalis, E., & Nakkula, M. J. (April 2012). *Motivation, engagement, and student voice.* Retrieved from Students at the Center website: http://www.studentsatthecenter.org/papers/motivation-engagement-and-student-voice

Tung, R., & Stazesky, P. (2010). *Including performance assessments in accountability systems: A review of scale-up efforts.* Boston: Center for Collaborative Education.

Webb, N. L. (1997). *Criteria for alignment of expectations and assessments in mathematics and science education.* Council of Chief State School Officers and National Institute for Science Education Research Monograph No. 6. Madison: University of Wisconsin, Wisconsin Center for Education Research.

Wiggins, G. (1989). A true test: Toward more authentic and equitable assessment. *Phi Delta Kappan,* 70(9), 703–711.

Wiggins, G. (2006). *Healthier testing made easy: The idea of authentic assessment.* Retrieved from Edutopia website: http://www.edutopia.org/healthier-testing-made-easy

Wiggins, G., & McTighe, J. (2005). *Understanding by design* (2nd ed.). Alexandria, VA: Association for Supervision and Curriculum Development.

Wood, G. H., Darling-Hammond, L., Neill, M., & Roschewski, P. (2007). *Refocusing accountability: Using local performance assessments to enhance teaching and learning for higher order skills.* A Briefing Paper Prepared for Members of the Congress of the United States. Retrieved from Forum for Education and Democracy website: http://www.forumforeducation.org/node/377.

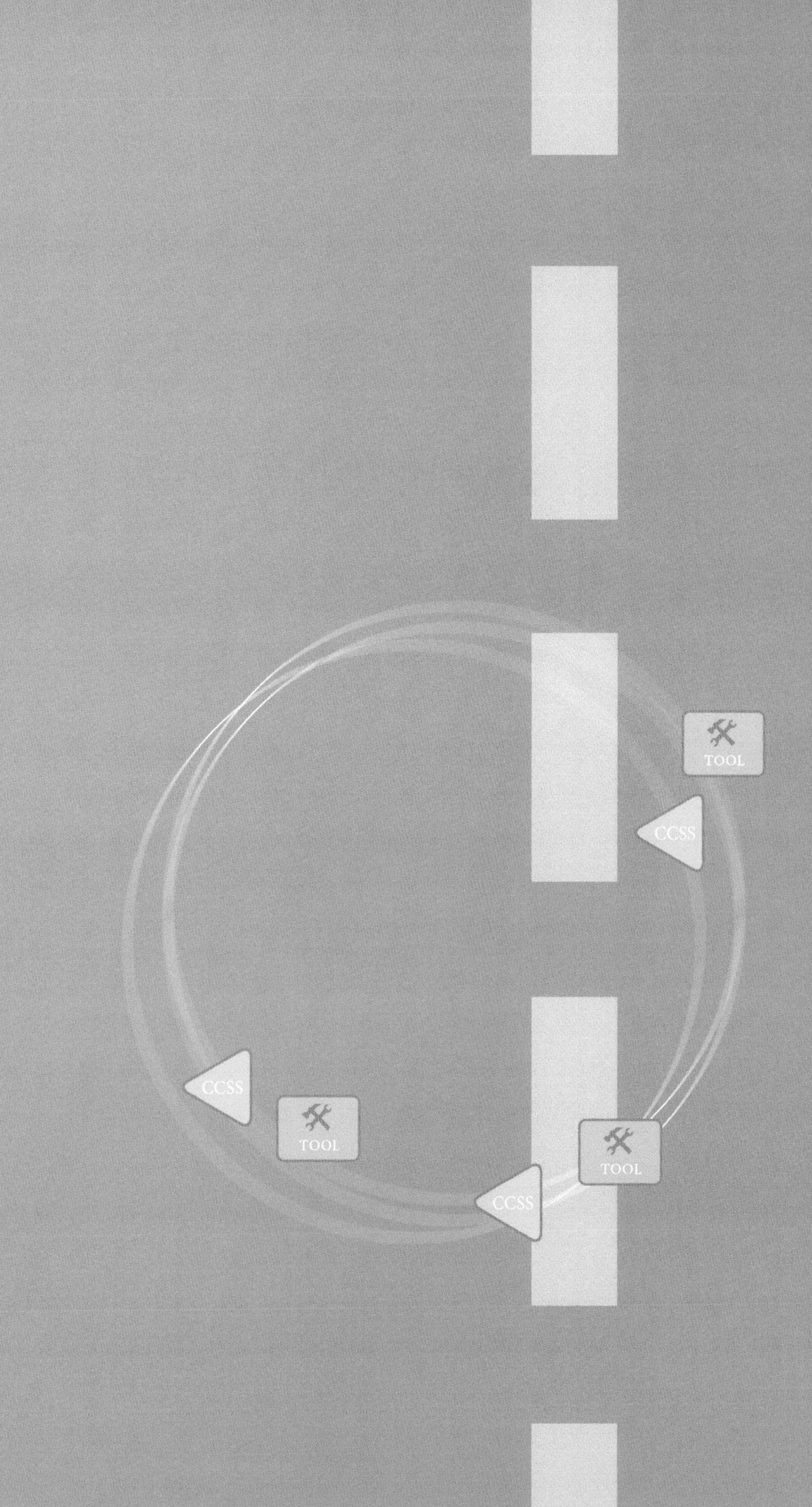
TOOL
CCSS
CCSS
TOOL
TOOL
CCSS

TOOLS

TOOLS

Tool #	Tool	Purpose	Page #
1	Assessment Validation Checklist	To review assessment plans for effective assessment design.	T3
2	Assessment Validation Cover Sheet	To share information about a task in preparation for assessment validation.	T6
3	Assessment Validation Protocol	To ensure assessments have technical quality in a formal setting.	T8
4	Calibration Protocol	To calibrate scoring of student work and explore the implications for instructional practice.	T9
5	Cognitive Rigor Matrix and Examples (ELA & Social Studies)	To examine ELA and Social Studies tasks for their level of complexity.	T10
6	Cognitive Rigor Matrix and Examples (Math & Science)	To examine Math and Science tasks for their level of complexity.	T11
7	Collaborative Cultures Survey	To assess the quality of team collaboration and identify areas needing improvement.	T12
8	Common Performance Assessment Curriculum Planning Template	To apply the QPA Framework to develop and implement a standards-based common performance assessment.	T13
9	Cookie Monster Protocol	To explore rubric creation and scoring, and apply learning to rubric use in schools and classrooms.	T17
10	Data Analysis Protocol	To guide practitioners as they collect, prepare, and use performance assessment data.	T19
11	Gradients in Complexity: Text Complexity Rubric for Informational Texts	To help practitioners select informational texts appropriate to their content and specific goals.	T21
12	Gradients in Complexity: Text Complexity Rubric for Literary Texts	To help practitioners select literary texts appropriate to their content and specific goals.	T22
13	Guidelines for Effective Meetings	To provide a list of guidelines for running effective meetings.	T23
14	Looking at Assessment Work Protocol	To help practitioners reflect on questions of assessment practice by analyzing student work.	T24
15	Mircolab Discussion Protocol	To use active listening skills and address a specific set of questions in small groups.	T26
16	Power Standards Protocol	To select the most important standards to guide common assessment work.	T27
17	QPA Common Analysis of Media Task	Tools 17-30: QPA Common Task Resources. Tasks: QPA model performance assessment tasks, adaptable to different content and with written, oral communication, and visual formats. Rubrics: Field-tested rubrics for scoring QPA common tasks. Scoring Guide: To use with QPA common writing rubrics. Teacher Directions: To support the use of QPA model tasks. For examples of common tasks used in QPA Network Schools see Samples of QPA Common Tasks on pages 73-78.	T28
18	QPA Common Analysis of Media Rubric		T29
19	QPA Common Literary Analysis Task		T31
20	QPA Common Literary Analysis Rubric		T32
21	QPA Common Oral Communication Task		T34
22	QPA Common Oral Communication Rubric		T35
23	QPA Common Position Paper Task		T37
24	QPA Common Position Paper Rubric		T38
25	QPA Common Research Task		T40
26	QPA Common Research Rubric		T41
27	QPA Common Task Scoring Guide		T43
28	QPA Common Task Teacher Directions		T45
29	QPA Common Visual or Media Task		T49
30	QPA Common Visual or Media Rubric		T50
31	Setting Norms Protocol	To guide teams in setting norms for collaborative work.	T51
32	Student Engagement Alignment Tool	To self-assess practitioner-developed performance assessments for attributes that maximize student engagement.	T53
33	Student Peer Editing Checklist	To provide a model for the scaffolding required to support effective peer editing and collaboration between students.	T54
34	Student Work Analysis Tool	To evaluate student work based on proficiency in order to plan next steps for instruction.	T57
35	Planning Worksheet: Analyzing Features of Text Complexity for Instruction and Assessment	To examine and select readings for scaffolding text complexity.	T59
36	Text-Based Discussion Protocol	To examine an issue using a short article or book excerpt.	T60
37	Training with Anchors Protocol	To score student compositions reliably using anchor papers, rubrics, scoring guidelines, and score reports.	T61
38	Tuning Protocol for Tasks	To receive feedback and fine-tune tasks.	T62
39	Vision of the Graduate Protocol	To develop a vision of what students should master by graduation.	T64

ASSESSMENT VALIDATION CHECKLIST

ASSESSMENT INFORMATION

Title of Assessment: ______________________ Date: __________

Grade/Subject: ______________________ Author: __________

Validation Team: ______________________

QUALITY ALIGNED INSTRUCTION — 6–8 MINUTES

1 Alignment

☐ Is clearly aligned to competencies and to specific content standards and habits.

☐ Is clearly aligned to 21st century skills.

☐ Is aligned to appropriate depth of knowledge (DOK) to assess the standard. Identify and check DOK levels assessed below. For example, an essay would mostly assess DOK 3, but some DOK 2 items might also be included. Check "most" for DOK 3 and "some" for DOK 2.

DOK 1: recall; memorization; simple understanding of a word or phrase

(☐ most of assessment/ ☐ some of the assessment/ ☐ none of the assessment)

DOK 2: Covers level 1 plus: paraphrase; summarize; interpret; infer; classify; organize; compare; and determine fact from fiction. There is a correct answer, but may involve multiple concepts.

(☐ most of assessment/ ☐ some of the assessment/ ☐ none of the assessment)

DOK 3: Students must support their thinking by citing references from text or other sources. Students are asked to go beyond the text to analyze, generalize, or connect ideas. Requires deeper knowledge. Items may require abstract reasoning, inferences between and across readings, application of prior knowledge, or text support for an analytical judgment about a text.

(☐ most of assessment/ ☐ some of the assessment/ ☐ none of the assessment)

DOK 4: Requires higher-order thinking, including complex reasoning, planning, and developing of concepts. Usually applies to an extended task or project. Examples: evaluates several works by the same author; critiques an issue across time periods or researches topic/issue from different perspectives; longer investigations or research projects.

(☐ most of assessment/ ☐ some of the assessment/ ☐ none of the assessment)

☐ Assesses what is intended to be assessed—will elicit what the student knows and can do related to the chosen standards and benchmarks. Any scaffolding provided (e.g., task broken into smaller steps: graphic organizer to preplan a response) does not change what is actually being assessed.

☐ The assessment is scheduled appropriately in the year, with enough teaching time provided to allow all students to successfully complete it.

Alignment Notes	

QUALITY TASK DESIGN — 10–12 MINUTES

2 Clarity and Focus

- ☐ Addresses an essential issue, big idea, or key concept or skill of the unit/course.
- ☐ Is linked to ongoing instruction (within a unit of study/course).
- ☐ Directions clearly indicate what the student is being asked to do.
- ☐ Includes what will be assessed individually by the student (even if it is a group task).

Clarity and Focus Notes	

3 Student Engagement

- ☐ Provides opportunity for ownership and decision making, requiring the student to be actively engaged.
- ☐ Focuses on significant content and addresses authentic problems and issues from the world outside the classroom.
- ☐ Includes multiple modalities for students to engage with content.

Student Engagement Notes	

4 Criteria and Levels

- ☐ Rubric(s) or scoring guide(s) assess identified competencies and content standards.
- ☐ Exemplars or models illustrate expectations aligned to identified competencies and standards.

Criteria and Levels Notes	

5 Fairness

- ☐ The task is fair and unbiased in language and design.
- ☐ Rubric or scoring guide is clear.
- ☐ Material is familiar to students from identifiable cultural, gender, linguistic, and other groups.
- ☐ The task is free of stereotypes.
- ☐ All students have access to resources (e.g., Internet, calculators, spell check, etc.).
- ☐ Assessment conditions are the same for all students.
- ☐ The task can be reasonably completed under the specified conditions.
- ☐ Allows for accommodations for students with IEPs/504 plans.

Fairness Notes	

6 Adherence to Principles of Universal Design

- ☐ Instructions are free of wordiness and irrelevant information.
- ☐ Instructions are free of unusual words students may not understand.
- ☐ Format/layout conveys focus of expected tasks and products.
- ☐ Format clearly indicates what actual questions and prompts are.
- ☐ Questions are marked with graphic cues (bullets, numbers, etc.).
- ☐ Format is consistent.

Adherence to Principles of Universal Design Notes	

QUALITY DATA ANALYSIS — 8–10 MINUTES

(This section occurs only if student work is presented.)

7 Student Work Analysis

- ☐ Student work sample demonstrates proficiency/mastery (with evidence of DoK level 3 or 4 performance) of the assessed competencies and standards for the grade level and discipline.
- ☐ If assessment is a common assessment or used for high-stakes decisions, student work can be scored reliably by all scorers using scoring guide and information provided.

Student Work Analysis Notes	

VALIDATION TEAM RECOMMENDATION — 8–10 MINUTES

- ☐ **Validation pending:** Please review feedback and make revisions.
- ☐ **Validation complete:** Please submit final edited version to team leader.

Overall Feedback	

ASSESSMENT VALIDATION COVER SHEET

ASSESSMENT INFORMATION

Title of Assessment: ______________________ Date: ______________

Grade/Subject: ______________________ Author: ______________

Validation Team: ______________________________________

ALIGNMENT INFORMATION

- Alignment to Common Core State Standard(s), competencies, habits, or other standards.

____

- Mission Alignment: How does this assessment fit into your school's local assessment system and align with your school's mission?

____

- What does this assessment intend to accomplish and how will results be used?

____

- How long do students spend on this unit and on this assessment, and when in the year/course do students complete it?

____

VALIDATION QUESTIONS

- What accommodations are available to students? Accommodations are commonly categorized in four ways: presentation, response, setting, and timing and scheduling.
  - ☐ Presentation accommodations: Allow students to access information in ways that do not require them to visually read standard print. These alternative modes of access are auditory, multisensory, tactile, and visual.
  - ☐ Response accommodations: Allow students to complete assessments in different ways or to solve or organize problems using some type of assistive device or organizer.
  - ☐ Setting accommodations: Change the location in which the assessment is given or the conditions of the assessment setting.
  - ☐ Timing and scheduling accommodations: Increase the allowable time to complete an assessment and perhaps change the way the time is organized.
- Are there student anchor papers provided to illustrate proficient work and other levels?

____

TYPE OF ASSESSMENT/ITEM TYPES (check all that apply)

- ☐ Selected response (multiple choice, true-false, matching, etc.)
- ☐ Short answer (short constructed response; fill in a graphic organizer or diagram; explain your thinking or solution; make and complete a table, etc.)
- ☐ Product (essay, research paper, editorial, log, journal, play, poem, model, multimedia, art products, script, musical score, portfolio pieces, etc.)
- ☐ Performance (demonstration, presentation, science lab, dance or music performance, athletic performance, debate, etc.)

SCORING GUIDE (please attach and check type below)

- ☐ Answer key, scoring template, computerized/machine scored
- ☐ Generalized rubric (e.g., for persuasive writing, for all science labs)
- ☐ Task-specific rubric (used only for this task)
- ☐ Checklist (e.g., with score points for each part)
- ☐ Teacher Observation Sheet/ Observation Checklist

THIS TASK INCLUDES (check all that are attached)

- ☐ Teacher directions
- ☐ Student directions
- ☐ Materials needed
- ☐ Estimated time
- ☐ Anchor papers or student exemplar(s)
- ☐ Other

ADDENDUM FOR TUNING

If you are still in the planning stages of your assessment, answer the following additional questions:

- What is our focusing question?
- On what aspect of our plan are we most hoping to receive feedback?
- What next steps do we anticipate taking that are not yet reflected in the current draft of our plan?
- How are we planning to scaffold for heightened student engagement?

ASSESSMENT VALIDATION PROTOCOL

Purpose

To ensure assessments have technical quality. This protocol can be used with performance assessments as well as traditional assessments. When we share our assessments with our colleagues, we are more likely to uncover our blind spots and assumptions.

Planning

- **Time:** 50–60 minutes (First round will take more time as group develops familiarity with questions. More time is also required if student work is being reviewed with assessment.)
- **Group size:** 4+
- **Roles:** Choose a facilitator, timekeeper, recorder, and reporter.

Setting Norms

- Honor our learning and be respectful of the work of the teacher and the student.
- Keep the conversation constructive; avoid judgmental language.
- Be appreciative of the facilitator's role and follow the guidelines and time constraints.
- Keep feedback crisp and to the point.
- Don't skip the debrief process.

Process

1. **Norms:** The facilitator reviews the protocol process, norms, and any additional questions or information if the assessment is being tuned. (2–5 minutes)
2. **Presentation:** Presenter briefly walks through the materials with the group and explains the context of the assessment. (3–5 minutes)
3. **Examination:** Group members silently examine the assessment materials. (7–10 minutes)
4. **Clarifying questions:** The group asks any clarifying questions they have about the materials and process. (2–7 minutes; round 1 may require more time for clarification)
5. **Validation guide:** While the presenter silently takes notes, the facilitator leads groups through each section of the Validation Checklist and seeks consensus for each item. The facilitator reads each numbered item aloud and asks the group to consider whether the answer is yes or no and to be prepared to explain their choice. Once consensus is reached (80% agreement), the group moves on to the next numbered item. Times are specified for each section, and each section can be modified to meet the needs of the group, as long as 7 minutes are left for the remaining steps of feedback and debrief. (20–30 minutes)
6. **Feedback and reflection:** The team reads the feedback from each section. After hearing all of the feedback, the presenter may ask clarifying questions, provide further information, and offer reflections based on the feedback, but DOES NOT need to justify! The facilitator reminds the presenter to resist the tendency to justify. (8–10 minutes)
7. **Debrief:** The facilitator leads the debrief. (4 minutes)
   - o Did the team honor the norms at all times?
   - o What went well? What could have gone better?
   - o What are the implications of what we've learned for instruction?

CALIBRATION PROTOCOL

Purpose

To calibrate our scoring of student work as we explore the instructional implications of the prompt/task, student work, and rubric.

Planning

- **Time:** 35-40 minutes
- **Group size:** 4–8
- **Materials needed** for each person:
  - o Sample work and prompt/task
  - o Task rubric
  - o Score sheet or task rubric can be used for scoring
  - o One extra score sheet is needed for the recorder, who will tally the scores for the whole group.
- **Roles:** Choose a facilitator, timekeeper, and recorder. (1 minute)

Setting Norms

- Honor our learning and be respectful of the work of the teacher and the student.
- Keep the conversation constructive; avoid judgmental language.
- Be appreciative of the facilitator's role and follow the guidelines and time constraints.
- Keep feedback crisp and to the point.
- Don't skip the debrief process.

Process

1. **Norms:** The facilitator reviews the protocol process and norms with the group. (2 minutes)
2. **Examination:** Group members silently examine the prompt, student work, the rubric, and the score sheet. (3 minutes)
3. **Clarifying questions:** The group asks any clarifying questions they have about the materials and process. (2 minutes)
4. **Read and score:** Using the rubric, group members independently and silently read and score the student work, recording their scores on the score sheet and making notes to justify their scores. (10 minutes)
5. **Score sharing:** One at a time, team members share their scores for each of the rubric categories—without explanation—as the recorder completes the group's score sheet. (2 minutes)
6. **Discussion:** Facilitator invites the group to consider where the differences in the scores occurred and why people scored differently for each rubric area—particularly the highest and lowest scores. (Approximately 2 minutes per criterion: 8 minutes)
7. **Debrief:** Discuss the following questions (approximately 2 minutes per question: 8 minutes):
   - o What did we notice about scoring student work and the rubric?
   - o What would be the next steps for instructing this student?
   - o What revisions should be made to the task and instructions?
   - o What are the implications for our instructional practice?

HESS' COGNITIVE RIGOR MATRIX & CURRICULAR EXAMPLES: Applying Webb's Depth-of-Knowledge Levels to Bloom's Cognitive Process Dimensions – ELA & Social Studies

REVISED BLOOM'S TAXONOMY	WEBB'S DOK LEVEL 1 RECALL & REPRODUCTION	WEBB'S DOK LEVEL 2 SKILLS & CONCEPTS	WEBB'S DOK LEVEL 3 STRATEGIC THINKING/ REASONING	WEBB'S DOK LEVEL 4 EXTENDED THINKING
Remember Retrieve knowledge from long-term memory, recognize, recall, locate, identify	o Recall, recognize, or locate basic facts, terms, details, events, or ideas explicit in texts o Read words orally in connected text with fluency & accuracy			
Understand Construct meaning, clarify, paraphrase, represent, translate, illustrate, give examples, classify, categorize, summarize, generalize, infer a logical conclusion), predict, compare/contrast, match like ideas, explain, construct models.	o Identify or describe literary elements (characters, setting, sequence, etc.) o Select appropriate words when intended meaning/definition is clearly evident o Describe/explain who, what, where, when, or how o Define/describe facts, details, terms, principles o Write simple sentences	o Specify, explain, show relationships; explain why (e.g., cause-effect) o Give non-examples/examples o Summarize results, concepts, ideas o Make basic inferences or logical predictions from data or texts o Identify main ideas or accurate generalizations of texts o Locate information to support explicit-implicit central ideas	o Explain, generalize, or connect ideas using supporting evidence (quote, example, text reference) o Identify/ make inferences about explicit or implicit themes o Describe how word choice, point of view, or bias may affect the readers' interpretation of a text o Write multi-paragraph composition for specific purpose, focus, voice, tone, & audience	o Explain how concepts or ideas specifically relate to other content domains (e.g., social, political, historical) or concepts o Develop generalizations of the results obtained or strategies used and apply them to new problem-based situations
Apply Carry out or use a procedure in a given situation; carry out (apply to a familiar task), or use (apply) to an unfamiliar task	o Use language structure (pre/suffix) or word relationships (synonym/antonym) to determine meaning of words o Apply rules or resources to edit spelling, grammar, punctuation, conventions, word use o Apply basic formats for documenting sources	o Use context to identify the meaning of words/phrases o Obtain and interpret information using text features o Develop a text that may be limited to one paragraph o Apply simple organizational structures (paragraph, sentence types) in writing	o Apply a concept in a new context o Revise final draft for meaning or progression of ideas o Apply internal consistency of text organization and structure to composing a full composition o Apply word choice, point of view, style to impact readers' /viewers' interpretation of a text	o Illustrate how multiple themes (historical, geographic, social, artistic, literary) may be interrelated o Select or devise an approach among many alternatives to research a novel problem
Analyze Break into constituent parts, determine how parts relate, differentiate between relevant-irrelevant, distinguish, focus, select, organize, outline, find coherence, deconstruct (e.g., for bias or point of view)	o Identify whether specific information is contained in graphic representations (e.g., map, chart, table, graph, T-chart, diagram) or text features (e.g., headings, subheadings, captions) o Decide which text structure is appropri-ate to audience and purpose	o Categorize/compare literary elements, terms, facts/details, events o Identify use of literary devices o Analyze format, organization, & internal text structure (signal words, transitions, semantic cues) of different texts o Distinguish: relevant-irrelevant information; fact/opinion o Identify characteristic text features; distinguish between texts, genres	o Analyze information within data sets or texts o Analyze interrelationships among concepts, issues, problems o Analyze or interpret author's craft (literary devices, viewpoint, or potential bias) to create or critique a text o Use reasoning, planning, and evidence to support inferences	o Analyze multiple sources of evidence, or multiple works by the same author, or across genres, time periods, themes o Analyze complex/abstract themes, perspectives, concepts o Gather, analyze, and organize multiple information sources o Analyze discourse styles
Evaluate Make judgments based on criteria, check, detect inconsistencies or fallacies, judge, critique			o Cite evidence and develop a logical argument for conjectures o Describe, compare, and contrast solution methods o Verify reasonableness of results o Justify or critique conclusions drawn	o Evaluate relevancy, accuracy, & completeness of information from multiple sources o Apply understanding in a novel way, provide argument or justification for the application
Create Reorganize elements into new patterns/ structures, generate, hypothesize, design, plan, produce	o Brainstorm ideas, concepts, problems, or perspectives related to a topic , principle, or concept	o Generate conjectures or hypotheses based on observations or prior knowledge and experience	o Synthesize information within one source or text o Develop a complex model for a given situation o Develop an alternative solution	o Synthesize information across multiple sources or texts o Articulate a new voice, alternate theme, new knowledge or perspective

HESS' COGNITIVE RIGOR MATRIX & CURRICULAR EXAMPLES: Applying Webb's Depth-of-Knowledge Levels to Bloom's Cognitive Process Dimensions – Math and Science

REVISED BLOOM'S TAXONOMY	WEBB'S DOK LEVEL 1 RECALL & REPRODUCTION	WEBB'S DOK LEVEL 2 SKILLS & CONCEPTS	WEBB'S DOK LEVEL 3 STRATEGIC THINKING/ REASONING	WEBB'S DOK LEVEL 4 EXTENDED THINKING
Remember Retrieve knowledge from long-term memory, recognize, recall, locate, identify	o Recall, observe, & recognize facts, principles, properties o Recall/ identify conversions among representations or numbers (e.g., customary and metric measures)			
Understand Construct meaning, clarify, paraphrase, represent, translate, illustrate, give examples, classify, categorize, summarize, generalize, infer a logical conclusion (such as from examples given), predict, compare/ contrast, match like ideas, explain, construct models	o Evaluate an expression o Locate points on a grid or number on number line o Solve a one-step problem o Represent math relationships in words, pictures, or symbols o Read, write, compare decimals in scientific notation	o Specify and explain relationships (e.g., non-examples/examples; cause-effect) o Make and record observations o Explain steps followed o Summarize results or concepts o Make basic inferences or logical predictions from data/observations o Use models /diagrams to represent or explain mathematical concepts o Make and explain estimates	o Use concepts to solve non-routine problems o Explain, generalize, or connect ideas using supporting evidence o Make and justify conjectures o Explain thinking when more than one response is possible o Explain phenomena in terms of concepts	o Relate mathematical or scientific concepts to other content areas, other domains, or other concepts o Develop generalizations of the results obtained and the strategies used (from investigation or readings) and apply them to new problem situations
Apply Carry out or use a procedure in a given situation; carry out (apply to a familiar task), or use (apply) to an unfamiliar task	o Follow simple procedures (recipe-type directions) o Calculate, measure, apply a rule (e.g., rounding) o Apply algorithm or formula (e.g., area, perimeter) o Solve linear equations o Make conversions among representations or numbers, or within and between customary and metric measures	o Select a procedure according to criteria/ problem and perform it o Solve routine problem applying multiple concepts or decision points o Retrieve information from a table, graph, or figure and use it solve a problem requiring multiple steps o Translate between tables, graphs, words, and symbolic notations (e.g., graph data from a table) o Construct models given criteria	o Design investigation for a specific purpose or research question o Conduct a designed investigation o Use concepts to solve non-routine problems o Use & show reasoning, planning, and evidence o Translate between problem & symbolic notation when not a direct translation	o Select or devise approach among many alternatives to solve a problem o Conduct a project that specifies a problem, identifies solution paths, solves the problem, and reports results
Analyze Break into constituent parts, determine how parts relate, differentiate between relevant-irrelevant, distinguish, focus, select, organize, outline, find coherence, deconstruct	o Retrieve information from a table or graph to answer a question o Identify whether specific information is contained in graphic representations (e.g., table, graph, T-chart, diagram) o Identify a pattern/trend	o Categorize, classify materials, data, figures based on characteristics o Organize or order data o Compare/ contrast figures or data o Select appropriate graph and organize & display data o Interpret data from a simple graph o Extend a pattern	o Compare information within or across data sets or texts o Analyze and draw conclusions from data, citing evidence o Generalize a pattern o Interpret data from complex graph o Analyze similarities/differences between procedures or solutions	o Analyze multiple sources of evidence o Analyze complex/abstract themes o Gather, analyze, and evaluate information
Evaluate Make judgments based on criteria, check, detect inconsistencies or fallacies, judge, critique			o Cite evidence and develop a logical argument for concepts or solutions o Describe, compare, and contrast solution methods o Verify reasonableness of results	o Gather, analyze, & evaluate information to draw conclusions o Apply understanding in a novel way, provide argument or justification for the application
Create Reorganize elements into new patterns/ structures, generate, hypothesize, design, plan, construct, produce	o Brainstorm ideas, concepts, or perspectives related to a topic	o Generate conjectures or hypotheses based on observations or prior knowledge and experience	o Synthesize information within one data set, source, or text o Formulate an original problem given a situation o Develop a scientific/mathematical model for a complex situation	o Synthesize information across multiple sources or texts o Design a mathematical model to inform and solve a practical or abstract situation

COLLABORATIVE CULTURES SURVEY

Purpose

To assess the quality of team collaboration and identify areas needing improvement.

Directions

For the following sets of questions, rate how you think your school is doing. Then discuss areas of weakness and ways to improve. Use this scale:

- 1 = No, or rarely, or only a few teachers
- 2 = Some, but not much, or not everyone
- 3 = Most teachers and teams do fairly regularly
- 4 = All teachers do regularly

DO WE:

_______ Look at student work in teams using defined protocols and use these discussions to take steps to improve learning, teaching, and assessment?

_______ Observe classrooms and have follow-up conversations with the teacher whose classroom is being observed to improve learning, teaching, and assessment?

_______ Work in teacher teams to plan and implement curriculum and assessments for shared students?

_______ Engage in text-based discussions?

_______ Use Critical Friends Groups to bring instructional dilemmas to the forefront and receive feedback on them?

_______ Work in study groups to examine data, conduct action research, and try new strategies for improving learning, teaching, and assessment?

_______ Serve on faculty panels to judge and assess student work that is presented through exhibitions, demonstrations, and portfolios?

_______ Work in teacher teams to develop rubrics for assessing student work?

_______ Collaboratively examine multiple sources of data to identify challenges and then use an inquiry process to develop schoolwide solutions?

HAVE WE:

_______ Set norms as a faculty for how we work with each other?

_______ Developed a shared vision and common agenda among the entire school community for moving the school forward?

_______ Developed schoolwide habits of mind?

_______ Created a shared decision-making governance structure that engages the entire faculty through teams, committees, and full faculty meetings to decide on key instructional, programmatic, and budgetary issues of the school?

COMMON PERFORMANCE ASSESSMENT CURRICULUM PLANNING TEMPLATE

Purpose

To apply the QPAFramework to develop and implement a standards-based common performance assessment, ensuring that technical quality and collaboration are built into the process. When teachers collaborate to design, implement, and score performance assessments, they are more likely to achieve technical quality and increase student achievement.

Planning

- Use professional development time or planning time to meet as a common performance assessment team to complete the form.
- Bring resources, standards, and curriculum materials to the planning session and create an agenda, goals, and roles for each session so time can be most productive.
- Continue to work on the template together and individually to complete sections. Remember, the learning plan is for the individual teacher, as common does not mean "the same."

Process

Work collaboratively to complete each section of the form, balancing the need for a common task and rubric while embedding the task in the curriculum and culture of each teacher's classroom.

ALIGN	
Thematic unit or topic	**Course/subject:** **Grade level:** **Teachers implementing common assessment:**
Established goals (standards, 21st century skills, and school-specific goals)	
Essential questions to guide learning, build enduring understanding, and make relevant connections	
Students will know (content)	**Students will be able to (skills)**

DESIGN	
Common performance task summary (see task for full details)	**Resources/texts (may vary by teacher)**
Key criteria for performance assessment. Which rubric(s) will you use?	**Possible accommodations (discuss in advance with SPED and ELL teachers)**
Common performance assessment schedule or approximate time needed	**Possible formative assessments**

Learning Plan: To be completed by individual teacher, as learning plan may vary by teacher

ANALYZE	
Schedule for collaborative scoring of performance assessment	**Plan for collaboration around revisions to task or rubric**
Next steps for teaching and learning	**Plan for analyzing student scores and data disaggregation**

COOKIE MONSTER PROTOCOL

Purpose

To explore rubric creation and scoring to better understand rubric use in schools and classrooms.

Planning

- **Time:** 45 minutes including completion of Cookie Mindset step.
- **Roles:** Facilitator, timekeeper, recorder (fills in chart), and reporter (shares data with group).
- **Preparation:** Bake, buy, or beg for 3–4 different kinds of chocolate chip cookies to sample, and label each cookie A, B, C, and D. Prepare a large chart for each reporting group.

Process

1. **Cookie Qualities—What makes a good cookie?** Brainstorm the qualities of a good chocolate chip cookie and write them on chart paper. (5 minutes)

2. **Cookie Rubric—What's essential?** Create a rubric using the three most important qualities the group has identified. Create performance levels for the three criteria using a 4-point scale and fill in as many levels as time allows, starting with the proficient level. Try to provide as much detail as possible for scoring the cookies. (10 minutes)

Level	4	3 (Proficient)	2	1
Cookie Quality:				

3. **Cookie Scoring—How good are they?** Each group uses the criteria created to score several different cookies, starting with A. Score as many cookies as time allows, coming to consensus on your scores. Recorder should chart all scores and be prepared to present the group's criteria and the score for each cookie. (10 minutes)

4. **Whole Group Sharing—What's the score?** The reporter shares the criteria and total score for each cookie out of the 12 possible points each cookie could earn for the three criteria on a 4-point scale. (60 seconds or less per group)

5. **Whole Group Debrief—How the cookie crumbles.** End with whole group debrief of the process and the implications for rubric creation.

COOKIE MONSTER MINDSET
Cookie Monster Protocol Part 2

Applying the chocolate chip cookie mindset (15-20 minutes)

After the group sharing, ask:

- Are all criteria equally important?
- How should uneven performance in different rubric criteria be addressed? For example, what if a cookie has a high score in number of chips or size, but a low score in taste? Does that matter?
- What are the implications for rubrics we use in our classes/courses?

There are five different types of criteria used in rubrics, and not all have to be included all of the time. When you create a rubric, keep these criteria types in mind, and consider whether some are more essential than others:

1. **Process criteria**—Did you follow the right steps (e.g., scientific investigation; data collection; developing an outline; following a routine)?
2. **Form criteria**—Did you apply correct formats and rules (e.g., handed in on time; correct citation format; correctly labeled; organized properly)?
3. **Accuracy of content criteria**—That is, is the answer correct; is the right relationship explained; is the concept understood or accurately applied?
4. **New knowledge criteria**—Did the student go beyond the accurate solution and correct process to gain new insights, raise new questions?
5. **Impact criteria**—Did the final product achieve its intended purpose (e.g., solved a problem; persuaded the audience; synthesized information)?

Now analyze your group's cookie rubric criteria using the above criteria types—and determine if some are more important, given the task. This might be an important consideration when determining the weighting of each rubric criterion.

DATA ANALYSIS PROTOCOL

Purpose

To guide practitioners as they collect, prepare, and use performance assessment data to drive student achievement and quality instruction.

Planning

- Select the data to analyze and the questions that will guide the analysis. Key to productive analysis is identifying appropriate data to look at and how to represent it. Suggestions:
  - o Recording student scores on each rubric criterion (e.g., Idea Development, Supporting Evidence) rather than keeping only the overall score on an essay, presentation, or project is one way to get more information about students' progress in developing specific content or skills.
  - o Include other student variables such as demographic information, English Language Learning status, and special needs classification in order to disaggregate by groups.
  - o Student work (or excerpts) from the performance assessment task may help with interpretation of the patterns that are observed in the score data.
- Plan the process. Questions to consider:
  - o Who will organize the data?
  - o How will data be organized?
  - o Which teams will analyze the data (e.g., teacher teams, leadership team)?
  - o What is the timeline for the process, including collection, organization, and analysis?
  - o What is the agenda for the meeting(s)?

Process

1 Choose a facilitator, timekeeper, and recorder.

- o For each step, the facilitator allows time for independent thinking, followed by group discussion.
- o The facilitator reviews the protocol process with the group.

2 Examine the data. Sample questions for examining score data:

- o Does the data reveal strengths or weaknesses in specific rubric criteria (e.g., Idea Development, Supporting Evidence, etc.)? In which criteria are students strongest? Weakest?
- o If you have data from assessments that use different modalities (e.g., writing and presentation), does the data reveal any patterns about student communication of their understanding in different modalities?
- o If you have data from different courses or class sections, does the data reveal any patterns between classes?
- o If you have data for student variables, are there differences in student subgroup scores by race/ethnicity, language, special education status, income, or gender?

3 Draw inferences from the data.

- o Are you surprised by anything you saw in the score data (or student work data, if used)?
- o What factors might contribute to the patterns you noticed? Possible factors to consider include:
  - Task design
    - Are there adjustments to the task and supporting materials that could assure more accurate student performance data in subsequent assessments?
    - How can students show what they know in a variety of ways without compromising the criteria for proficient attainment of the learning target(s) or benchmark(s)?
  - Instruction
    - Did students have ample opportunity to learn the skills and content needed to succeed?
    - What formative assessments provided students feedback on their progress?
- o What might account for any differences between groups of students?
- o *Tip:* You may want to use the Student Work Analysis Tool to deepen your understanding of patterns in the score data (see Tool 34).

4 Use your analysis to inform instruction and plan next steps.

- o Thinking about your answers to each of the above questions, what do you see as the implications for instruction?
- o What formative or interim assessments could help students build the skills and content knowledge required to succeed in the task?
- o What are the learning needs of the students at the proficient, just below proficient, and far below proficient levels? How might the learning needs of students at different levels vary? As you plan your next steps for instruction, consider each of the following:
  - Whole class instruction
  - Targeted instruction for subgroups
  - Individual instruction

GRADIENTS IN COMPLEXITY: Text Complexity Rubric for Informational Texts

	SIMPLE TEXTS [1]	SOMEWHAT COMPLEX TEXTS[2]	COMPLEX TEXTS [3]	VERY COMPLEX TEXTS [4]
Layout	Consistent placement of text, regular word and line spacing, often large plain font	May have longer passages of uninterrupted text, often plain font	Longer passages of uninterrupted text may include columns or other variations in layout, often smaller more elaborate font	Very long passages of uninterrupted text that may include columns or other variations in layout, often small densely packed print
	• Graphics, captioned photos, labelled diagrams that directly support and help interpret the written text	• Graphs, photos, tables, charts, diagrams that directly support the text	• Essential integrated graphics, tables, charts, formulas (necessary to make meaning of text)	• Extensive/complex, intricate, essential integrated tables, charts, formulas necessary to make connections or synthesize concepts presented
	• Simple indexes, short glossaries	• Indexes, glossaries, occasional quotes, references	• Embedded quotes, concluding appendices, indexes, glossaries, bibliography	• Abstracts, footnotes, citations and detailed indexes, appendices, bibliography
	• Supportive signposting and enhancements	• Reduced signposting and enhancements	• Minimal signposting and/or enhancements	• Integrated signposting conforming to disciplinary formats. No enhancements
Purpose and Meaning	A single or simple purpose conveying clear or factual information	Purpose involves conveying a range of ideas with more detailed information or examples	Purpose includes explaining or interpreting information, not just presenting it	Purpose may include examining/evaluating complex, sometimes theoretical and contested information
	• Meaning is clear, concrete with a narrow focus	• Meaning is more involved with a broader focus	• Meaning includes more complex concepts and a higher level of detail	• Meaning is intricate, with abstract theoretical elements
Structure/ Discourse	The discourse style & organization of the text is clear or chronological and/or easy to predict	The organization of the text may include a thesis or reasoned explanation in addition to facts	The organization of the text may contain multiple pathways, more than one thesis and/or several genres	The organization of the text is intricate or specialized for a particular discipline or genre.
	• Connections between ideas, processes or events are explicit and clear.	• Connections between some ideas, processes or events are implicit or subtle	• Connections between an expanded range ideas, processes or events are deeper and often implicit or subtle.	• Connections between an extensive range ideas, processes or events are deep, intricate and often implicit or subtle.
	• One primary text structure is evident (e.g., sequence, description)	• Includes a main text structure with 1-2 embedded structures	• Includes different text structure types of varying complexity	• Includes sustained complex text structure types and/or specialized, hybrid text types
Language Features	Mainly simple sentences	Simple and compound sentences with some more complex constructions	Many complex sentences with increased subordinate phrases and clauses or transition words	Mainly complex sentences, often containing multiple concepts
	• Simple language style, sometimes with narrative elements	• Increased objective style and passive constructions with higher factual content	• Objective/passive style with higher conceptual content and increasing nominalization	• Specialized disciplinary style with dense conceptual content and high nominalization
	• Vocabulary is mostly familiar	• Includes some unfamiliar, context-dependent or multiple meaning words	• Includes much academic (nuanced) vocabulary and/or some domain specific (content) vocabulary	• Includes extensive academic (nuanced, precise) and/or domain specific (content) vocabulary
Bk Knowledge Demands Informational	General topic is familiar, with details known by reader	General topic is familiar, with some details new to reader (cultural, historical, literary, political, legal, etc.)	General topic is somewhat familiar but with many details unknown to reader (cultural, historical, literary, political, legal, etc.)	General topic is mostly unfamiliar with most details unknown to reader (cultural, historical, literary, political, legal, etc.)
	• Simple, concrete ideas	• Both simple and more complicated, abstract ideas	• A range of recognizable ideas and challenging abstract concepts	• Many new ideas, perspectives and/or complex, challenging, abstract and theoretical concepts

GRADIENTS IN COMPLEXITY: Text Complexity Rubric for Literary Texts

	SIMPLE TEXTS [1]	SOMEWHAT COMPLEX TEXTS[2]	COMPLEX TEXTS [3]	VERY COMPLEX TEXTS [4]
Layout	Consistent placement of text, regular word and line spacing, often large plain font	May have longer passages of uninterrupted text, often plain font	Longer passages of uninterrupted text may include columns or other variations in layout, often smaller more elaborate font	Very long passages of uninterrupted text that may include columns or other variations in layout, often small densely packed print
	• Numerous illustrations that directly support and help interpret the written text	• A range of illustrations that support selected parts of the text	• A few illustrations that support the text OR includes images that require some interpretation	• Minimal or no illustrations that support the text OR includes images/text layout that require deeper interpretation (e.g., symbolism or recursive reading)
	• Supportive signposting and enhancements	• Reduced signposting and enhancements	• Minimal signposting and/or enhancements	• Integrated signposting conforming to disciplinary formats. No enhancements
Purpose and Meaning	Purpose usually stated explicitly in the title or in the beginning of the text	Purpose tends to be revealed early in the text, but may be conveyed with some subtlety	Purpose is implicit and may be revealed over the entirety of the text	PPurpose implicit or subtle, is sometimes ambiguous and revealed over the entirety of the text
	• One level of meaning	• More than one level of meaning, with levels clearly distinguished from each other	• Several levels of meaning that may be difficult to identify/separate	• Several levels and competing elements of meaning that are difficult to identify/separate and interpret
	• Theme is obvious and revealed early in the text	• Theme is clear and revealed early in the text, but may be conveyed with some subtlety	• Theme may be implicit or subtle, is sometimes ambiguous and may be revealed over the entirety of the text	• Theme is implicit or subtle, is often ambiguous, and is revealed over the entirety of the text
Structure/ Discourse	The discourse style & organization of the text is clear, chronological and/or easy to predict or follow	The organization of the text may have additional characters, two or more storylines and is occasionally difficult to predict	The organization of the text may include, subplots, time shifts and more complex characters	The organization of the text is intricate with regard to elements such as narrative viewpoint, time shifts, multiple characters, storylines and detail
	• Connections between events or ideas are explicit and clear.	• Connections among events or ideas are sometimes implicit or subtle	• Connections among events or ideas are often implicit or subtle	• Connections among events or ideas are implicit or subtle throughout the text.
	• One primary text structure is evident (e.g., chronology)	• Includes a main text structure with 1-2 embedded structures	• Includes different text types of varying complexity	• Includes sustained complex text types and hybrid or non-linear texts
Language Features	Mainly short, simple sentences	Simple and compound sentences with some more complex constructions	Many complex sentences with increased subordinate phrases and clauses	Many complex sentences, often containing intricate detail or concepts
	• Simple, literal language; predictable	• Mainly literal, common language	• Some figurative or literary language	• Much figurative language or use of literary devices (metaphor, analogy, connotative language literary allusion, etc.)
	• Vocabulary is mostly familiar for grade level; frequently appearing words	• Some unfamiliar or context-dependent, multiple meaning words	• Includes much academic vocabulary and some domain specific (content) vocabulary	• Includes extensive academic and domain specific (content) vocabulary, and possibly archaic language
Bk Knowledge Demands Literary/Fiction	Minimal assumed personal experience or background knowledge needed	Some assumed personal experience and/or knowledge of cultural or historical or ideas	Much assumed personal experience and/or explicit references to cultural, historical, literary, or political knowledge	Extensive, demanding, assumed personal experience and implied cultural, historical, literary, or political knowledge
	• Simple, straightforward ideas	• Both simple and more complex ideas	• A range of recognizable ideas and challenging concepts or themes	• Many new ideas, perspectives, and/or complex, challenging concept.

GUIDELINES FOR EFFECTIVE MEETINGS

Purpose

To provide a list of guidelines for running effective meetings.

Directions:

When a team is first established, it is helpful to distribute the following guidelines for discussion. You may adapt them to fit the needs of individual teams and revisit these guidelines as necessary.

GUIDELINES

- The agenda is distributed with sufficient time for members to prepare for the meeting.
- Members arrive on time for meetings.
- Meetings start and end at the scheduled times.
- Each meeting has an assigned facilitator, recorder, and timekeeper. (Often these are rotating positions.)
- Teams follow norms they have established together. These may include:
    - o Trusting that members can say what they truly feel about an issue;
    - o Keeping confidentiality when members agree to do so;
    - o Asking clarifying questions when in doubt about an issue;
    - o Having a chance to consider more than one solution to an issue;
    - o Thoroughly understanding an issue before reaching consensus;
    - o Encouraging participation by everyone, even the quietest members.
- There are set time limits for the meeting (and for individual agenda items when possible).
- At the end of each meeting, the facilitator summarizes what has been accomplished. Plans on "who will do what by when" are finalized and recorded in the minutes.
- The recorder distributes minutes of meetings to all team members in a timely fashion.
- Someone takes responsibility to communicate regularly with the Leadership Team and other interested groups. (This may be a rotating position.)
- Periodically, teams evaluate meeting efficiency, productivity, and use of time.

LOOKING AT ASSESSMENT WORK PROTOCOL

Purpose

To help practitioners to reflect on question(s) of assessment practice, the Common Core State Standards, and Webb's Depth of Knowledge (DoK) framework by analyzing student assessment work.

Planning

Time: Approximately 40–50 minutes.

Roles:

Presenter: Provides student work, supporting documents, and a focusing question.

Facilitator: Makes sure the group stays focused on the particular issue/question addressed in each step. The facilitator may choose to participate.

Timekeeper: Provides facilitator with time cues to make sure that the group stays on the protocol schedule, adheres to the one-minute-per-person limit in the rounds, and that everyone participates fully.

Process

Presenting teacher gathers student work for presentation and meets with facilitator to hone the focusing question.

1 Presentation of Student Work (1 minute to share question, plus 5–9 minutes to read student work)

- o Presenter shares the focusing question, student work, and supporting documents with the group, but says nothing about it until step 5.

Question:

____

____

____

- o Participants observe or read the work in silence, making brief notes. Note: Steps 2, 3, and 4 are conducted in rounds where each member of the group goes in turn for approximately one minute. Rounds continue until comments have been exhausted, as long as time remains. Keep the presenter's question in mind, but focus deeply on the assessments.

2 Describing the Work (5 minutes)

- o Facilitator asks, "What do you see?"
- o Next, group members provide answers without making judgments about the work. If the facilitator interprets a statement as a judgment, he or she redirects attention to description by asking, "Where is the evidence?"

3 Asking Questions about the Work (5 minutes, depending on group size)

- o The facilitator asks, "What questions does this work raise for you?"
- o Next, group members state any questions they have about the work, the student(s), the assessments, or the circumstances under which it was carried out, etc.
- o The presenting teacher makes notes about these questions (but does not answer them yet).

Modified from the Collaborative Assessment Conference. Developed by Steve Seidel and modified by Christina Brown.

4 Speculating about What Standards the Student Is Working On (10 minutes)

- The facilitator asks, "What standards do you think the student is working on, and how are they reflected in the assessment?" (Feel free to refer to the Common Core State Standards during the discussion.)
- Next, group members use Webb's DOK framework below to reflect on the level of rigor of the standards the student is working on.

DOK 1:	Recall; memorization; simple understanding of a word or phrase
DOK 2:	Basic Application: Covers level 1 plus paraphrase, summarize, interpret, infer, classify, organize, compare, and determine fact from fiction. There is a correct answer, but it may involve multiple concepts.
DOK 3:	Strategic Thinking: Students must support their thinking by citing references from text or other sources. Students are asked to go beyond the text to analyze, generalize, or connect ideas. Requires deeper knowledge. Items may require abstract reasoning, inferences between and across readings, application of prior knowledge, or text support for an analytical judgment about a text.
DOK 4:	Extended Thinking: Requires higher-order thinking, including complex reasoning, planning, and developing of concepts. Usually applies to an extended task or project. Examples: evaluates several works by the same author; critiques an issue across time periods or researches topic/issue from different perspectives; conducts longer investigations or research projects.

5 Hearing from the Presenting Teacher (5 minutes)

- Facilitator invites the presenting teacher to speak.
- Next, the presenting teacher provides he/she perspective on the assessment work, describing what he/she sees in it, responding to the questions raised, and adding any other information that he/she feels is important to share with the group.
- Next, the presenting teacher comments on anything surprising or unexpected that he/she heard during the describing, questioning, and speculating phases.
- Finally, the presenting teacher reminds the group of his/her question.

6 Discussing Implications for Assessment Practice (10–12 minutes)

- Facilitator invites group members and the presenting teacher to discuss the presenting teacher's question in light of the earlier phases.
- Group members discuss implications for increasing the level of rigor of the assessment and address the Common Core State Standards.

7 Reflecting on the LAAW Conference (3 minutes)

- The facilitator leads a brief conversation about the group's experience and reactions to the protocol as a whole or to particular parts of it. The facilitator thanks the presenter and all group members for their participation.

MICROLAB DISCUSSION PROTOCOL

Purpose

To use active listening skills and address a specific set of questions in small groups. The Microlab is useful for team building and for democratizing participation because it asks that participants equalize communication and withhold judgment. It affirms people's ideas and builds community while addressing specific content issues.

Planning

- **Time allotted:** Individual writing time: 3 minutes; Microlab time: 9 minutes; debrief time: 3 minutes.
    - o Allow 3 minutes per question, with one minute per person per question.
    - o Read each question out loud at the start of each round.
    - o On the first question, begin with person #1, then #2, then #3.
    - o On the second question, begin with #2, then #3, then #1.
    - o On the third question, begin with #3, then #1, then #2.
    - o Each person has one minute per question.

Process

MICROLAB QUESTIONS

1 Give an example of an effective performance assessment that you have given or taken that you feel was an effective assessment of learning and explain why.

____

____

____

____

2 What skills, content, and/or knowledge was that performance assessment actually assessing?

____

____

____

____

3 What evidence was captured in the performance assessment that distinguished poor performance from best performance, and how was feedback given?

____

____

____

____

DEBRIEF QUESTIONS

- How did this go for you? What worked well, and what was difficult? Why?
- What are the implications of the Microlab conversation for our work together?

POWER STANDARDS PROTOCOL

Purpose

To select the most important standards to guide common assessment work.

Planning

- **Time:** 60 minutes
- **Group size:** Discipline team
- **Materials needed:**
  - o Chart paper for recorder to write standards
  - o Prioritized list of standards for subject
  - o Stickers for participants
- **Roles:** Choose a facilitator, timekeeper, reporter, and recorder.

Process

1. **Norms:** The facilitator reviews the protocol process and norms with the group. (2 minutes)
2. **Clarifying questions:** The group asks any clarifying questions they have about the standards and process. (2 minutes)
3. **Examination:** Discipline team members in contiguous grades (or other pairing) pair up and silently examine each other's standards using *LESS* criteria and have a short conversation about where they agree and disagree. (5 minutes)
   - *Leverage:* Knowledge and skills of value in multiple disciplines.
   - *Endurance:* Knowledge and skills beyond the test date or time in school.
   - *Success in:* Essential knowledge and skills for success in next grade level.
   - *School:* Essential knowledge and skills for the school/district's mission.
4. **Report out:** Each group shares the standards that had three letters, and charts them on a piece of chart paper. Then, standards that had two or more letters, and that are not included on the first chart, are recorded on a second piece of chart paper. The group posts any remaining standards that have one letter, and that they feel are essential, on a third piece of paper. (15–20 minutes)
5. **Voting:** Each participant votes with a dot for their top 15 standards on the collection of standards on all three pieces of chart paper. (5–10 minutes)
6. **Discussion:** The facilitator invites the group to consider the following questions (12 minutes):
   - What did we agree were the **power standards** for our discipline?
   - What does a **graduate** of our school/district look like in our discipline?
   - What agreements did we come to about our discipline's **coherence from grade to grade**?
   - What are the next steps?
7. **Debrief:** What did we notice about the standards and our process? What questions arise? What are the implications for our instructional practice? Are we prepared for our report out? (8 minutes)

QPA COMMON ANALYSIS OF MEDIA TASK

Learning Goals

In this task you will be working on:

- **CCSS Writing:** Write effective informative texts to examine and convey complex ideas for a variety of purposes and audiences.
- **CCSS Reading:** Analyze and critique a variety of increasingly complex print and non-print informational texts.
- **Additional Modes of Communication:** Oral or Visual Communication *(specified by teacher).*
- **Content Standards:** *(specified by teacher).*

Student Directions

- Carefully read the student directions and rubrics. Ask your teacher if you have any questions.
- Work on this task independently. However, your teacher will build in checkpoints for peer and teacher feedback.
- Cite your sources using a standard citation method as directed by your teacher (e.g., MLA, APA) and include a Works Cited/References page.

Task *(parts to be specified by teacher)*

Compare and contrast how multiple types of media portrayed an event or story from literature, current events, or history. Analyze how words, sounds, and still or moving images are used in each medium.

CONSIDER THE FOLLOWING TYPES OF MEDIA:

- Print media (newspapers, magazines, books, pamphlets, documents, etc.)
- Online media (online newspapers and magazines, websites, blogs, Twitter, etc.)
- Audio and visual media (radio, podcasts, CDs, TV, webcasts, film, art, photographs, slides, etc.)
- Emerging technologies (media not listed above)

SUMMARY:

- **Topic:** Specify the content, background information, or scenario.
- **Genre:** Informational writing: The goal of this paper is to compare and contrast at least two pieces of media and provide analysis and textual evidence that demonstrate understanding of the media.
- **Evidence sources:** To support your thesis, you must evaluate at least two different types of media portraying the same event specified by teacher. Include direct citations from the media.
- **Audience:** The intended reader including the level of knowledge of this specific audience so that the product is appropriate.
- **Products and Rubrics:** For written work, include the approximate number of words or pages; for oral communication include the number of minutes; etc.
- **Time frame:** How long students will have to complete task.

SAMPLE VARIATIONS

- Compare and contrast the message and impact of a current or historical political cartoon with 1-2 other types of media, such as newspaper editorials, news broadcasts and personal accounts.
- Analyze the varied effects of a story/book/play and its television or film adaptation.
- Critique how newspapers, radio, television, and internet news outlets cover the same story, such as the Boston Marathon or a day in a political campaign.

QPA COMMON ANALYSIS OF MEDIA RUBRIC

Student Name: Scorer: Date:

Subject: ☐ ELA ☐ Social Studies ☐ Science ☐ Mathematics ☐ Other:

	ADVANCED – 4	PROFICIENT – 3	DEVELOPING – 2	BEGINNING – 1
IDEA DEVELOPMENT (ID) (weighted x 2) *The main thesis the student conveys to his/her audience and the way the thesis and analysis are expressed.*	***I've done everything to earn a score of Proficient, plus 2 of 3:***			
	a. I use my own voice and perspective in presenting my analysis.	a. My thesis is important, clear, and defensible.	a. My paper has a topic, but my thesis is not important, not clear, or not defensible.	a. My paper has a topic, but not a thesis.
	b. My analysis includes different points of view and develops the reasoning, evidence, strengths, and limitations for each point of view.	b. My analysis shows that I understand the media I am analyzing because I explain and show the reason for each idea used to support my thesis.	b. My analysis is confusing, OR it only partly shows that I understand the meaning of the media I am analyzing because I mainly summarize the information instead of explaining how my ideas relate to my thesis.	b. My ideas are not clearly related to my topic because I only list information rather than connect my ideas about the media to my topic. *OR* I make inappropriate connections between the media and my topic.
	c. I make connections between the essay and myself, other media, history, pieces of evidence, and/or the world.	c. I explain the significance of my thesis/analysis (the "so what?" of my essay).	c. I attempt to explain the significance of my thesis/analysis, but it is not clear.	c. I do not explain the significance of my topic.
	ADVANCED – 4	**PROFICIENT – 3**	**DEVELOPING – 2**	**BEGINNING – 1**
SUPPORTING EVIDENCE (SE) *The facts, quotations, definitions, descriptions, examples, and/or scenarios used to support the main thesis*	***I've done everything to earn a score of Proficient, plus 2 of 3:***			
	a. In my analysis, I distinguish fact from opinion and show that I know how to identify and use each appropriately.	a. I use sufficient evidence that is relevant to my thesis/topic and that effectively elaborates on my point.	a. I use evidence to support my thesis/topic, but it is insufficient, not fully relevant, or repeats rather than elaborates on my point.	a. I use limited evidence, or my evidence contradicts or does not connect to my thesis/topic.
	b. I consistently and effectively integrate well-chosen citations to create a cohesive analysis.	b. I use accurate evidence with enough detail to support my thesis/topic.	b. Most of my evidence is related to my thesis/topic, but some of it may be too general, inaccurate, or misinterpreted.	b. I use evidence that is too general, is inaccurate, or is misinterpreted.
	c. I anticipate my audience's knowledge level, including concerns, values, and possible biases.	c. I cite supporting evidence from my sources appropriately, even when paraphrasing.	c. I sometimes cite my supporting evidence appropriately.	c. I do not include citations from the media I am analyzing. OR I use direct quotations but do not identify where they are from.

QPA COMMON ANALYSIS OF MEDIA RUBRIC

	ADVANCED – 4	PROFICIENT – 3	DEVELOPING – 2	BEGINNING – 1
ORGANIZATION (O)	***I've done everything to earn a score of Proficient, plus 2 of 3:***			
The logic, structure, and clarity of the essay.	a. My introduction hooks and orients the reader to the topic in a thoughtful and engaging way.	a. My introduction orients the reader to my topic and provides an overview of the analysis in the rest of the paper.	a. My paper begins with an introduction that only partly orients the reader to the rest of my paper.	a. My paper begins presenting information without an introduction.
	b. My body paragraphs build in significance and enhance the clarity and engagement of my essay.	b. My body paragraphs are logically ordered.	b. Most, but not all, of my body paragraphs are logically ordered.	b. The order of my body paragraphs is confusing and distracting.
	c. My conclusion is interesting and ties up my analysis, leaving the reader with a new perspective.	c. My topic sentences are clearly stated for each paragraph and develop my paper's logic.	c. My topic sentences are sometimes underdeveloped or unclear.	c. My topic sentences are mostly missing, unclear, or do not relate to the rest of the paragraph.
		d. My essay's structure and transitions are logical and help the reader understand my essay.	d. My transitions between sentences and ideas are inconsistent.	d. The transitions between my sentences and ideas are non-existent or hard to follow.
		e. My conclusion summarizes my analysis and reflects upon the thesis.	e. My conclusion does not fully close/summarize my analysis.	e. My paper lacks a conclusion.
	ADVANCED – 4	**PROFICIENT – 3**	**DEVELOPING – 2**	**BEGINNING – 1**
CONVENTIONS & STYLE (CS)	***I've done everything to earn a score of Proficient, plus 2 of 3:***			
The word choice, fluency, spelling, mechanics, usage, and grammar.	I maintain the audience's interest by doing at least two of the following: • varying syntax and sentence structure • using figures of speech • choosing precise language	a. I have only a few errors, and my errors do not interfere with the reader's interpretation of my message.	a. I have many different types of errors. *OR* My errors interfere somewhat with the reader's interpretation of my message.	a. My errors seriously interfere with the reader's interpretation of my message.
		b. The style of my writing and my use of vocabulary is academic and appropriate for the intended audience and topic.	b. The style of my writing and my use of vocabulary is not consistently academic and appropriate for the intended audience or topic.	b. The style of my writing is not academic; it is too informal.
		c. I demonstrate control of Standard English.	c. I have some control of Standard English, but it is not consistent.	c. I have little control of Standard English conventions, sentence structure, and grammar.

QPA COMMON LITERARY ANALYSIS TASK

Learning Goals

In this task you will be working on:

- **CCSS Writing:** Write effective informative texts to examine and convey complex ideas for a variety of purposes and audiences.
- **CCSS Reading:** Analyze and critique a variety of increasingly complex print and non-print literary texts.
- **Additional Modes of Communication:** Oral or Visual Communication *(specified by teacher).*
- **Content Standards:** *(specified by teacher).*

Student Directions

- Carefully read the student directions and rubrics. Ask your teacher if you have any questions.
- Work on this task independently. However, your teacher will build in checkpoints for peer and teacher feedback.
- Cite your sources using a standard citation method as directed by your teacher (e.g., MLA, APA) and include a Works Cited/References page.

Task *(parts to be specified by teacher)*

Choose one or more pieces of fiction and write a literary essay that compares and contrasts one or more character(s), literary device(s), theme(s), or historical context(s) of the works.

SUMMARY:

- **Topic:** Specify the content, background information, or scenario.
- **Genre:** Literary analysis: The goal of your paper is to use evidence from the text(s) to inform the reader.
- **Evidence sources:** Choose one or more works of literature. Include direct citations from the texts.
- **Audience:** Specify the intended reader including the level of knowledge of this specific audience so that the product is appropriate.
- **Products and Rubrics:** For written work, include the approximate number of words or pages; for oral communication include the number of minutes; etc.
- **Time frame:** Specify how long students will have to complete task.

SAMPLE VARIATIONS

- Compare Mark Twain's *The Adventures of Huckleberry Finn* and Rudyard Kipling's *Kim* as cross-cultural examples of a similar theme.
- Analyze the character(s), literary device(s), theme(s), or historical context(s) of John Steinbeck's *Of Mice and Men* and another work we have read.
- Using Sandra Cisneros' *The House on Mango Street* and Anne Frank's *The Diary of a Young Girl,* write a literary essay that compares and contrasts the characters Esperanza and Anne Frank.

QPA COMMON LITERARY ANALYSIS RUBRIC

Student Name: Scorer: Date:

Subject: ☐ ELA ☐ Social Studies ☐ Science ☐ Mathematics ☐ Other:

	ADVANCED – 4	PROFICIENT – 3	DEVELOPING – 2	BEGINNING – 1
IDEA DEVELOPMENT (ID) (weighted x 2) *The main thesis the student conveys to his/her audience and the way the thesis and analysis are expressed.*	***I've done everything to earn a score of Proficient, plus 2 of 3:***			
	a. I use my own voice and perspective in presenting my analysis.	a. My thesis is important, clear, and defensible.	a. My paper has a topic, but my thesis is not important, not clear, or not defensible.	a. My paper has a topic, but not a thesis.
	b. My analysis includes different points of view and develops the reasoning, evidence, strengths, and limitations for each point of view.	b. My analysis shows that I understand the literary work(s) I am analyzing because I explain and show the reason for each idea used to support my thesis.	b. My analysis is confusing, *OR* it only partly shows that I understand the meaning of the literary work(s), because I mainly summarize the information instead of explaining how my ideas relate to my thesis.	b. My ideas are not clearly related to my topic because I only list information rather than connect my ideas about the literary work(s) to my topic. *OR* I make inappropriate connections between the literary work(s).
	c. I make connections between my analysis and myself, other texts, history, pieces of evidence, and/or the world.	c. I explain the significance of my thesis/analysis (the "so what?" of my essay).	c. I attempt to explain the significance of my thesis/analysis, but it is not clear.	c. I do not explain the significance of my topic.
	ADVANCED – 4	**PROFICIENT – 3**	**DEVELOPING – 2**	**BEGINNING – 1**
SUPPORTING EVIDENCE (SE) *The facts, quotations, definitions, descriptions, examples, and/or scenarios used to support the main thesis*	***I've done everything to earn a score of Proficient, plus 2 of 3:***			
	a. In my analysis, I distinguish between the text(s) and my interpretation, and show that I know how to use each appropriately.	a. I use sufficient evidence that is relevant to my thesis/topic and that effectively elaborates on my point.	a. I use evidence to support my thesis/topic, but it is insufficient, not fully relevant, or repeats rather than elaborates on my point.	a. I use limited evidence, or my evidence contradicts or does not connect to my thesis/topic.
	b. I consistently and effectively integrate well-chosen citations to create a cohesive analysis.	b. I use accurate evidence with enough detail to support my thesis/topic.	b. Most of my evidence is related to my thesis/topic, but some of it may be too general, inaccurate, or misinterpreted.	b. I use evidence that is too general, is inaccurate, or is misinterpreted.
	c. I anticipate my audience's familiarity with the literary work(s) and their values and possible biases.	c. I cite supporting evidence from my sources appropriately, even when paraphrasing.	c. I sometimes cite my supporting evidence appropriately.	c. I do not include citations from the media I am analyzing. *OR* I use direct quotations but do not identify where they are from.

QPA COMMON LITERARY ANALYSIS RUBRIC

	ADVANCED – 4	PROFICIENT – 3	DEVELOPING – 2	BEGINNING – 1
ORGANIZATION (O)	***I've done everything to earn a score of Proficient, plus 2 of 3:***			
The logic, structure, and clarity of the essay.	a. My introduction hooks and orients the reader to the topic in a thoughtful and engaging way.	a. My introduction orients the reader to my topic and provides an overview of the analysis in the rest of the paper.	a. My paper begins with an introduction that only partly orients the reader to the rest of my paper.	a. My paper begins presenting information without an introduction.
	b. My body paragraphs build in significance and enhance the clarity and engagement of my essay.	b. My body paragraphs are logically ordered.	b. Most, but not all, of my body paragraphs are logically ordered.	b. The order of my body paragraphs is confusing and distracting.
	c. My conclusion is interesting and ties up my analysis, leaving the reader with a new perspective.	c. My topic sentences are clearly stated for each paragraph and develop my paper's logic.	c. My topic sentences are sometimes underdeveloped or unclear.	c. My topic sentences are mostly missing, unclear, or do not relate to the rest of the paragraph.
		d. My essay's structure and transitions are logical and help the reader understand my essay.	d. My transitions between sentences and ideas are inconsistent.	d. The transitions between my sentences and ideas are non-existent or hard to follow.
		e. My conclusion summarizes my analysis and reflects upon the thesis.	e. My conclusion does not fully close/summarize my analysis.	e. My paper lacks a conclusion.

	ADVANCED – 4	PROFICIENT – 3	DEVELOPING – 2	BEGINNING – 1
CONVENTIONS & STYLE (CS)	***I've done everything to earn a score of Proficient, plus 2 of 3:***			
The word choice, fluency, spelling, mechanics, usage, and grammar.	I maintain the audience's interest by doing at least two of the following: • varying syntax and sentence structure • using figures of speech • choosing precise language	a. I have only a few errors, and my errors do not interfere with the reader's interpretation of my message.	a. I have many different types of errors. *OR* My errors interfere somewhat with the reader's interpretation of my message.	a. My errors seriously interfere with the reader's interpretation of my message.
		b. The style of my writing and my use of vocabulary is academic and appropriate for the intended audience and topic.	b. The style of my writing and my use of vocabulary is not consistently academic and appropriate for the intended audience or topic.	b. The style of my writing is not academic; it is too informal.
		c. I demonstrate control of Standard English.	c. I have some control of Standard English, but it is not consistent.	c. I have little control of Standard English conventions, sentence structure, and grammar.

QPA COMMON ORAL COMMUNICATION TASK

Learning Goals

In this task you will be working on:

- **CCSS Listening:** Students will demonstrate the ability to listen and view critically for variety of purposes.
- **CCSS Speaking:** Students will demonstrate the ability to speak purposefully and effectively - strategically making decisions about content, language use, and discourse style.
- **Additional Modes of Communication:** Written or Visual Communication *(specified by teacher).*
- **Content Standards:** *(specified by teacher).*

Student Directions

- Carefully read the student directions and rubrics. Ask your teacher if you have any questions.
- Work on this task independently. However, your teacher will build in checkpoints for peer and teacher feedback.
- Cite your sources using a standard citation method as directed by your teacher (e.g., MLA, APA) and include a Works Cited/References page.

Task *(parts to be specified by teacher)*

Prepare and deliver an oral presentation that expresses the analysis and arguments you have set forth in your written work. Select a format for your oral communication presentation that will best allow you to communicate your argument and conclusions.

- ☐ Exhibition
- ☐ Oral presentation
- ☐ Speech
- ☐ Debate
- ☐ Simulation
- ☐ Panel discussion
- ☐ Group presentation
- ☐ Song or short play
- ☐ Radio broadcast or podcast
- ☐ Other: ____________________

SUMMARY:

- **Topic:** Specify the content, background information, or scenario.
- **Genre:** Oral communication: The goal of the oral presentation is to incorporate evidence in support of the speaker's analysis and argument and to demonstrate effective communication skills in selected format.
- **Evidence sources:** Specify the evidence to be incorporated in the oral presentation, which should be similar to that for written work.
- **Audience:** The intended reader including the level of knowledge of this specific audience so that the product is appropriate.
- **Products and Rubrics:** For oral communication, include the number of minutes; for written work, include the approximate number of words or pages; etc.
- **Time frame:** Specify how long students will have to complete task.

SAMPLE VARIATIONS

- Exhibition: Students present multiple times to students from other classes, teachers, families, and community members.
- Presentation in small groups: Students form small groups, each with a teacher who volunteers as a scorer and facilitator, and take turns presenting to each other and asking questions. This allows more students to present within a single class period.

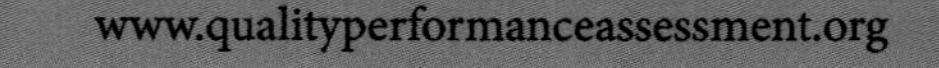

QPA COMMON ORAL COMMUNICATION RUBRIC

Student Name: Scorer: Date:

Subject: ☐ ELA ☐ Social Studies ☐ Science ☐ Mathematics ☐ Other:

Type of Oral Communication: ☐ Oral Presentation ☐ Speech ☐ Debate ☐ Simulation ☐ Other:

	ADVANCED – 4	PROFICIENT – 3	DEVELOPING – 2	BEGINNING – 1
PERFORMANCE (P) (weighted x 3) *The manner in which a student communicates through speaking*	***I've done everything to earn a score of Proficient, plus:***			
	a. I change my voice and language for expressive purposes in a compelling and genuine manner. *AND/OR*	a. I use appropriate language, style, and tone to engage and maintain the audience's attention.	a. I sometimes use language, style, or tone that is not appropriate for this presentation or audience.	a. I do not use the right words or tone to engage my audience.
	b. I adapt my presentation to different contexts or purposes, or depending on my audience's reactions.	b. I use appropriate body language, gestures, and eye contact with the audience.	b. I fidget AND/OR avoid eye contact in a way that somewhat interferes with the listener's interpretation of my analysis.	b. I fidget AND/OR avoid eye contact in a way that seriously interferes with the listener's interpretation of my analysis.
		c. I speak clearly at an appropriate volume and pace.	c. I speak quickly AND/OR quietly in a way that somewhat interferes with the listener's interpretation of my analysis.	c. I speak too quickly AND/OR quietly in a way that seriously interferes with the listener's interpretation of my analysis.
		d. My presentation is well paced and I use the allotted time effectively.	d. I meet the minimum time requirements without going over time.	d. I do not meet the time requirements for the presentation.
		e. I respond to questions thoughtfully and concisely using formal English.	e. I respond to some questions inaccurately/ inappropriately for this setting.	e. I respond to questions inaccurately or inappropriately for this setting.
	ADVANCED – 4	**PROFICIENT – 3**	**DEVELOPING – 2**	**BEGINNING – 1**
IDEA DEVELOPMENT (ID) *The main thesis the student conveys to his/her audience and the way the thesis and analysis are expressed.*	***I've done everything to earn a score of Proficient, plus:***			
	My own voice, style, and unique perspective are evident in my analysis and presentation.	a. My thesis is important, clear, and defensible.	a. My presentation has a thesis, but it is not important, not clear, or not defensible.	a. My presentation does not have a thesis.
		b. My analysis is logical and well developed for the type of presentation I am giving.	b. I include information about my topic without explaining my ideas enough or providing enough detail.	b. I include information that is unrelated to my topic.
		c. My presentation mode is appropriate for the intended audience.	c. My presentation mode is not an effective way to convey my analysis and information.	c. My presentation mode detracts from my analysis and information.

QPA COMMON ORAL COMMUNICATION RUBRIC

	ADVANCED – 4	PROFICIENT – 3	DEVELOPING – 2	BEGINNING – 1
SUPPORTING EVIDENCE (SE)	***I've done everything to earn a score of Proficient, plus:***			
The facts, descriptions, examples, and/or scenarios used to support the main message/thesis.	a. I use evidence to address questions and counterclaims.	a. The evidence I use to support my thesis/analysis is relevant, specific, and accurate.	a. Most of my evidence is related to my thesis/topic, but some of it may not be relevant, specific, accurate, or correctly interpreted.	a. I use evidence related to topics other than my thesis/topic; OR I use evidence that is too general, is inaccurate, or is misinterpreted.

	ADVANCED – 4	PROFICIENT – 3	DEVELOPING – 2	BEGINNING – 1
ORGANIZATION (O)	***I've done everything to earn a score of Proficient, plus 2 of 3:***			
The structure and flow of the presentation.	a. My introduction hooks and orients the audience to the topic in a thoughtful and engaging way.	a. My introduction orients the reader to my topic and provides an overview of the analysis in the rest of my presentation.	a. My presentation begins with an introduction that only partly orients the reader to the rest of my presentation.	a. My presentation begins delivering information without an introduction.
	b. I anticipate my audience's knowledge level, concerns, values, and possible biases.	b. My presentation's structure and transitions are logical and help the audience to understand my analysis.	b. My presentation's structure and transitions are inconsistent.	b. My presentation is difficult to follow and lacks structure.
	c. My conclusion is interesting and ties up my analysis, leaving the audience with a new perspective.	c. My conclusion summarizes my analysis and reflects upon the thesis.	c. My conclusion does not fully close/summarize my analysis.	c. My presentation lacks a conclusion.

QPA COMMON POSITION PAPER TASK

Learning Goals

In this task you will be working on:

- **CCSS Writing:** Write arguments to analyze and critique texts or topics and support claims and reasoning with sufficient evidence for intended purpose and audience.
- **CCSS Reading:** Analyze and critique a variety of increasingly complex print and non-print informational texts.
- **Additional Modes of Communication:** Oral or Visual Communication *(specified by teacher).*
- **Content Standards:** *(specified by teacher).*

Student Directions

- Carefully read the student directions and rubrics. Ask your teacher if you have any questions.
- Work on this task independently. However, your teacher will build in checkpoints for peer and teacher feedback.
- Cite your sources using a standard citation method as directed by your teacher (e.g., MLA, APA) and include a Works Cited/References page.

Task *(parts to be specified by teacher)*

Take a position on an issue that matters to people living in our American democracy. Write an evidence-based argument to convince your audience of your position with an important, clear, precise, and defensible thesis. Use relevant, specific, and accurate evidence from research, real life, and your prior knowledge to support your argument and address alternative viewpoints.

SUMMARY:

- **Topic:** Specify the content, background information, or scenario.
- **Genre:** Argument writing: The goal of the paper is to use evidence to create a compelling argument.
- **Evidence sources:** Cite at least three sources, using at least two different types of the following works: books, journals, magazine articles, online materials, expert interviews, visual and audio materials, and public documents.
- **Audience:** Specify the intended reader including the level of knowledge of this specific audience so that the product is appropriate.
- **Products and Rubrics:** For written work, include the approximate number of words or pages; for oral communication, include the number of minutes; etc.
- **Time frame:** Specify how long students will have to complete task.

SAMPLE VARIATIONS

- Take on either Mary Mallon's or the New York City Board of Public Health's point of view. Write an evidence-based letter to the other party that explains and supports your position on Mary's quarantine on North Brother Island.
- Does Andrew Jackson deserve to be on the twenty dollar bill?
- Are students or schools responsible for high school drop outs?

QPA COMMON POSITION PAPER RUBRIC

Student Name: Scorer: Date:

Subject: ☐ ELA ☐ Social Studies ☐ Science ☐ Mathematics ☐ Other:

	ADVANCED – 4	PROFICIENT – 3	DEVELOPING – 2	BEGINNING – 1
IDEA DEVELOPMENT (ID) (weighted x 2)	***I've done everything to earn a score of Proficient, plus 2 of 3:***			
The main thesis the student conveys to his/her audience and the way the thesis and analysis are expressed.	a. I use my own voice and perspective in presenting my argument.	a. My thesis is important, clear, and defensible.	a. My paper has a topic, but my thesis is not important, not clear, or not defensible.	a. My paper has a topic, but not a thesis.
	b. My argument includes different points of view and develops the reasoning, evidence, strengths, and limitations for each point of view.	b. My argument demonstrates my understanding of the topic. I explain and show the reason for each idea used to support my thesis and I address different points of view.	b. My argument is confusing, OR it only partly shows that I understand the topic. I mainly summarize the information instead of explaining how my ideas relate to my thesis.	b. My ideas are not clearly related to my topic. I only list information rather than connect it to my argument. *OR* I make inappropriate connections between the evidence and my topic.
	c. I make connections between the topic of my paper and the impact of my argument's presentation on myself and/or the world.	c. I explain the significance of my thesis/argument (the "so what?" of my paper).	c. I attempt to explain the significance of my thesis/argument, but it is not clear.	c. I do not explain the significance of my topic.
	ADVANCED – 4	**PROFICIENT – 3**	**DEVELOPING – 2**	**BEGINNING – 1**
SUPPORTING EVIDENCE (SE)	***I've done everything to earn a score of Proficient, plus 2 of 3:***			
The facts, quotations, definitions, descriptions, examples, and/or scenarios used to support the main thesis	a. In my analysis, I distinguish fact from opinion and show that I know how to identify and use each appropriately.	a. I use sufficient evidence that is relevant to my argument and that effectively elaborates on my point.	a. I use evidence to support my argument, but it is insufficient, not fully relevant, or repeats rather than elaborates on my point.	a. I use limited evidence, or it contradicts or does not connect to my argument.
	b. I consistently and effectively integrate well-chosen citations to create a cohesive analysis and to address questions and counterclaims.	b. I use accurate evidence with enough detail to support my argument.	b. Most of my evidence is related to my argument, but some of it may not be accurate, detailed, or correctly interpreted.	b. I use evidence that is inaccurate or misinterpreted.
	c. I anticipate my audience's knowledge level, including concerns, values, and possible biases.	c. I cite supporting evidence from multiple sources appropriately, even when paraphrasing.	c. I sometimes cite my supporting evidence appropriately.	c. I do not include citations from my research. *OR* I use direct quotations but do not say where they are from.

QPA COMMON POSITION PAPER RUBRIC

	ADVANCED – 4	PROFICIENT – 3	DEVELOPING – 2	BEGINNING – 1
ORGANIZATION (O)	***I've done everything to earn a score of Proficient, plus 2 of 3:***			
The logic, structure, and clarity of the essay.	a. My introduction hooks and orients the reader to the topic in a thoughtful and engaging way.	a. My introduction orients the reader to my topic and provides an overview of the analysis in the rest of my paper.	a. My paper begins with an introduction that only partly orients the reader to the rest of my paper.	a. My paper begins presenting information without an introduction.
	b. My body paragraphs build in significance and enhance the clarity and engagement of my paper.	b. My body paragraphs are logically ordered.	b. Most, but not all, of my body paragraphs are logically ordered.	b. The order of my body paragraphs is confusing and distracting.
	c. My conclusion is interesting and ties up my analysis, leaving the reader with a new perspective.	c. My topic sentences are clearly stated in each paragraph and develop my paper's logic.	c. My topic sentences are sometimes underdeveloped or unclear.	c. My topic sentences are mostly missing, unclear, or do not relate to the rest of the paragraph.
		d. My paper's structure and transitions are logical and help the reader better understand my thesis/topic.	d. My transitions between sentences and ideas are inconsistent.	d. The transitions between my sentences and ideas are non-existent or hard to follow.
		e. My conclusion summarizes my analysis and reflects upon the thesis.	e. My conclusion does not fully close/summarize my analysis.	e. My paper lacks a conclusion.
	ADVANCED – 4	**PROFICIENT – 3**	**DEVELOPING – 2**	**BEGINNING – 1**
CONVENTIONS & STYLE (CS)	***I've done everything to earn a score of Proficient, plus:***			
The word choice, fluency, spelling, mechanics, usage, and grammar.	I maintain the audience's interest by doing at least two of the following: • varying syntax and sentence structure • using figures of speech • choosing precise and content-specific language	a. I have only a few errors, and my errors do not interfere with the reader's interpretation of my message.	a. I have many different types of errors. *OR* My errors interfere somewhat with the reader's interpretation of my message.	a. My errors seriously interfere with the reader's interpretation of my message.
		b. The style of my writing and my use of vocabulary is academic and appropriate for the intended audience and topic.	b. The style of my writing and my use of vocabulary is not consistently academic and appropriate for the intended audience or topic.	b. The style of my writing is not appropriate.
		c. I demonstrate control of Standard English.	c. I have some control of Standard English, but it is not consistent.	c. I have little control of Standard English conventions, sentence structure, and grammar.

QPA COMMON RESEARCH TASK

Learning Goals

In this task you will be working on:

- **CCSS Writing:** Write effective informative texts to examine and convey complex ideas for a variety of purposes and audiences.
- **CCSS Reading:** Analyze and critique a variety of increasingly complex print and non-print informational texts.
- **Additional Modes of Communication:** Oral or Visual Communication *(specified by teacher)*.
- **Content Standards:** *(specified by teacher)*.

Student Directions

- Carefully read the student directions and rubrics. Ask your teacher if you have any questions.
- Work on this task independently. However, your teacher will build in checkpoints for peer and teacher feedback.
- Cite your sources using a standard citation method as directed by your teacher (e.g., MLA, APA) and include a Works Cited/References page.

Task *(parts to be specified by teacher)*

Write a research paper about a topic of your own choosing

SUMMARY:

- **Topic:** Decided by student or specified by teacher.
- **Genre:** Informational writing: The goal of the research paper is to use evidence to educate the reader about the topic.
- **Evidence sources:** Cite at least four (4) sources for 8th grade (at least five (5) sources for 10th grade), using at least three (3) different types of the following works: books, magazine articles, online materials, expert interviews, visual and audio materials, functional documents, and public documents. Some or all of these sources may be provided by the teacher.
- **Audience:** Specify the intended reader including the level of knowledge of this specific audience so that the product is appropriate.
- **Products and Rubrics:** For written work, include the approximate number of words or pages; for oral communication, include the number of minutes; etc.
- **Time frame:** Specify how long students will have to complete task.

SAMPLE VARIATIONS

- What is the most important way that the United States expanded during the 1800s – politically, geographically or economically?
- Research the allusion(s) made to specific events, eras, movements, artifacts, works of literature or art, etc. in a novel, short story, work of poetry, or lyrics of a song.
- Research an issue related to water scarcity in the 21st century.

QPA COMMON RESEARCH RUBRIC

Student Name: Scorer: Date:

Subject: ☐ ELA ☐ Social Studies ☐ Science ☐ Mathematics ☐ Other:

	ADVANCED – 4	PROFICIENT – 3	DEVELOPING – 2	BEGINNING – 1
IDEA DEVELOPMENT (ID) (weighted x 2) *The main thesis the student conveys to his/her audience and the way the thesis and analysis are expressed.*	***I've done everything to earn a score of Proficient, plus 2 of 3:***			
	a. I use my own voice and perspective in presenting my argument.	a. My thesis is important, clear, and defensible.	a. My paper has a research topic, but my thesis is not important, not clear, or not defensible.	a. My paper has a topic, but not a thesis.
	b. My analysis develops the reasoning, evidence, strengths, and limitations for different interpretations.	b. My analysis of my research makes sense and demonstrates my understanding. I explain the reason for each idea used to support my thesis.	b. My analysis of my research is confusing, *OR* it only partly shows that I understand my topic. I mainly summarize the information instead of explaining how my ideas relate to my thesis.	b. My ideas are not clearly related to my topic because I only list information rather than connect it to my research topic. OR I make inappropriate connections between the evidence and my research topic.
	c. I make connections between the research findings and the impact of my research on myself and/or the world.	c. I explain the significance of my research (the "so what?" of my paper).	c. I attempt to explain the significance of my research, but it is not clear.	c. I do not explain the significance of my research topic.

	ADVANCED – 4	PROFICIENT – 3	DEVELOPING – 2	BEGINNING – 1
SUPPORTING EVIDENCE (SE) *The facts, quotations, definitions, descriptions, examples, and/or scenarios used to support the main thesis*	***I've done everything to earn a score of Proficient, plus 2 of 3:***			
	a. In my analysis, I distinguish fact from opinion and show that I know how to identify and use each appropriately.	a. I use sufficient evidence that is relevant to my thesis/topic and that effectively elaborates on my point.	a. I use evidence to support my thesis/topic, but it is insufficient, not fully relevant, or repeats rather than elaborates on my point.	a. I use limited evidence, or my evidence contradicts or does not connect to my thesis/topic.
	b. I consistently and effectively integrate well-chosen citations to create a cohesive analysis.	b. I use accurate evidence with enough detail to support my thesis/topic.	b. Most of my evidence is related to my thesis/topic, but some of it may not be accurate, detailed, or correctly interpreted.	b. I use evidence that is inaccurate or misinterpreted.
	c. I anticipate my audience's knowledge level, including concerns, values, and possible biases.	c. I cite supporting evidence from multiple sources appropriately, even when paraphrasing.	c. I sometimes cite my supporting evidence appropriately.	c. I do not include citations. OR I use direct quotations but do not say where they are from.

QPA COMMON RESEARCH RUBRIC

	ADVANCED – 4	PROFICIENT – 3	DEVELOPING – 2	BEGINNING – 1
ORGANIZATION (O)	***I've done everything to earn a score of Proficient, plus 2 of 3:***			
The logic, structure, and clarity of the paper.	a. My introduction hooks and orients the reader to the research topic in a thoughtful and engaging way.	a. My introduction orients the reader to my research topic and provides a roadmap for the analysis in the rest of the paper.	a. My paper begins with an introduction that only partly orients the reader to the rest of my paper.	a. My paper begins presenting information without an introduction.
	b. My body paragraphs build in significance and enhance the clarity and engagement of my paper.	b. My body paragraphs are logically ordered.	b. Most, but not all, of my body paragraphs are logically ordered.	b. The order of my body paragraphs is confusing and distracting.
	c. My conclusion is interesting and ties up my analysis, leaving the reader with a new perspective.	c. My topic sentences are clearly stated in each paragraph and develop my paper's logic.	c. My topic sentences are sometimes underdeveloped or unclear.	c. My topic sentences are mostly missing, unclear, or do not relate to the rest of the paragraph.
		d. My paper's structure and transitions are logical and help the reader better understand my paper.	d. My transitions between sentences and ideas are inconsistent.	d. The transitions between my sentences and ideas are non-existent or hard to follow.
		e. My conclusion summarizes my analysis and reflects upon the thesis.	e. My conclusion does not fully close/summarize my analysis.	e. My paper lacks a conclusion.
	ADVANCED – 4	**PROFICIENT – 3**	**DEVELOPING – 2**	**BEGINNING – 1**
CONVENTIONS & STYLE (CS)	***I've done everything to earn a score of Proficient, plus:***			
The word choice, fluency, spelling, mechanics, usage, and grammar.	I maintain the audience's interest by doing at least two of the following: • varying syntax and sentence structure • using figures of speech • choosing precise and content-specific language	a. I have only a few errors, and my errors do not interfere with the reader's interpretation of my message.	a. I have many different types of errors. *OR* My errors interfere somewhat with the reader's interpretation of my message.	a. My errors seriously interfere with the reader's interpretation of my message.
		b. The style of my writing and my use of vocabulary is academic and appropriate for the intended audience and topic.	b. The style of my writing and my use of vocabulary is not consistently academic and appropriate for the intended audience or topic.	b. The style of my writing is not academic; it is too informal.
		c. I demonstrate control of Standard English.	c. I have some control of Standard English, but it is not consistent.	c. I have little control of Standard English conventions, sentence structure, and grammar.

QPA COMMON TASK SCORING GUIDE

Please remember to follow the guidelines below when scoring QPA common tasks:

a. Read the entire paper and make notations and markings for each criterion as listed below. Once you have a sense of the paper as a whole, begin your scoring.

b. When scoring with the rubric, start with the proficient (3) column and go to the left to the advanced (4) column if the paper is stronger than the proficient descriptors, or to the right to the developing (2) column if the paper is weaker than the proficient descriptors.

c. For the proficient level (3), an essay must have every bullet present. For all other levels (1, 2, and 4), the essay must have most of the bullets in the level to earn that score.
   - o If a paper has a single bullet in multiple categories, default to the middle score.
   - o The advanced level requires all criteria in level 3 plus two of the three criteria in advanced (4).

d. Scorers must select a score point; 2.5 or 1.5 is not an acceptable score.

e. Keep each criterion separate in your mind to avoid double-counting mistakes.

f. When questions arise while using the rubric, refer to anchor works and their corresponding rubrics, annotations, and score reports for clarity.

g. Tasks are aligned to the Common Core State Standards. Scorers should be aware of that alignment when interpreting the work and should follow the anchors and not an internal or school standard.

Criteria-Specific Rules

SUMMARY OF SUGGESTED ANNOTATIONS

TS+ or TS-	strong or weak Thesis Statement
T+ or T-	strong or weak Topic Sentences
A+ or A-	strong or weak Analysis
T+ or T-	strong or weak Transition
SE+ or SE-	strong or weak Supporting Evidence
V	Vocabulary
C	Conventions Error

IDEA DEVELOPMENT:

The thesis the student conveys to his/her audience and the way the thesis and analysis are expressed.

1. **Mark Thesis:** Underline and label the thesis statement, as doing so will help you to make sure that you can track the idea development in the essay based on the thesis.
2. **Importance:** The thesis must be deemed important by specifically answering a question for which the answer is not obvious and can be disputed. For example, "These two stories are similar and different" is obvious and can't be disputed, making it a weak thesis statement.
3. **Mark Analysis:** Identify analysis in the paper with an "A+" for where it is working and an "A-" for where it is not working so that you can identify how the analysis develops throughout the paper.
4. **So What:** The "so what" criterion ensures that students can connect their writing to big ideas and enduring understandings as they explain why the topic is significant. The student must explain the "so what" to make the importance of the thesis/topic obvious to the reader.
5. Be careful when scoring for idea development, as poor organization can obscure a good idea. Keep each category separate in your mind to avoid double-counting mistakes.

SUPPORTING EVIDENCE:

The facts, quotations, definitions, descriptions, examples, and/or scenarios used to support the main thesis/topic.

1. **Mark Evidence:** Mark instances of evidence provided by citations or quotations with an "SE+" for where it is relevant and elaborates the point or "SE-" where evidence is weak. Citations indicate references to texts, images, films that have been shared by the teachers, while quotations present the actual words of the texts in quotation marks. Students can also paraphrase, but must cite the source.
2. **Elaboration:** Supporting evidence should be used to elaborate on a point, not to merely repeat it. This example repeats: "The caption of the photo states, 'That is the blame for this war.' This image explains that the man in the photo is to blame for the war."
3. **Accuracy:** Scorers who are unfamiliar with a text or topic should focus on relevance and specificity rather than assess the accuracy of content and/or literature with which they are unfamiliar.
4. **Support of thesis/topic:** Consider whether the evidence is in support of the topic if the thesis is not clear. If a student has not developed an effective thesis, this should only count against him or her in idea development and not in other criteria.

ORGANIZATION:

The logic, structure, and clarity of the essay.

1. **Mark Topic Sentences:** Underline the topic sentence of each paragraph, as doing so will help you make sure that topic sentences are effective.
2. **Mark Transitions:** Mark transition words with a "T" to indicate that the transitions are logical and help the reader understand the essay.
3. **Cohesion:** Organization does not mean just the existence of five paragraphs and a topic sentence for each. It refers to the level of cohesion of the whole document.
4. **Paragraph order:** Paragraphs should be logical and should build in either chronology, significance, or another way that clearly adds to the clarity and logic of the essay.
5. **Support of thesis/topic:** Consider whether the organization is in support of the topic if the thesis is not clear. If a student has not developed an effective thesis, this should only count against him or her in idea development and not in other criteria.

CONVENTIONS:

The word choice, fluency, spelling, mechanics, usage, and grammar.

1. **Mark Convention Errors:** Identify convention errors in the paper with a "C" so that you can look over the whole paper and get a sense of how many errors there are for criteria A at levels 1, 2, and 3.
2. **Errors:** Define types of errors in conventions: grammar, spelling and typos, mechanics, and usage. Students need to have made different types of errors and not merely have repeated the same error to earn a score of 2.
3. **Mark Vocabulary:** Underline literary, media, or content-specific terms as you see them and mark them as "V."
4. **Academic writing style:** Consider the level of formality of the writing. Style should also be academic and avoid a conversational tone, slang, contractions, or other informal language. Students should use third-person pronouns and not pronouns such as we, you, or I. (Exception: Pronoun use may vary in Position Paper Task as long as it is appropriate for the audience.)
5. **Control of Standard English:** Consider the coherence of sentence structure and freedom from error. In a paper that lacks control, errors and sentence structure interrupt the paper's flow.

QPA COMMON TASK TEACHER DIRECTIONS

Purpose

The QPA Common Task Teacher Directions are intended to support the implementation of the QPA Common Performance Tasks in grades 6-12. The tasks model the type of consistency required for teachers to implement common assessments when creating new common tasks.

Task Administration

Carefully read the teacher directions, student directions, student tasks, and rubrics when planning where in the curriculum this assessment will be administered.

- *Common* does not mean "the same." The performance assessment tasks are designed to allow teachers to select the content for the task that is most appropriate for the course curriculum.

- Teachers must also create tasks that are most appropriate for the course curriculum. QPA strongly encourages that students complete a written task and presentation task.

WRITTEN TASK:

- **Written task summary:**
  - o **Topic:** Content
  - o **Genre:** Specify genre-specific features.
  - o **Evidence sources:** Specify evidence sources and requirements.
  - o **Audience:** Specify the audience and the level of knowledge of this specific audience.
  - o **Time frame:** Specify how long students will have to complete task.

- **Written tasks:** The teacher has the option of changing the highlighted elements in the written tasks in order to embed this task into his/her curriculum by incorporating curriculum-relevant content. Additionally, the tasks are designed in such a way that teachers can customize them for the level of complexity they wish to assess. If the teacher keeps the task in its generic given form, s/he can choose to leave it open ended or include examples and/or sample thesis statements. If the teacher decides to provide the students with specific texts they must use, s/he can choose whether or not to include sample thesis statements and/or issues to consider.

PRESENTATION TASK:

- There are two **purposes for including the presentation component:**
  - o To provide multiple entry points for students to demonstrate their skills.
  - o To provide opportunities for students to develop **21st century and higher-order thinking skills** by asking students to take what they learned in the process of researching and writing the written task and to convey that learning in an oral presentation or a visual/multimedia format.

- **Presentation tasks:** Two options are provided for the presentation component (oral or visual/multimedia). Teachers have the option of changing each task by allowing students to choose their medium or by selecting it for them.

ORAL TASK:

- **Oral task options:** The oral communication task can be completed in a variety of formats. Students do not need to present individually, and formats that promote student engagement and discussion with each other as they plan and present are opportunities for deepening student understanding. For example, all students might take part in a debate or simulation structured by the teacher. Time requirements can also be changed to accommodate different class sizes and lengths. Presentations should be videotaped whenever possible so students can learn from others and critique their own performances. Listed below are suggested oral communication task options (teachers should feel free to create other ways for students to communicate orally, beyond this list):
    - o Exhibition
    - o Oral presentation
    - o Speech
    - o Debate
    - o Simulation
    - o Panel discussion
    - o Group presentation
    - o Song or short play
    - o Radio broadcast or podcast

For the exhibition option, students present simultaneously, and teacher circulates to score using rubric and asking questions. Students can also circulate and complete rubric for their peers.

VISUAL TASK:

- **Visual task options:** Work submitted for the visual task must be accompanied by an artistic statement. In the statement, the student should clearly explain the creative decisions made in creating the product and provide convincing evidence in support of the thesis. The artistic statement should be one or two pages in length. Multiple drafts are not required for the artistic statement. Listed below are suggested visual task options (teachers should feel free to create other ways for students to communicate visually, beyond this list):
    - o Booklet or pamphlet
    - o Poster
    - o Webpage, blog, or wiki
    - o PowerPoint
    - o Public service announcement
    - o TV show, webcast, or movie
    - o Graphic comic
    - o Picture book

TASK GUIDLINES:

- **Task guidelines:** Provided below are guidelines for the process of task creation for both written and presentation tasks.
    - o The task sparks students' imaginations and creativity. Use words or phrases that invite a variety of interpretations and responses and that connect to an essential question.
    - o The task includes an authentic audience for the writing task. Students understand the audience's familiarity with the topic. The task specifies the level of formality of writing style appropriate to the audience.
    - o When specifying an authentic, beyond-school audience for a performance assessment, always include the evaluator, who is typically the teacher. (Some audiences require less sophisticated writing than we want to see in our assessments.)
    - o Directions are clear and provide expectations for genre, length, sources, and format, and call attention to aspects of the rubric by which their work will be judged.
    - o Directions are succinct. Too much direction in a task can stifle originality in students' compositions.
    - o If sources are not provided by the teacher, the task should include expectations about how students find and use evidence sources.
    - o The task is appropriate in content and form to the grade level of the students being assessed.
    - o The task is designed for both the student and the scorer, so they can clearly interpret the rubric in light of the task, especially in terms of audience, evidence requirements, or genre-specific features.

THESIS DEVELOPMENT:

- **Thesis development:** Developing a strong thesis, or claim, for the written task is essential for students to perform well on both the written and presentation tasks. Supporting students in the thesis development process through instruction, discussion, and feedback is critical. The following criteria can help students understand how to create a thesis.

A thesis statement:

- o Makes a claim.
- o Is specific.
- o Communicates what the reader can expect in the rest of the paper.
- o Is the author's opinion of the significance of the subject matter.
- o Takes the form of one sentence in the first paragraph.
- o Connects all the evidence and analysis of the rest of the paper.

ADDITIONAL PROCESSES:

- **Optional components for instruction or assessment:** Teachers are welcome to include additional processes when implementing the task. For example:
  - o Hold a reflective class discussion about the differences between the mediums of writing a position paper and delivering an oral presentation or creating a visual/multimedia product about the same topic.
  - o Have students write individual reflections about the learning process, how s/he applied his/her skills, or why s/he chose one type of presentation or one kind of multimedia product over another.
  - o Include a self-assessment and/or peer assessment of performance in oral communication using the performance component of the rubric or a rubric the teacher creates. To assess listening skills, encourage students to ask each other questions and to evaluate each other's performances, reasoning, and use of evidence.
  - o Conduct a preassessment on important skills such as thesis development or selecting supporting evidence. Preassessments can inform teaching prior to task administration to make sure all students have the skills to be successful.

- The teacher should make sure students have read the student directions, student tasks, and rubrics.
  - **o Discuss** these documents with the students. The teacher should talk about expectations for the task and define terms on the rubric, using the task and their own expectations and norms. Teachers can use the tools in the guide—anchor papers, curriculum samples, products—as aids to understanding common expectations across classrooms and schools.
  - **o Provide** time for students to self-assess and revise, using the student version of the rubric as a guide. This should be done before the teacher reads a full draft.
  - **o Feedback** is important, so build in checkpoints with students where teachers use the rubric to guide their work, ask questions to push their thinking, and use scaffolding strategies to support students. These checkpoints should include peer feedback. A Student Peer Editing Checklist is provided in tool section of this guide.

- Students should complete the work for this task during class over a 2- to 4-week period, depending on how many hours the class meets and the amount of research required.

- In the planning phase, teachers are encouraged to review the task with a special educator or ELL teacher to establish **modifications** for ELL students and those with individual educational plans or 504 plans. Modifications should be documented, as they will provide useful guidance for teachers who use the task in the future.

Prerequisite Skills and Student Support

Before administering the assessment, the teacher should make sure s/he has **provided opportunities in class** for students to learn and practice the knowledge and skills necessary to complete the task successfully. Students should have direct instruction and experience with the elements in the list below prior to the administration of the task:

- Reading and following directions for written tasks
- Using a rubric to evaluate their written work and presentations
- Writing and revising written work using teacher feedback
- Using a specific citation format (MLA, APA, etc.)
- Thesis development and thesis-driven essay writing
- Finding resources and choosing appropriate evidence
- Giving oral presentations in class

Although students must work on this task independently, teachers should consult with and provide feedback to students prior to completion. Teachers are encouraged to ask prompting questions, refer students to the rubric criteria, and share models, but not to correct or revise student papers.

Teachers should reflect on when they plan to provide teacher feedback to students or provide opportunities for peer feedback.

	Teacher Feedback to All	Targeted Teacher Feedback (e.g., ELLs, students with IEPs)	Peer Editing Feedback
Research Process (e.g., selection of sources)			
Thesis Development			
Paper			
Paper Draft			
Presentation Component			

QPA COMMON VISUAL OR MEDIA TASK

Learning Goals

In this task you will be working on:

- **CCSS Technology:** Use the tools of technology (including digital media and the Internet) to gather, interpret, and analyze information and create sharable products.
- **Additional Modes of Communication:** Written or Oral Communication *(specified by teacher).*
- **Content Standards:** *(specified by teacher).*

Student Directions

- Carefully read the student directions and rubrics. Ask your teacher if you have any questions.
- Work on this task independently. However, your teacher will build in checkpoints for peer and teacher feedback.
- Cite your sources using a standard citation method as directed by your teacher (e.g., MLA, APA) and include a Works Cited/References page.

Task *(parts to be specified by teacher)*

Create a visual or media product that expresses your analysis, argument, and/or point of view. Select a format for your visual or media product that will best allow you to communicate your argument and conclusions.

- ☐ Booklet or pamphlet
- ☐ Poster
- ☐ Webpage, blog, or wiki
- ☐ PowerPoint
- ☐ Public Service Announcement
- ☐ TV show, webcast, or movie
- ☐ Graphic comic
- ☐ Picture book
- ☐ Other: ____________________

Write an artistic statement that must be submitted with your product that clearly and effectively supports the analysis and argument presented in your product. In your statement, clearly explain the creative decisions that have shaped your product and provide convincing evidence in support of your thesis. The artistic statement should be 1–2 pages in length.

SUMMARY:

- **Topic:** Specify the content, background information, or scenario.
- **Genre Visual:** The goal of the visual product's design is to incorporate evidence in support of the product's analysis and argument and to demonstrate the ability to use the visual medium effectively.
- **Evidence sources:** Specify the evidence to be incorporated in the visual or media products, which should be similar to that for written work.
- **Audience:** The intended reader including the level of knowledge of this specific audience so that the product is appropriate.
- **Products and Rubrics:** For visual or media products specify design requirements; for the artist statement or other written work, include the approximate number of words or pages; etc.
- **Time frame:** Specify how long students will have to complete task.

QPA COMMON VISUAL OR MEDIA RUBRIC

Student Name: Scorer: Date:

Subject: ☐ ELA ☐ Social Studies ☐ Science ☐ Mathematics ☐ Other:

	ADVANCED – 4	PROFICIENT – 3	DEVELOPING – 2	BEGINNING – 1
COMMUNICATION THROUGH VISUAL AND/OR MULTIMEDIA FORMATS (C) (weighted x 3) *The manner in which a student communicates through artistic, visual, or multimedia formats.*	***I've done everything to earn a score of Proficient, plus 2 of 3:***			
	a. My choice of medium expresses my unique perspective in a compelling manner that engages my audience with my research topic.	a. My thesis is important, precise, clear, defensible, and clearly conveyed in my chosen medium.	a. I include information about my research topic, but my thesis is not clearly conveyed in my chosen medium.	a. I include some information about my topic, but I do not have a thesis.
	b. My product is designed in such a way as to enhance the audience's understanding of my research topic.	b. My product engages the audience's interest using artistic and multimedia techniques (textural, graphic, audio, visual, or interactive elements) to enhance the thesis, evidence, and reasoning.	b. The artistic and/or multimedia techniques that I have chosen do not always engage the audience or enhance my thesis/topic.	b. My product is too simple or too confusing to engage my audience.
	c. When I use my product in an oral presentation, it provides additional context and perspective(s).	c. My product is well designed and organized for its intended purpose.	c. My product is well designed but not for its intended purpose. *OR* My choice of medium fits the purpose, but my product is poorly designed.	c. My product is poorly designed or organized. *AND* My product does not fit the intended purpose.
		d. When I use my product in an oral presentation, it helps my audience under-stand my research topic and line of reasoning.	d. When I use my product in an oral presentation, it somewhat distracts my audience from understanding my thesis/topic.	d. When I use my product in an oral presentation, it distracts my audience from understanding my thesis/topic.
	ADVANCED – 4	**PROFICIENT – 3**	**DEVELOPING – 2**	**BEGINNING – 1**
SUPPORTING EVIDENCE (SE) *The facts, descriptions, examples, and/or scenarios used to support the main message/thesis and the quality of the artistic statement.*	***I've done everything to earn a score of Proficient, plus:***			
	My written artistic statement adds clarity to the research presented in my product by clearly articulating the creative decisions I have shaped my product.	a. The evidence I use to support my thesis/analysis is relevant, specific, and accurate.	a. Most of my evidence is related to my thesis/topic, but some of it may not be relevant, specific, accurate, or correctly interpreted.	a. I use evidence related to topics other than my thesis/topic; OR I use evidence that is too general, is inaccurate, or is misinterpreted.
		b. My written artistic statement is clear, and it effectively supports the research presented in my product by articulating the creative decisions that have shaped my product.	b. My written artistic statement is not clear and does not effectively support the research presented in my product.	b. My written artistic statement provides inaccurate information AND/OR provides information that contradicts my product.

SETTING NORMS PROTOCOL

Purpose

To guide teams in setting norms and to set norms for collaborative work.

Directions

Have groups read the following before doing the activity to set norms. What are norms? Norms are ways of working together that can help groups be more thoughtful and productive. They fall into two categories: procedural and interpersonal. Once norms have been established, it is important that the entire group, not just the facilitator, takes responsibility for making sure that the norms are respected, and for redirecting the group when they are not. Norms can change and evolve as the group develops and matures.

Operating as a Team

Norms need to be set in many different areas, including: decision making, logistics, how to give feedback, how to treat other members of the team, how the norms will be monitored, and the roles team members will take. Within each area, the essential question is "How do we want to operate as a team?" Following are some key components:

- **Logistics:** These are the nuts and bolts of how the team operates. Examples of logistical issues include meeting schedule, start time, end time, lateness, and attendance. Although they seem like small matters, many of these items can become much larger issues unless they are spelled out clearly and accepted by all team members.
- **Timeliness:** Start time, finish time, lateness, and attendance.
- **Courtesy:** People have different styles of participating and different levels of tolerance for discussion, disagreement, and interruption. The norms set in these areas are designed to help team members communicate with each other in a respectful and caring fashion. Setting norms on how to listen, participate, and handle conflict allows team members to discuss and decide how they want to treat each other.
- **Decision-making process:** How will we make decisions? Reach agreements? How will we show agreement? Any significant decisions that affect the entire team should be decided by consensus, because this method is most effective for incorporating differing viewpoints and for creating the discourse that contributes to a collaborative culture. Consensus requires that all members express opinions on any decision and agree that they can live with the decision that is being considered. Any decision a team makes should be judged on two criteria: (1) how well the decision deals with the matters at hand, and (2) how committed the group members are to carrying it out.
- **Workload assignment:** How will work be assigned? How will conflicts with existing workloads be settled?
- **Setting priorities:** How will we discharge responsibility for on-time completion and equal distribution?
- **Enforcement of norms:** How will we make sure the norms are followed?

SAMPLE WAYS TO EXPRESS OPINIONS

Thumbs up: I'm in favor of the decision.

Thumbs down: I don't agree with the decision.

Thumbs in neutral: I'm not 100% behind the decision, but I can live with it.

To reach consensus, there should be no thumbs down. In order to build consensus, sometimes groups table decisions to allow time for collecting more data and information, and take a vote at a subsequent meeting.

Activity for Setting Norms/Setting Community Agreements

In this activity, members of a team write statements about how they want their team to operate and then categorize the statements into procedural norms and interpersonal norms. The group discusses the statements and reaches consensus on norms for their group.

Directions

1. The facilitator passes out Post-It notes to each team member.
2. Each person writes a norm, or a statement about how he or she wants the group to work together, on a Post-It.
3. The team shares its individual notes and divides them into the two categories—procedural norms and interpersonal norms.
4. Within each category, group the suggestions that are similar (e.g., take turns speaking and make sure everyone speaks should be grouped together).
5. Give a name to the norm for each group. (From the example above, the norm could be "Make sure everyone is heard.")
6. The group discusses the norms that have been suggested and checks to see whether or not the group is in agreement. The group should reach consensus on the norms it accepts.

Notes

- The team will work with greater commitment if they generate their norms themselves.
- Post the norms during each meeting.
- Reflect on norms at the end of each meeting.
- Add new norms as the team develops and new situations arise.

STUDENT ENGAGEMENT ALIGNMENT TOOL

This tool is designed for the self-assessment of practitioner-developed performance assessments for attributes that maximize student engagement.

ASSESSMENT INFORMATION

Title of Assessment: ______________________ Date: __________

Grade/Subject: ______________________ Author: __________

STUDENT ENGAGEMENT ALIGNMENT

- ☐ Assessment includes multiple modalities for students to engage with content.
- ☐ Assessment addresses an essential issue, big idea, or key concept or skill of the unit/course.
- ☐ Directions clearly indicate what the student is being asked to do.
- ☐ Assessment provides for ownership and decision making, requiring the student to be actively engaged.
- ☐ Students clearly understand, and engage in applying, significant content and skills to authentic problems and issues in the world outside the classroom through discussion, reflection, or presentations.
- ☐ Plan has been made for teacher feedback to be provided to students at key checkpoints throughout the project to ensure that all students stay on track and can make midcourse corrections to maximize their success and engagement.
- ☐ Students are introduced to the project by an activity or question that captures their attention and initiates the process of inquiry.
- ☐ Students are challenged to think deeply around a complex, open-ended question and are encouraged to generate further questions, answers, and solutions.
- ☐ Peer feedback is used to improve student work.
- ☐ Students must present new solutions or unique ideas, using critical and creative thinking.
- ☐ Students have opportunities to practice and develop their collaborative working skills with their peers.
- ☐ Presentation skills are taught and practiced.
- ☐ Students self-assess work using rubric criteria before submission and reflect on their performance on the assessment, identifying strengths and weaknesses and targeting areas for growth.
- ☐ Rubric(s) or scoring guide(s) are reviewed with students and used to guide the instruction.

Student Engagement Next Steps	

STUDENT PEER EDITING CHECKLIST

Purpose:

To provide a model for the scaffolding required to support effective peer editing and collaboration between students. The Student Peer Editing Checklist is aligned with the QPA rubric criteria and designed to support the implementation of the QPA Common Performance Tasks.

Date: ______________________________

Author: ______________________ Peer Editor: ______________________

Student Directions: Please provide a check mark (✓) next to each question the author has successfully completed. If the writing does not fulfill the requirement(s) below, mark an (X) and write notes in the comment box for each section, describing what the author needs to improve for his/her next draft. As you go through the peer editing process, edit the paper directly. Be as clear as possible in your editing and comments so the author can understand your feedback. Guidelines are provided to assist you in the feedback process.

FORMAT

- ☐ 1. Is the work labeled with name, date, and class?
- ☐ 2. Is there a title?
- ☐ 3. Are paragraphs indented? (Draw an arrow where paragraphs need to be indented.)
- ☐ 4. Is there a Works Cited page with appropriately cited sources for those not provided by your teacher?

I. IDEA DEVELOPMENT

- ☐ 5. Does the paper have a clear thesis statement? (Underline the thesis statement.)
- ☐ 6. Does the thesis statement appear early in the paper so the audience can understand what the paper will be about?
- ☐ 7. Does the thesis statement cover the entire scope of the paper's content?
- ☐ 8. Does the thesis statement explain the importance of the thesis/analysis (the "so what") of the essay?

Idea Development Comments:	

II. SUPPORTING EVIDENCE

- ☐ 11. Does each body paragraph contain supporting evidence? (Number the evidence in each paragraph.)
- ☐ 12. Is the evidence presented relevant to the topic being discussed?
- ☐ 13. Does the author distinguish fact from opinion when presenting evidence?
- ☐ 14. Does the author offer his/her own analysis of the evidence presented?
- ☐ 15. Does the paper cite direct evidence from the supporting source or materials in each body paragraph? (Write "DE" next to sentences that need more support.)
- ☐ 16. Does the paper properly integrate direct quotations by introducing them within the context of another sentence, being sure to establish speaker or context?
- ☐ 17. Does the paper properly integrate direct quotations by following them up with analysis that explains direct meaning derived from the quote? (Write "INT" next to any quotes that need further attention.)
- ☐ 18. Does the paper properly integrate direct quotations by having proper parenthetical citation format? Example: "Quote . . ." (39).

Supporting Evidence Comments:	

III. ORGANIZATION

- ☐ 19. Does the introduction provide a roadmap for what the rest of the paper will be about?
- ☐ 20. Does each paragraph's topic sentence control the content covered in that paragraph? (Write "TS" where this is lacking.)
- ☐ 21. Does the topic sentence for each paragraph contain a controlling idea that is presented in the thesis? (Double underline the controlling idea in each of the topic sentences.)
- ☐ 22. Does the paragraph order follow the sequence that is laid out in the introduction?
- ☐ 23. Does the conclusion offer a "take away" point and deepen the analysis, but stay away from going too far into a new thought?

Organization Comments:	

IV. CONVENTIONS (AND STYLE)

- ☐ 24. Does the paper have appropriate spelling? (Circle spelling errors.)
- ☐ 25. Does the paper have appropriate grammar? (Circle grammar errors.)
- ☐ 26. Does the paper have appropriate punctuation? (Circle punctuation errors.)
- ☐ 27. Is the writing style appropriate for the intended audience?
- ☐ 28. Does the paper vary in syntax and sentence structure to make the paper more interesting?
- ☐ 29. Does the paper choose precise language and terms specific to the topic being discussed?

Conventions and Style Comments:	

NEXT STEPS: FOR THE AUTHOR

I plan to resubmit my paper with all of the appropriate edits from the Student Peer Editing Checklist and my own revisions on (date):

____

From the Student Peer Editing Checklist, what edits will you make in your next draft? How will you address the Idea Development, Supporting Evidence (including citations), Organization, and Conventions feedback from the Student Peer Editing Checklist? Please describe at least three significant revisions (in addition to minor formatting and editing changes) you will incorporate based on the feedback you have received here.

1. ______________________________

2. ______________________________

3. ______________________________

4. ______________________________

5. ______________________________

***Please return the Student Peer Editing Checklist to your teacher with your paper after both the peer editor AND the author have fully completed the form. Please sign the bottom of this form before returning this document.
I have read and commented on the Student Peer Editing Checklist to the best of my knowledge.

Signature of Author: ______________________ Date: ______________

Signature of Peer Editor: ______________________ Date: ______________

STUDENT WORK ANALYSIS — A FORMATIVE ASSESSMENT TOOL

Subject Area: ______________________ Grade Level: ______________

Formative or Performance Task: ______________________

Aligned to CC Standards: ______________________

1 Using district/classroom assessment or rubric, describe expectations for performance:
(See wording of prompt, genre-specific rubric wording, and related CC standards for determining expectations for this assessment)

____

____

2 Quickly "sort" (do not score) students' work by general degree of objectives met (list student names in each category in order to monitor progress over time with each performance task). Start by sorting 2 larger piles: met OR not met objectives. You may also need a "not sure" pile. Then re-sort each of those piles into two: not met-partially met/close, AND met and met and exceeded. Any remaining papers that you were not sure about can now be matched with" typical" papers in one of the other existing piles.

OBJECTIVES NOT MET	*OBJECTIVES PARTIALLY MET*	*OBJECTIVES FULLY MET*	OBJECTIVES FULLY MET AND EXCEEDED
________% of class	________% of class	________% of class	________% of class

3 Choose a few samples from each group/category and describe "typical" performance, or specific performance of selected students

OBJECTIVES NOT MET	*OBJECTIVES PARTIALLY MET*	*OBJECTIVES FULLY MET*	OBJECTIVES FULLY MET AND EXCEEDED

4 Describe the NEXT learning needs of identified students (or students in each targeted group)

OBJECTIVES NOT MET	*OBJECTIVES PARTIALLY MET*	*OBJECTIVES FULLY MET*	OBJECTIVES FULLY MET AND EXCEEDED

5 Identify differentiated strategies to move ALL groups of students forward. Note any patterns or trends.

___

Whole class needs/will benefit from:

___

Some students need/will benefit from:

___

PLANNING WORKSHEET: ANALYZING FEATURES OF TEXT COMPLEXITY FOR INSTRUCTION & ASSESSMENT

Text or text passage: ______________________ Genre: ______________________

Approximate reading time: (indicate silent ________ or oral ________) Lexile ________ or Level: ________

CCSS suggested Lexile range for this grade level ________ (see also page 8, CCSS Appendix A): ________

Factors that Influence Text Complexity	Characteristics of this Text	Identify Best/Appropriate CC standards for assessment & instructional supports
Length of Text		
Format and Layout of Text: to what degree does the text layout support comprehension? (e.g., bold key words, visuals, inset text with definitions, white space, signposts=quotation marks, sub heading)		
Genre & Characteristic Features of Genre		CC standards Supports/scaffolding
Level of Meaning & Reasoning Required by Reader (sophistication or complexity of themes or ideas presented)	*Theme(s)/Key Concept(s)* *Explicit-Implied Purposes*	CC standards Supports/scaffolding
Text Structure (sequence, chronology, description, definition, compare-contrast, cause-effect, problem-solution, proposition-support, judgment/critique, inductive-deductive) **Discourse Style** (sarcasm, satire, irony, humor, etc.)	*Text Structure(s)* *Semantic cues/signal words* *Discourse style(employs use of literary devices)*	CC standards Supports/scaffolding
Words, Language Features, & Structure • Word length, word frequency • Sentence length; transitions • Potential levels of meaning (single-multiple; explicit-implicit; literal-figurative) • Precise/nuanced meaning • Domain-specific	*Tier 2 words-academic words (precise, contextual, literal-figurative, archaic)* *Tier 3 words (technical, content/domain-specific)*	CC standards Supports/scaffolding (before-after reading)
Background Knowledge Demands or Degree of Familiarity with Content Required (prior knowledge, multiple perspectives, embedded citations)	*Embedded references (literary, historical, cultural, economical, political, etc.)*	CC standards Supports/scaffolding (before-after reading)

TEXT-BASED DISCUSSION PROTOCOL

Purpose

To examine a relevant issue in depth using a short article or excerpt from a book.

Directions

This seminar helps build a culture of discourse in a school by allowing for enlargement of intellectual understanding. In a text-based seminar of 40 minutes to 1 hour, a team examines an issue from an outside point of view. Participants read a short article or excerpt from a book that is related to teaching and learning and then engage in a discussion about the text. The purpose of the discussion is not to persuade other group members of a particular point of view, but to clarify, build upon, and enhance understanding of the text. Text-based seminars give participants an opportunity to extract different meanings and ideas from a text and to discuss important issues related to the text.

1. **Select the text:** Choose an article or book excerpt that will have implications for teaching and learning. The article may be selected by the team facilitator or by an individual member of the team.

2. **Read the text:** If the text is long, the facilitator may distribute it before the meeting, or a shorter text may be read for the first time during the meeting. If participants have already read the text, allow 5 minutes of seminar time to review it. If a short article is to be read during the seminar, 10–15 minutes should be enough. While reading, participants may take notes, underline or highlight important ideas, and record questions the text raises for them.

3. **Begin the discourse:** There are two effective ways to begin the discourse. Each member of the seminar may take turns reading aloud a sentence or two that has particular significance to them and share why they responded to that particular excerpt. Or, the facilitator may present a framing question to start the discussion.

4. **Discuss the text:** The facilitator leads a 20- to 30-minute discussion. He or she should remind participants to refer to the text to support their comments. Groups may want to follow these guidelines:
   Listen actively.
   Build on what others say.
   Expose/suspend your assumptions.
   Don't step on others' talk. Silences and pauses are OK.
   Emphasize clarification, amplification, and implications of ideas.
   Converse directly with each other, not through the facilitator.
   As much as possible, let the conversation flow without raising hands.
   Make references to the text and encourage others to do the same.
   Watch your airtime for how often you speak and how much you say when you speak.

5. **Close the discussion:** The facilitator closes the discussion about the text, highlighting two or three main points of discussion and thanking participants for their perspectives. The result is that all participants leave the seminar with a deeper understanding of the text. Many times this leads to agreement for further exploration of the topic.

Source: Gene Thompson-Grove 1/03 "Text-Based Seminar Guidelines." Adapted from National School Reform Faculty (NSRF), Harmony Education Center, Bloomington, IN. http://www.nsrfharmony.org/protocol/doc/text_based_guidelines.pdf

TRAINING WITH ANCHORS PROTOCOL

Purpose

To learn how to score student work reliably and accurately using anchor papers, rubrics, scoring guidelines.

Planning

- **Time:** varies based on the number of papers—approximately 30 minutes per paper
- **Group size:** 5–8
- **Materials needed** for each person:
    - o Sample work and task (see QPA website for additional samples)
    - o Task rubric
    - o Scoring guidelines (if applicable)
    - o Two anchors of student work with corresponding rubrics, annotations, and score reports
    - o Score sheet or task rubric can be used for scoring
    - o One extra score sheet is needed for the recorder, who will tally the scores for the whole group.
- **Roles:** Choose a facilitator, timekeeper, and recorder. (1 minute)

Process

1. **Norms:** The facilitator reviews the protocol process and norms with the group. (2 minutes)
2. **Examination:** Group members silently examine the rubric, scoring guidelines, and one anchor with the corresponding rubric, annotations, and score report. (12 minutes)
3. **Clarifying questions:** The group asks any clarifying questions they have about the materials and process. (3 minutes)
4. **Read and score:** Read the prompt and the essay independently and silently. Using the rubric, score the essay at each criterion point and overall. Underline the words, sentences, or phrases that provide evidence for your scores. (10 minutes)
    a. **Use a ✓** to indicate that a specific criterion on the rubric is evident or present.
    b. **Use a ?** to indicate that you are unsure if a criterion is present.
    c. **Circle** the score for each criterion.
5. **Score sharing:** One at a time, team members share their scores for each criterion—without explanation—as the recorder completes the group's chart. (1 minute)
6. **Discussion:** The facilitator invites the group to consider where the differences in the scores occurred and why people scored differently for each rubric criterion—particularly the highest and lowest scores. Group members use their notes and underlined examples within the essay to justify their scores. ***All comments need to be evidence based.*** The group comes to consensus (at least 80%) for scores in each criterion and overall. (5–10 minutes)
7. **Review anchor score:** Review the rubric, annotations, and score report explaining how the anchor was scored. (Note: Annotations are for training purposes and are not a model for what should be provided to students as feedback.) The facilitator records the consensus scores on the group's chart for comparison, then opens a conversation around the following questions. (10–15 minutes)
    a. Where were we aligned and where were we out of alignment?
    b. What should be the feedback for the teacher on the prompt or other prompt-related questions or comments?
    c. What is the next step for this student's instruction?
8. **Repeat steps 4–7:** Use the shortest allotted time for step 7.
9. **Debrief:** The facilitator leads the debrief. (4 minutes)
    a. Did the team honor the norms at all times?
    b. What went well?
    c. What could have gone better?
    d. What will I take back to my classroom from this process?

TUNING PROTOCOL FOR TASKS

Purpose

To receive feedback and fine-tune tasks.

Planning

- **Time:** 40 minutes
- **Group size:** 4–6
- **Preparation:** Presenter gathers task contextual materials (if any) and focusing question.
- **Roles:** Facilitator, presenter, timekeeper, and recorder/reporter

Process

1. **Norms:** The facilitator reviews the protocol process and norms with the group. (3 minutes)
2. **Presentation:** The presenter shares the context for the task (i.e., information about the students, the class, student learning goals, etc.), a focusing question, and the task itself. (5 minutes)
3. **Clarifying questions:** The facilitator invites participants to ask clarifying questions in order to better understand the context for the question and the instructional task. Clarifying questions are matters of fact and generally elicit quick answers. The facilitator reminds participants that thinking or probing questions are better left for the feedback section. (5 minutes)
4. **Examination of the task and any contextual materials:** Participants silently examine the presenter's materials and the guidelines for effective tasks and take notes, with a focus on the presenter's question. The presenter also remains silent. It is sometimes helpful for the presenter to slide his or her chair back to observe while being slightly removed from the group. (5 minutes)
5. **Feedback and group discussion:** Participants share feedback with each other, reflecting collaboratively for the benefit of the presenter. The presenter takes notes, but continues to remain silent as the group thinks for him or her. (12 minutes)
   a. In what ways is the task aligned—or in tune—with the presenter's goals?
   b. What aspects of the task make it effective?
   c. In what ways is the task not aligned with the presenter's goals?
   d. What aspects of the task may lessen its effectiveness?
   e. How would we answer the presenter's focusing question?
   f. What have we learned about instructional tasks from examining this one?
6. **Reflection:** The facilitator invites the presenter to reflect aloud on the feedback and to comment on ideas or questions that were particularly interesting, reminding the presenter that the group's feedback is offered in service to the presenter, so there is no need to defend or explain. (5 minutes)
7. **Debrief:** The facilitator asks the group to comment on their experience with the Tuning Protocol. (4 minutes)
   a. Did the team honor the norms at all times?
   b. What went well?
   c. What could have gone better?

Modified from the National School Reform Faculty's Tuning Protocol.

Guidelines for QPA Common Tasks

- The task sparks students' imaginations and creativity. Use words or phrases that invite a variety of interpretations and responses and that connect to an essential question.
- The task includes an authentic audience for the writing task. Students understand the audience's familiarity with the topic. The task specifies the level of formality in writing style appropriate to the audience.
- When specifying an authentic, beyond-school audience for a performance assessment, always include the evaluator, who is typically a teacher. (Some audiences require less sophisticated writing than we want to see in our assessments.)
- Directions are clear and provide expectations for genre, length, sources, and format and call attention to aspects of the rubric by which the work will be judged.
- Directions are succinct. Too much direction in a task can stifle originality in students' compositions.
- If sources are not provided by the teachers, the task should include expectations about how students find and use evidence sources.
- The task is appropriate in content and form to the grade level of the students being assessed.
- The task is for both the student and the scorer, so they can clearly interpret the rubric in light of the task, especially in terms of audience, evidence requirements, or genre-specific features.

VISION OF THE GRADUATE PROTOCOL

Purpose

To develop a vision of what a graduate from our school should know, understand, and be able to do.

Planning

- **Time:** 135 minutes
- **Roles for group of 25–30 participants:** 1 whole group facilitator and 1 whole group recorder; small group facilitators, recorders, and timekeepers. (If possible, include students, parents, and community members in this process, integrating them into all of the groups.)

Preparation

- *Prior to the meeting,* **create** a large silhouette of a student on chart paper.
- *Prior to the meeting,* **create** charts to separately represent the head, heart, hands, feet, and eyes of a student, and post them in "stations" around the room with plenty of space between them. (Note: Guiding questions to be written on or next to the charts are listed at the end of this protocol.)
- Form groups of 5–6 participants for "vision teams."
- Give the recorder for each vision team a marker whose color will be used only for their group.
- Identify a place for each team to post their free writes.
- Give sticky notes to each team for the Gallery Walk.

Process

1 **Decide** who will be the vision team facilitator, recorder, and timekeeper.

2 **Protocol review:** Facilitator reviews the protocol with the group. (3 minutes)

3 **Journal:**

a. Facilitator reviews the school's mission statement with the group.

b. Facilitator reads the question "What should a graduate from our school know, understand, and be able to do?" and team members free-write their individual responses to the question. (8 minutes)

c. Share responses with vision team members, then post. (2 minutes)

4 **Carousel:** (30 minutes)

a. Each team goes to a station that represents one "part" of the student—head, heart, hands, feet, or eyes—and the recorder charts the group's responses to the questions posed on the chart. (5 minutes)

b. Each group rotates to the next station, representing another "part" of the student, reads what the previous group wrote, and builds on the existing comments by using the symbols below and adding ideas or posting questions. (5 minutes)

c. Groups continue to rotate at 5-minute intervals and build on the previous groups' work until each student "part" has comments from all groups.

Symbol	Meaning
✓	Agree
!	Strongly agree
?	Questions
X	Strongly disagree

Adapted by Christina Brown and Susan Westlund from Future Protocol "Back from the Future," a National School Reform Faculty protocol by Scott Murphy, August 2001.

5 **Break (varies)**

6 **Synthesis and product:** Each group returns to the station where it began, reviews the comments by all the groups, consolidates the ideas, writes them as "essential" ideas, and prioritizes them to produce a "clean," synthesized representation of each part to exhibit in the gallery. Each group posts its final work. (35 minutes)

7 **Gallery Walk:** Participants circulate among the gallery of charts, taking notes and leaving "Wows" (impressive ideas) or "Wonders" (ideas that make you think or raise questions) sticky notes in response to what they see. (15 minutes)

8 **Whole group sharing:** The facilitator for the whole group poses the following questions while the recorder for the whole group charts the comments (15 minutes):

a. What did you notice?

b. What seems important?

c. Do our ideas promote equity in our schools?

d. Do our ideas align with what we know about teaching and learning?

e. How do you hope the information will be used?

f. What worked about the process, and what didn't work so well?

9 **What next?** Extensions and next steps: The whole group facilitator and recorder lead the group in completing the chart below. Pair shares or journaling may be appropriate for 2 minutes of the total time. (15 minutes)

Consider the following questions:

a. How coherent is our vision at this moment? What will it take to make it readable and understandable?

b. Who needs to know? How do we communicate our vision to all members of the school community?

c. How do we celebrate and make it public to the whole school community?

d. How often do we need to revisit it?

e. How can we tell if the vision is embedded in all the work of the school?

What needs to happen?	Who needs to be involved?	When does it need to happen?	Where does it need to take place?	What resources are needed?

10 **Owning the plan:** The whole group facilitator thanks the group for their thoughtful work, tells them what she will do with it and when they can next expect to hear about it, and asks them to thank each other as well.

ADVANCE PREPARATION OF CHARTS

1. Cut outs or drawings that represent each "part" of the student make the process visually more interesting as well as easier to identify and remember the focus.
2. Guiding questions: Beside or on each of the following charts, write the questions suggested for that chart.
   - **Head**—What should every graduate know? Consider general and specific facts, concepts, and ideas. What should they understand? What thinking skills should they have?
   - **Heart**—What traits, qualities, or characteristics should every graduate embody?
   - **Hands**—What should graduates be able to do and produce? What skills should they have?
   - **Eyes**—What perspectives should graduates have? How discriminating should their vision be regarding arts and sciences?
   - **Feet**—How would we most like to see our students moving in the world? Where should their education take them?
3. It may be helpful to post this small chart beside each of the "part" charts.

✓	Agree
!	Strongly agree
?	Questions
X	Strongly disagree

Notes

Notes

Notes